D1571886

lessons
in gourmet cooking

lessons
in gourmet cooking

By LIBBY HILLMAN

Drawings by Ivy Bottini

HEARTHSIDE PRESS, INCORPORATED
PUBLISHERS • NEW YORK

For Herb, David,
Don and Betty

Acknowledgments

Many thanks to Ruth Kreiger and Rena Gold, my class assistants; to Harold Seiden, for the color transparencies, and to family, friends and students, whose enthusiasm and encouragement have been a constant source of inspiration.

Table of Contents

Editor's Foreword

It is always a pleasure for a publisher to present a book which is not only widely appealing—and what is of greater interest than the subject of food?—but also unusual in its approach. *Lessons in Gourmet Cooking* is a course in good food, written by a practicing teacher who has been exceptionally successful in her field. This distinguishes it from the cookbooks written by professional chefs whose procedures are often quite complicated . . . from the cookbooks written by magazine staffs aimed to please a quantity, not usually a quality, audience . . . and from the cookbooks (these are the best ones I think) written by talented homemakers whose frame of reference is necessarily narrow. I do not include in this comparison the bound books issued by flour and food companies. To me, they are glorified advertising pieces paid for by the consumer.

For the last ten years, Libby Hillman has taught cooking in the Adult Program of the Great Neck (N.Y.) Public Schools. Of a hundred-odd courses offered annually to adults, hers have been the most popular for eight years in a row. Brides, working wives, expert party-givers, professional restaurateurs and many men (only men may register for barbecuing lessons) are among the students. A high percentage enroll for the whole series of five courses at a cost of about sixty dollars. This popularity reflects Mrs. Hillman's skill as a teacher, her extraordinary gastronomic knowledge, and her collection of superb and unusual recipes. Homemade Danish pastries, stuffed boned chicken, Dobostortes, unusual pilafs, a marvelous shrimp beignet . . . these are just a few of the specialties easily mastered in Libby Hillman's classes.

To present the best of her material, usefully and simply even for new cooks, we developed the book as a series of informal lessons. Each lesson gives the salient facts of the subject, "teacher says" sections, questions and answers, and marvelous recipes. Menus, buying advice, freezing and defrosting notes, and cook-ahead ideas for party givers with or without a freezer are included. The explanatory drawings by Ivy Bottini, like herbs in an omelet, add a final grace note.

Many of my neighbors and friends have taken Libby Hillman's courses, so personal knowledge supports my thesis that the accumulated wisdom presented in this book can make you gourmet *cum laude* and a hostess (or host) *extraordinaire*. We are proud to present this book under our imprint.

NEDDA CASSON ANDERS

Great Neck, New York

lessons
in gourmet cooking

★ ★ ★

All the recipes in this book are good but, with a bow towards the *Guide Michelin*, we have given a special accolade, three stars, to the very best ones.

LESSON 1

The Appetizer

Most dinners and many luncheons begin with an appetizer, so let us make it the starting point for our lessons. The French word for appetizer, hors d'oeuvre, literally translated means outside the work, in other words, not a regular course of the meal. Choose your appetizer carefully whether it is served in the living room apart from the meal or as a first course at the table. Decide on the main course then select the appetizer.

Cooking is an art and like all arts it has basic rules. Here we apply these rules to our first lesson:

Scale: Keep a sense of proportion in what you serve; appetizers should whet the appetite, not satiate it. Unless served with forks and individual plates, creamy appetizers should be small enough to be eaten in one bite; solid foods in two. Many recipes in this book, if made bite-sized in scale, can be offered as hors d'oeuvres.

Contrast: Use varieties, textures and colors that contrast with other courses of the meal. Before a main course of fish, serve a cheese appetizer or tiny hot pastry. Before hot beef, consider cold sea-food. Serve a creamy appetizer if no creamed dishes are repeated. Use pastry for a first course if it does not reappear later in the menu. Serve a cold appetizer salad when the main course is hot.

13

Unity: To unify a party, some hostesses enjoy developing a theme. For instance, an antipasto might lead to an Italian main course, Guacamole to a Mexican one. Often these themes are not so defined, but rather the unifying element is the formality or informality of the party. Dunks and dips are informal in character, well suited to barbecues, buffets and similar types of entertaining. Hot hors d'oeuvres, a simple pâté, or caviar served out of the tin (perfectly permissible), set in cracked ice and accompanied by lemon, minced egg yolk, whites and onion, are appropriate to the most ceremoniously formal affair.

Balance: So many kinds of balance are involved! Do have a balanced array of colors, shapes and quantities on your hors d'oeuvre platters. At large parties provide enough tables so that guests won't have to balance cocktails, ashtrays, and plates on their laps.

Rhythm: The rhythm of the party is smoother if the hors d'oeuvre period gives the hostess time for a breather. Allow half an hour from the time set for dinner for late comers. During this grace period, if you do not have help, select a first course that does not need last-minute attention. Use this half hour to take care of necessary kitchen detail. Then your dinner can be kept moving in a rhythmic sequence from course to course.

THE COLD HORS D'OEUVRE

The simplest but still among the tastiest of appetizers are the dunks and spreads. These are especially practical for large informal parties, because they can be made in bulk and finished well in advance.

Bleu Cheese Dunk

8 ounces cream cheese
4 ounces bleu cheese
4 tablespoons heavy sweet cream

1 teaspoon Worcestershire sauce
1 tablespoon chopped chives

Allow cheese to come to room temperature. Blend all ingredients together. This may be done by hand or with the electric mixer. Serve with potato chips or raw crisp vegetables, such as celery, carrots, radishes, cucumbers, green pepper, cauliflower. Yield: 1½ cups.

...store cheese mixture in crock!

...if you can't find 'soft' cheddar...

...grate 'hard cheddar' and soften with liquid in recipe.

Wine Cheese Pot

½ pound soft cheddar cheese
4 ounces cream cheese
¼ cup port wine

1 teaspoon Worcestershire sauce
2 teaspoons Dijon or Dusseldorf
    mustard

Bring cheeses to room temperature. Blend all ingredients by hand or with the electric mixer. Store in a covered cheese crock or a jar. It keeps well in the refrigerator; however serve it at room temperature. Good with crackers. Yield: 1½ cups.

Shrimp Catalina

4 hard-cooked eggs, sieved
1 pound cooked shrimp, diced fine
3 tablespoons mayonnaise
2 tablespoons chile sauce
1 tablespoon lemon juice

1 teaspoon Worcestershire sauce
1 tablespoon chopped parsley
pinch of cayenne
½ teaspoon salt
¼ teaspoon pepper

Mash eggs with fork or put through sieve. Combine all ingredients until well mixed. Place in a two- to three-cup bowl. Refrigerate at least 2 hours in bowl. Unmold on a chilled crystal platter. Garnish with paper thin slices of cucumber and sweet onion. Serve with thin-sliced rye bread. Yield: 2 cups.

~~~~~~~

My pâté recipe is lengthy but not tricky. Line up your ingredients, follow the steps in order and it is all yours. Of course the inspiration is French but as far as I know the only "maison" this comes from is mine.

Pâté Maison　★ ★ ★

7 slices bacon
6 slices bacon, cut into 1″ pieces
3 onions, diced
1 pound calves' liver, cut into
　1″ pieces
1 pound chicken livers, cut in halves
1 teaspoon salt
½ teaspoon pepper
3 egg yolks
2 eggs

¼ cup Madeira wine
¼ teaspoon salt
½ teaspoon pepper
½ teaspoon chervil or parsley
⅓ teaspoon tarragon
½ teaspoon cinnamon
¼ teaspoon allspice
1 truffle, sliced thin and soaked in
　2 tablespoons Madeira Wine
½ cup freshly rendered chicken fat

1. Set seven 1-cup terrines in an oblong pan at least 2 or 3 inches deep. Place one slice of raw bacon across the bottom and up the sides of each terrine. Preheat oven set to 375°F.

2. In a skillet, render remaining pieces of bacon. Add diced onion and cook until brown. Add the liver, 1 teaspoon salt and ½ teaspoon pepper. Sauté for 3 or 4 minutes. Cover and cook for 3 minutes.

3. Purée the entire mixture either through a grinder or blender, using all juices. Add yolks and eggs one at a time if blender is used.

4. Place liver mixture in a large bowl. Mix with all the other ingredients, reserving the 7 nicest pieces of truffle and the chicken fat.

5. Fill each terrine with liver mixture to ½-inch from the top. Place a slice of truffle on each one and cover with aluminum foil. Pour hot water into pan around terrines to fill the pan half way.

6. Bake for 2 hours. Remove from oven. When totally cool, cover with chicken fat. Set cover on each terrine and refrigerate. Each terrine amply serves 8 as a do-it yourself spread for canapés. Yield: Seven 1-cup terrines.

Teacher says:

Inexpensive onion-soup casseroles make good terrines. For serving larger groups this can be baked in two 8″ x 3″ loaf pans. Since the pâté is rich it goes a long way. Refrigerated, it keeps well for 3 weeks. In the freezer, it will keep 2 months. There is a slight change in texture after freezing but not enough to detract from the flavor.

If pâté is baked in loaf size, unmold it after it has been refrigerated. Serve with the bacon strips. Garnish it with a full border of watercress, large ripe olives and cherry tomatoes.

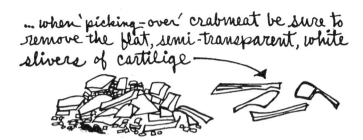

... when 'picking-over' crabmeat be sure to remove the flat, semi-transparent, white slivers of cartilige —

After his recent vacation from school, my son David carried back a jar of Crabmeat Rémoulade because the boys at college adore it; you don't need college training to like this—just an educated palate. For an elegant beginning make the Sole Laurentian (see index). Serve the ring cold with Crabmeat Rémoulade poured into the center. This was first course at the Hillman's latest Thanksgiving dinner.

Crabmeat Rémoulade ★ ★ ★

1 7-ounce can crab meat
1 cup mayonnaise
¼ cup olive oil
2 tablespoons lemon juice
2 cloves garlic crushed

1 teaspoon celery seed
2 stalks celery, finely chopped
¼ teaspoon salt
⅛ teaspoon pepper

Pick over and shred crab meat. Blend all ingredients by hand. Refrigerate. Serve with crackers, chips and raw vegetables. Yield: 3 cups.

~~~~~~~~

Two special recipes have come from a student and friend. Essie Davis'
favorite hors d'oeuvre is very, very good! Later, I'll give you her second
recipe, the wonderful Danish elephant ears.

Artichoke and Shrimp Bowl

1 egg yolk
¾ cup olive oil
¼ cup wine vinegar
2 tablespoons prepared mustard,
   Dijon or Dusseldorf
1 shallot, chopped fine, or
   2 tablespoons minced onion

2 tablespoons parsley, finely
   chopped
2 tablespoons chives
1 package frozen artichoke hearts,
   cooked
1 pound medium shrimps, cooked
   and cleaned

Use blender or hand beater. Using blender place egg yolk in container and blend for 10 seconds. With hand beater, mix for 2 minutes. Add oil, vinegar and mustard. Beat only until mixture is creamy. Place dressing in a bowl with shallots, herbs, artichoke hearts and shrimps. Marinate for a few hours or overnight; looks lovely served in a silver bowl. Serves 8.

Deviled Egg Orleans

See index for recipe.

~~~~~~~~

Vegetables á la Grecque are usually cooked in a broth seasoned with
olive oil, lemon juice and herbs. One vegetable or a combination as
below makes a tasty appetizer salad.

Artichokes à la Grecque

1 package frozen artichoke hearts
1 package frozen mixed vegetables
1 onion, chopped fine
1 cup water
¼ cup oil
1 tablespoon lemon juice
1 clove garlic, crushed

1 tablespoon chopped parsley
1 tablespoon chopped fresh tarragon
   (1 teaspoon dried)
1 teaspoon salt
¼ teaspoon coarsely ground pepper
2 tablespoons flour blended smooth
   with 2 tablespoons water

Place all ingredients except the flour and water into a covered saucepan. Cook for 7 minutes. Remove vegetables to a shallow serving bowl with a slotted spoon. Thicken juices in pan with flour and water. Cook for 2 minutes. Pour sauce onto vegetables and refrigerate. Serve very cold.

For another arrangement, mound the chilled salad in the center of a flat platter and surround with sliced tomatoes. Sprinkle tomatoes with capers and garnish all with watercress and Greek olives. Yield: 6 servings.

I've always found that the best things in food are often the most expensive, but here is an elegant Romanian recipe for poor man's caviar, as prepared by the mother of my friend, Alton Allen.

Ikra

1 cup fresh whitefish roe,
  washed well
1 to 2 teaspoons salt
1 tablespoon olive oil
lemon wedges

Spanish onion, diced fine
1 egg yolk, cooked and sieved
1 egg white, cooked and
  chopped fine

Place whitefish roe in a colander over a large bowl. Run very cold water through the roe allowing the tiny beads to run through the openings of the colander into the bowl. Pour off excess water in bowl and turn roe into a clean container. Keep washing remainder of roe until all the membranes are removed. When the pale orange beads are clean, strain off excess water. Salt caviar well and store in refrigerator overnight. On the next day pour oil over caviar and taste for an adjustment of salt. Serve Ikra just as you would Russian caviar. Set bowl on ice, accompanied by lemon wedges, diced onion, egg yolk and egg white. Bring on the black pumpernickel and champagne! Yield: 1 cup. Serves 8.

I wish you could hear the sighs of admiration and delight when students and guests see this beautiful "flower" for the first time! You will hear them too if you follow the easy directions. Be sure to use only fruits in season, when they are at the peak of quality. Incidentally, although the name sounds Oriental, I must admit it was my own invention.

Flower of Goodness

1 perfect head Boston lettuce
1 recipe Guacamole
2 pink grapefruits, segmented

2 white grapefruits, segmented
1 pound large shrimp, cooked
   and cleaned

Wash lettuce carefully without tearing it apart. Dry it well, store greens in a covered container in the refrigerator. It takes anywhere from 2 to 12 hours to crisp greens. Place lettuce on 12″ round tray. Keep the head intact but flatten and open the leaves to spread over platter. Cut out center core of lettuce. Place bowl of Guacomole in the center. Grapefruit sections and shrimps should now be tucked in the crisp green petals. Serves 6 to 8.

~~~~~~~~

Guacamole

1 large ripe avocado
1 small onion, chopped fine
1 clove garlic, crushed
1 tablespoon olive oil
1 tablespoon wine vinegar

1 tomato, peeled and diced
1 tablespoon lemon juice
¼ teaspoon salt
⅛ teaspoon pepper

Mash avocado, but leave it slightly lumpy. Add other ingredients. Serve with crackers. Yield: 1½ cups.

~~~~~~~~

My students delight in the combination of colors and textures which result from this recipe. Nor are they disappointed by the taste test. Although it seems long, it is no trouble to prepare. After the many dozens of times I have done this tray, I still find it rewarding.

Holiday Hors D'oeuvres Tray ★ ★ ★

LOBSTER ASPIC

1 envelope unflavored gelatin
¼ cup water
¾ cup mayonnaise
¼ cup sour cream
1 tablespoon chile sauce
1 tablespoon tarragon vinegar
2 tablespoons lemon juice

1 tablespoon capers
10 stuffed olives, sliced fine
¼ teaspoon celery seed
½ teaspoon salt
⅛ teaspoon white pepper
4 lobster tails, cooked and diced
  (reserve 2 lobster shells)

Rinse 9-inch loaf pan in water. Soften gelatin in ¼ cup cold water. Place cup in a saucepan holding 1 inch of water. Place over low heat and allow gelatin to liquefy. In the meantime mix all other ingredients in a bowl. When gelatin becomes a clear liquid, cool for 1 minute. Mix gelatin thoroughly into lobster mixture. Pour into pan and refrigerate. This aspic jells rapidly but to do away with last-minute work, prepare it 24 hours in advance.

DEVILED EGGS

1 dozen hard-cooked eggs
3 ounces cream cheese
¼ cup mayonnaise
¾ teaspoon salt
¼ teaspoon pepper

¼ teaspoon powdered mustard
¼ teaspoon curry
½ teaspoon monosodium glutamate
½ teaspoon Worcestershire sauce

Cut each egg in half (vertically). Remove egg yolks and sieve or mash thoroughly. Reserve egg whites. Combine yolks with other ingredients to make a smooth mixture. If eggs are to be used within a few hours, fill egg white with a decorating bag or merely with a spatula. If preparing in advance, store the yolk mixture separately from whites. When ready to use allow egg yolk mixture to soften to room temperature. If egg whites have become slightly moist, wipe them with paper toweling. Fill egg whites 1 or 2 hours before using or fill them earlier in the day and cover well with Saran Wrap.

CUCUMBER AND ONION RELISH

2 cucumbers
2 medium onions or
 1 large Spanish onion
1 teaspoon salt

2 tablespoons vinegar
4 tablespoons water
1 teaspoon sugar

Score the cucumbers with the tines of a fork (do not peel). Slice the cucumbers and onions very thin. Place in a bowl with salt. Allow to stand for 30 to 40 minutes. Pour off water that settles. Add vinegar, water and sugar. Adjust seasoning, which may vary with size of cucumber. If you enjoy cucumber slightly crisp, this relish must be made a few hours before use. Most people enjoy wilted cucumbers, so make this a day in advance.

GARNISHES

2 pounds cooked and cleaned shrimp
1 cantaloupe (in season)
 sliced in wedges
1 honeydew melon (in season)
 sliced in wedges
  (substitute segments of 2 pink
  and 2 white grapefruits, when
  melon is not available)
1 large ripe avocado

1 dozen flat anchovies, drained of oil
6 rolled anchovies with capers,
 drained of oil
1 ounce black caviar
chives, fresh and uncut
1 bunch fresh parsley (or chicory)
large ripe olives
2 lobster shells

Fruits may be cut and stored even a day in advance. Cover tightly. Avocado must be sliced when tray arrangement is made. Its lovely green will darken if sliced in advance. Greens can be washed and crisped days in advance. Chicory may be used with, or instead of, parsley.

ARRANGEMENT

1. Choose a tray 2 to 3 feet long and at least 18 inches wide. If it is not decorative, cover it with heavy foil. If the tray is silver you might want to line it with Saran or foil anyway.

2. Unmold aspic on to a sheet of heavy foil. Place in center of tray. It would be difficult to unmold aspic in the center of such a large tray and hit the right spot.

3. Stand shrimp up around aspic as to cover sides of aspic. Place extra shrimp in foreground. On either side of aspic set deviled eggs in two lines.

4. Using 2 relish dishes, place cucumber and onions on both sides of eggs.

5. Alternate fruits and avocado along either sides of tray and around the corners. Fill in all empty spaces with greens (parsley, or chicory).

6. Garnish every other egg with a strip of anchovy. (Some people, I find, do not care for anchovy.)

7. Starting from bottom to top, 1 inch from left, place 6 rolled anchovies, 1 inch apart, on to aspic. Cut 6 chives 2 inches long. Place chive under anchovy to resemble a stem. Cut 6 chives ½ inch long. Place these on to main stem to resemble a branch. With a tiny spoon place a few grains of caviar on to outer stem. Take a deep breath now and enjoy your handiwork—it's not too good to eat! Serves 18. This tray is illustrated in color.

this is how the decoration on the Aspic should look when it is finished →

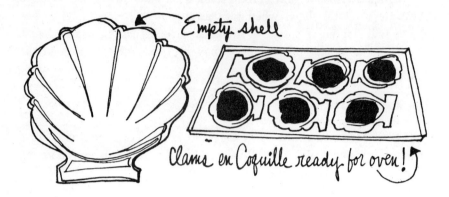

Empty shell

Clams en Coquille ready for oven!

THE HOT HORS D'OEUVRE

It's wise to stock your pantry shelf with a few cans of minced clams, crab meat, lobster, anchovies, tuna and salmon. These can be the base for many quick hot appetizers. In the following recipe, no salt is added because canned clams are well salted. If you use fresh clams, allow 1½ cups finely minced clams and include a little juice; adjust seasoning.

Clams en Coquille

2 tablespoons butter or oil	½ teaspoon oregano
2 onions, diced fine	¼ cup bread crumbs
1 clove garlic	⅛ teaspoon pepper
2 8-ounce cans minced clams (drain off ¼ cup juice)	2 tablespoons bread crumbs combined with 2 tablespoons
1 tablespoon chopped fresh parsley	Parmesan cheese

Set 6 natural 4-inch shells or ramekins on a cooky sheet. Preheat oven to 400° F. Heat butter or oil in skillet and sauté onions with garlic. When onions are golden, discard garlic. Remove from flame. Add all other ingredients except crumb mixture. Divide clam mixture in 6 individual shells. Sprinkle with combined crumbs and Parmesan. Bake in oven at 400° F. for 10 minutes. Serves 6.

For a variation, add a slice of Gruyere or grated Swiss cheese on top of each clam. At the end of cooking time, place under broiler until bubbly and brown.

Baked Whole Clams

2 doz. Little Neck clams
 on the half shell
4 tablespoons butter, melted
1 shallot, minced or
 2 tablespoons minced onion
6 mushrooms, minced
2 cloves garlic, crushed
¾ cups bread crumbs
½ teaspoon anchovy paste

2 tablespoons Parmesan cheese
2 tablespoons white wine
1 tablespoon chopped parsley
½ teaspoon oregano
½ teaspoon salt
⅛ teaspoon freshly ground pepper
½ cup clam juice or water
2 tablespoons oil

Preheat oven to 425° F. Place clams on a baking pan. Mix together all other ingredients except juice and oil. Spread a spoon of paste over each clam, easily done by hand. Before baking pour a little clam juice or water into pan. Sprinkle drops of oil over all the clams. Bake for 10 minutes at 425° F. Serves 6.

A long time ago my friend Bert Greenhut, an ex-Baltimorean, confessed that many natives used just mayonnaise to moisten the crab. No cream sauce had to be prepared, especially if fresh crab was available. I was skeptical until I tried it myself. True enough, it is most delicious!

Imperial Crab Baltimore

1 pound crab meat (fresh, frozen or
 canned and picked over)
½ green pepper, minced
½ pimento, minced
1 tablespoon lemon juice
1 teaspoon Worcestershire sauce
½ cup mayonnaise

3 drops Tabasco sauce
½ teaspoon dry mustard
¼ teaspoon salt
¼ teaspoon white pepper
4 tablespoons bread crumbs
2 tablespoons butter

Preheat oven to 375° F. Combine all ingredients except the last two. Combine bread crumbs and butter by rubbing butter into crumbs with your fingers. Divide the mixture into 8 scallop shells or ramekins or use a casserole. Top with bread crumb mixture. Set shells on a baking sheet and bake at 375° F. for 15 minutes. Serves 8.

Teacher says:

Crab must be picked over carefully for bones. This can be done with your hand. The best "lump" crab meat need not be used here but if you do splurge, there are the least amount of crab bones in this type.

Variations:

Heat mixture in a chafing dish; accompany with toast points.

Add a beaten egg and 4 tablespoons bread crumbs. Use as a stuffing for fish or sea food.

Add 2 tablespoons of sherry and spread on to 3 dozen crackers, place under broiler for 30 seconds.

Blend mixture with 2 cups cooked elbow #3 macaroni. Top with grated Parmesan cheese. Bake at 350° F. for 20 minutes.

Substitute other fish such as halibut, cod or assorted shellfish.

Use cold as a salad or a spread.

Two-Minute Shrimp in a Chafing Dish

1 tablespoon butter	½ teaspoon tomato paste
1 shallot, diced fine	¼ teaspoon salt
or 2 tablespoons minced onion	⅛ teaspoon pepper
1 pound medium shrimp, cooked	¼ cup sherry
and cleaned (22 to 26 shrimp)	1 tablespoon chopped parsley
½ cup heavy sweet cream	1 tablespoon chopped chives

Place butter in blazer pan, directly on flame. Sauté shallots in butter for 30 seconds. Add shrimp, cream, tomato paste, salt and pepper. Allow cream to cook down for 1 minute, then add sherry. Sprinkle parsley and chives over all. Stir for 30 seconds and serve on toast points or pastry shells. Serves 6.

Five-Minute Shrimp in a Chafing Dish

2 tablespoons butter
2 cloves garlic, crushed
1 pound shrimp,
  cleaned and uncooked
1 tablespoon lemon juice

¼ cup dry vermouth
2 tablespoons mixed chopped herbs
  (parsley, chervil, tarragon)
½ teaspoon salt
⅛ teaspoon pepper

Melt butter in blazer, directly over flame. Add garlic and shrimp. Wait for shrimp to turn pink and opaque white. Blend in lemon juice, vermouth, herbs, salt and pepper. Heat thoroughly and serve. Serves 6.

These mushrooms are similar to those served at the Belle Terrasse in Tivoli Gardens, Copenhagen, but I've adjusted the recipe for easier handling. Should you want to duplicate it exactly, dip the mushrooms in a batter before deep-frying. Serve with fine black caviar, heavy sour cream and fried parsley.

Mushrooms Copenhagen

1 bunch fresh parsley, stemmed
1 cup sour cream
1 small jar red caviar
2 to 4 tablespoons butter

1 pound large mushroom caps
½ teaspoon salt
¼ teaspoon freshly ground pepper

1. Wash parsley, dry very well and refrigerate in a covered container. This will make it very crisp.

2. Blend sour cream and caviar together lightly in an attractive bowl. Completely cover a round tray with crisp parsley. Set bowl of sour cream mixture in the center.

3. Heat skillet until hot enough for a drop of butter to sizzle immediately. Add remainder of butter. Sauté mushrooms on high heat. Season with salt and pepper. Brown mushrooms no more than 2 minutes allowing them to remain slightly firm. Serve immediately by placing them on the bed of parsley around bowl of caviar cream.

4. Guests may help themselves by topping the mushrooms with a dollop of caviar cream. Serves 4 to 6.

Teacher says:

Mushrooms take a short time to cook. If you prefer you may sauté them in the blazer pan of a chafing dish. Sauté 6 or 8 mushroom caps at a time, directly over flame and in full view of guests.

Keep an extra pound of mushrooms, cleaned and ready. You may need them for second helpings!

If you plan to serve a fine caviar, serve it separately from the sour cream (2 dishes).

Beignet ★ ★ ★

1 recipe Pâté a Chou (cream puff paste), unbaked (see index).

Cheese Beignets: Add ¼ pound grated sharp cheddar cheese, 2 tablespoons Parmesan cheese, ¼ teaspoon salt to 1 cup cream puff paste.

Shrimp Beignets: Dice fine 1 pound cooked shrimp. Add 1 tablespoon finely minced scallion, 1 tablespoon chopped parsley, 1 teaspoon soy sauce. Blend mixture into 1 cup of cream puff paste.

1. Grease a cooky sheet with oil. Use a decorating bag fitted with a plain tube from #5 to #9. Fill bag with cheese mixture and pipe ¾″ puffs onto cooky sheet. Do the same with shrimp. Refrigerate for 30 minutes or all day.

2. Heat 1 quart of oil in a deep kettle for frying. Oil should be 400° F.

3. Prepare a serving dish covered with shredded lettuce. Lay out a double thickness of absorbent paper toweling.

4. Just before serving time, remove beignets from refrigerator. Slide one at a time into the hot fat. Do not fry more than 1 dozen at one time. When beignets start puffing up and become light brown, they are finished. Allow 3-4 minutes for each batch.

5. Remove beignets from the oil. Blot them on the paper toweling and arrange them on the shredded lettuce. Serve immediately. Yield: 24 cheese beignets or 24 shrimp beignets.

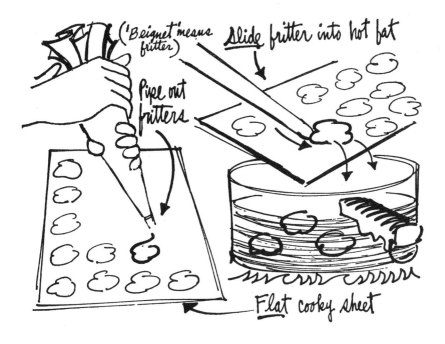

('Beignet' means fritter)

Pipe out fritters

Slide fritter into hot fat

Flat cooky sheet

The onion and the cheese pie are cousins of the "quiche Lorraine." All are excellent as appetizers or main courses for light meals. Preparation is quick because the ingredients are simple. Skip over to Lesson 13; learn the basic pie crusts and you'll forever stock them in your freezer. This onion pie, tremendously popular as accompaniment for broiled steak or roast beef, is always a hit with the men of the house.

Onion Pie

1 tablespoon butter
3 large onions, sliced
3 tablespoons flour
½ cup light cream
¼ teaspoon salt

¼ teaspoon pepper
2 eggs
1 unbaked 8-inch pie pastry
  (see index)

Preheat oven to 400° F. Melt butter in skillet. Sauté onions until they are translucent. Sprinkle flour on onions and stir. Blend in light cream and seasonings and remove from flame. Beat eggs. Add eggs to the onions and pour mixture into pie pastry. Bake for 45 minutes at 400° F. Serves 8.

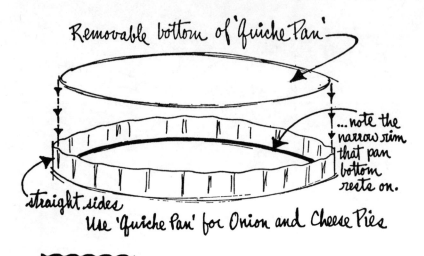

Removable bottom of 'quiche Pan'

...note the narrow rim that pan bottom rests on.

straight sides

Use 'Quiche Pan' for Onion and Cheese Pies

Cheese Pie

½ pound sharp cheddar cheese
1 tablespoon flour
3 eggs
1 cup cream
½ teaspoon salt

¼ teaspoon pepper
1 unbaked 9-inch pie pastry
  or 10-inch flat scalloped quiche
  pan, pastry lined

Preheat oven to 400° F. Grate cheese and stir in flour. Beat eggs. Stir cream and seasonings into eggs. Line the bottom of pastry with the cheese. Pour on eggs and cream. Bake at 400° F. for 35 minutes. Serves 8.

Cheese Tartlettes

1 recipe Basic Pie Pastry (see index)
4 eggs
6 ounces Swiss cheese
  (grated or thinly diced)
4 ounces sharp cheddar cheese,
  grated

2 tablespoons Parmesan, grated
1 teaspoon flour
⅔ cup milk
¾ teaspoon salt
¼ teaspoon pepper
¼ teaspoon nutmeg

Preheat oven to 425° F. Roll dough quite thin. Line tiny (1½") muffin tins with pastry. Refrigerate or freeze. Beat eggs slightly. Add all the other ingredients and stir briskly. Fill shells ⅔ full. Bake 15 minutes at 425° F. If pastry was frozen allow another five minutes in oven. Yield: 4 dozen tartlettes.

APPETIZER QUESTIONS ANSWERED

Q *How long will the wine cheese pot keep?*
A Refrigerated, it keeps well up to 3 weeks. The cheese mixtures that contain sharp cheese keep well for a long period. Freshen them with a small amount of sharp cheese as the supply runs down.

Q *What do you think of frozen sea food and fish?*
A Freezing causes some loss of flavor in fish. Frozen products may be used to advantage in salads or in hot hors d'ouevres where they are mixed in dressings or sauces.

Freezing is an advantage in the summer. For the preparation of any of my buffet platters using shrimp, I cook the shrimp, cool them rapidly and freeze them (only for one or two days). When ready to arrange my tray, I place the frozen shrimp and allow them to defrost on the platter before serving.

Q *Which crabmeat is best in appetizers?*
A Our own Maryland crabmeat is certainly superior. However, when it is not available use the best canned or frozen crabmeat.

Q *Can the beignets be prepared for guests well in advance?*
A No. However, they may be individually placed raw on a pan 24 hours in advance if desired, ready to be slid into the hot fat. They cannot be fried until they are ready to be eaten.

Q *Can the Artichokes á la Grecque be served hot?*
A Yes, they make a good hot appetizer as served from a chafing dish. They may also be used as a hot vegetable, excellent with a lamb dinner.

Q *When pepper is mentioned in a recipe does it mean white or black?*
A When pepper is called for in my recipes, I always mean black unless white is specified. White pepper is the inner kernel of the black and is used for white sauces and stocks. In both cases, I use a grinder. Freshly ground pepper has considerably more flavor.

LESSON 2

The Soup

Let us turn our thoughts to the old-fashioned soup pot which has literally disappeared from the back of the stove. No other food (except yeast bread) lends such warmth and satisfying aroma to a home. Also no other food is more essential to fine cooking than the broth or soup stock.

The basic soup stock is father and mother to all of the wonderful sauces and gravies in classic French cuisine. On its own, soup stock can be turned into a simple vegetable broth, a hearty chowder or a delicate sparkling clear consommé.

In our American kitchens, where the *saucier, potager* and *chef de cuisine* are the same woman who drives Junior to Cub Scout meetings, it may often be more practical to rely on canned broths and stocks. Canned and dehydrated stocks all vary in flavor but the good ones are excellent substitutes for homemade broths. They may be used successfully for the soup recipes in this lesson.

Making stock

    1. Supply yourself with a 6- or 8-quart covered soup pot.
    2. A good-flavored homemade stock will depend on the propor-

Skim with spoon lightly.

Remove the 'scum' that forms after soup has cooked for a short time.

tion of meat or chicken to water used. The seasoning should be subtly enhanced with vegetables such as onions, leeks, carrots, celery and parsley (Italian parsley is very good). Be light-handed with the green vegetables; do not add more than the recipe calls for; they have a tendency to color the soup!

3. Only a small amount of salt is added at the start because in cooking the liquid reduces somewhat and so the soup becomes saltier. It is always best to adjust the salt before serving.

4. Stock is always started with cold water. The flavor of the meat or chicken is extracted by lightly salted cold water. Hot water seals the surface of the meat or chicken preventing the release of its full flavor.

5. As the water comes to a boil a certain insoluble substance called scum rises to the top. If a very clear soup is desired, carefully remove the scum. These substances actually have nutritional value so in making hearty soups, do not skim.

6. After soup comes to a boil, cover it and bring it to a simmer.

7. Broths may be made stronger and more delicious if a combination of beef, veal and chicken is used.

8. Even in the smallest household, chicken necks, wings, gizzards and backs can be accumulated little by little. Freeze them as they collect. They make excellent additions to every soup pot. By themselves they will make a fine chicken broth.

9. Veal knuckles, marrow bones, chicken bones and chicken feet give soups tremendous flavor. They also provide the gelatinous substance necessary for aspics. These broths, when clarified, will jell without the use of gelatin.

10. To prepare a light or white stock, use only veal and chicken with their bones.

11. To prepare a brown stock it is best to use some beef. On a baking pan, brown the bones (some beef too if you wish), sliced carrots and onions (400° F.) for 45 minutes. Proceed with the basic directions for beef broth but be sure to deglaze (extract brownness from) the browned pan with 1 cup (reserved from recipe) of boiling water.

〜〜〜〜〜

Beef Broth

2 pounds shin of beef, lean flank,   1 stalk celery, with top leaves
   chuck or round, if you plan to   1 onion, studded with 2 cloves
   eat the beef   2 leeks, cut lengthwise
2 beef bones   for easy cleaning
2 veal bones   1 bay leaf
1 quart cold water   1 teaspoon salt
1 carrot   ¼ teaspoon white pepper
2 sprigs curly parsley
   or Italian parsley

1. Place everything in a heavy soup pot that has a tight cover. With pot uncovered, bring to a boil.

2. As scum comes to the top, skim it off with a large spoon. If you are not seeking a totally clear soup, allow scum to remain because it contains valuable nutrients.

3. Cover pot, reduce heat to a simmer and cook for 3 hours. If meat is to be eaten, remove it when it is tender.

4. Strain soup to discard bones and vegetables. If soup is too concentrated you may have to add water. If not concentrated enough, cook it down slightly.

5. Always adjust seasoning before ready to serve. Soup improves when reheated the second or third day after cooking. Serves 6.

Pot au Feu

After ten centuries, Frenchmen still acclaim Pot-au-Feu as one of their great soups. Literally it is a Basic Beef Broth. Use the better cut of beef (as listed in the recipe) if you are planning to make a meal of it. Twenty minutes before dining you may wish to add potatoes, green beans or other vegetables to the soup pot. Meat and vegetables may be served in one large soup bowl or separately from the soup.

Petite Marmite

In the French home, the quantity of Basic Beef Broth could easily be doubled or tripled, for, on the following day, a fresh chicken would be cooked in the beef broth. This soup becomes the well known Petite Marmite. With the timesaving element always in mind, my first instinct would be to cook the chicken with the beef. Refrigerate the chicken for another day's dinner (Chicken with Almonds, Festive Chicken Salad, etc.).

The one-course soup meal is simple for the cook and a great gift for busy women. It needs attention only at the beginning, until the water comes to a boil. Always slow the boiling liquid down to a simmer, cover it and you are free for several hours; best of all your dinner is complete!

Consommé

4 cups strained beef broth (fat removed)	¼ cup wine (red or white)
¼ cup ground beef	1 fresh tomato, cut up
	1 cup cold water

Place all ingredients except water into a soup pot. Bring to a boil and skim. Cover pot, simmer for 1 hour. Add cold water. Bring to a boil uncovered. Skim again. Cover and cook 30 minutes. Strain through a fine strainer covered with triple thickness cheese cloth.

To clarify consommé: First adjust seasoning. Beat 1 egg white till frothy. Add egg white and broken shell to soup. Beating constantly, bring soup to a boil. Cook for a few minutes. Strain again as above. The soup should now be clear. Serves 6 to 8.

Onion Soup

4 tablespoons butter
4 large onions, sliced thin
4 cups beef broth, hot
2 slices Swiss or gruyere cheese,
  cut in strips

⅓ cup freshly grated Parmesan
  cheese
4 ½-inch slices toasted French bread

Melt butter in skillet and brown onions. Add hot broth to onions. Hot broth extracts the flavor and color from the onions to make the soup very tasty. Add Swiss cheese and 1 tablespoon Parmesan cheese. Divide into 4 oven soup bowls. Bake in 350° F. oven for 30 minutes. Soup may also be baked in one casserole and divided later. Serve topped with toasted croutons. Pass the Parmesan! Serves 4 generously.

Vegetable Barley Soup, a Robust Winter Meal

4 cups beef broth
¼ cup medium barley, washed
1 stalk celery, finely diced
1 carrot, finely diced
4 pieces dried mushroom
1 onion finely diced

1 potato, finely diced
1 turnip, finely diced
1 cup mixed green vegetables
  (peas, green beans)
1 teaspoon salt
½ teaspoon pepper

Place all ingredients into soup pot except peas and green beans. Bring to a boil and skim off scum. Add green vegetables and simmer for 20 minutes more. Taste and adjust seasoning before serving. Serves 6.

Black Mushroom Soup for a Diet Luncheon

6 Chinese black mushrooms,
  soaked 1 hour in ⅓ cup
  warm water
4 cups strong, clear beef broth

⅓ cup Madeira wine
1 tablespoon cornstarch diluted with
  2 tablespoons cold water
  (optional)

When mushrooms are soft, slice thin. (Do not use water that mushrooms soaked in. Save to use another time for a soup or sauce.) Boil up broth with mushrooms and wine for 30 minutes. Thicken soup slightly with cornstarch mixture if desired. Serves 6.

Chicken Broth

4- to 6-pound fowl or
   roasting chicken
extra necks, backs and gizzards
2 veal bones
4 cups water
1 stalk celery with leaves

2 sprigs parsley
1 onion
1 carrot
1 teaspoon salt
4 peppercorns

Place everything in a large soup pot. Bring to a boil slowly. Skim off the scum if you desire a clear soup. Cook chicken until tender (1 hour for roaster). Fowl may take 2 to 3 hours. Remove chicken when tender. Cook soup for 3 hours. Strain through a strainer covered with triple-thickness cheesecloth. Discard vegetables, bones and chicken extras. Adjust seasoning when ready to serve. Serves 6.

Teacher says:

Chicken broth makes a superior base for most cream soups. A cup of puréed vegetable, 2 cups of chicken broth, 2 egg yolks (or 3 table-spoons flour), 1 cup cream, heat, and presto, a delicious soup is born!

Chestnut Soup ★ ★ ★

2 tablespoons butter
1 onion diced fine
1 pound cooked chestnuts
   (2 cups canned purée of chestnut)
4 cups chicken soup, hot
1 stalk celery

1 carrot, cut in slices
1 sprig parsley
2 tablespoons of Madeira
   or sherry wine
2 tablespoons heavy cream

Melt butter in soup pot. Sauté onions until golden brown. Add cooked or canned chestnuts and sauté for 2 minutes. Pour hot soup into pot. Add celery, carrot and parsley. Cover and simmer for 45 minutes. Put entire mixture in blender or through a Foley food mill. Heat again in soup pot. Blend in wine and heavy cream before serving. Have more wine on the table for those who wish! Serves 8.

~~~~~~~

Cheddar Soup, a Meal in Itself

2 tablespoons butter
1 onion, finely diced
1 carrot, finely diced
1 stalk celery, finely diced
3 tablespoons flour
1 tablespoon cornstarch
2 cups chicken stock,
  combined and heated

  with 2 cups milk
1 cup grated cheddar cheese
⅛ teaspoon baking soda
¾ teaspoon salt
⅛ teaspoon pepper
1 tablespoon chives, chopped
1 tablespoon parsley, finely chopped

Melt butter in a heavy soup pot. Add vegetables and sauté until vegetables are golden and slightly cooked. Add flour and cornstarch to vegetables. Stir well and gradually add combined stock and milk. Cook until mixture thickens. Blend in cheese, baking soda, seasonings and herbs. Heat to melt cheese. Serve immediately with freshly made melba toast. Serves 8.

For a complete meal: Serve Cheddar Soup with hot crusty bread, a chef's salad, fruit, cookies and coffee.

~~~~~~~

This next soup is enough to baffle the most detecting palate. Some of my students look rather shocked at the thought of walnut soup but after the first taste, the shock turns into a demand for a second helping.

Walnut Soup

2 tablespoons butter
3 tablespoons flour
4 cups chicken broth
½ teaspoon salt
⅛ teaspoon pepper

1 bay leaf
¼ teaspoon curry powder
¾ cup chopped walnuts
1 cup medium cream

Melt butter in soup pot. Stir in flour. Add broth gradually and then seasonings. Add walnuts and cream. Cook for 20 minutes. Serve immediately or set aside to reheat. Serves 8.

Fill scooped-out pumpkin with soup

Replace top before setting on table

Pumpkin soup is hearty fare through fall and winter. It too is built on the chicken soup base and is surprisingly delicious!

Pumpkin Soup

2 tablespoons butter
1 onion, finely diced
2 stalks celery, finely diced
1 carrot, sliced
2 tablespoons flour
1 cup cooked and puréed pumpkin

3 cups chicken broth
½ teaspoon salt
⅛ teaspoon white pepper
pinch of sugar
½ cup whipped cream

Melt butter in a soup pot. Sauté onion until golden brown. Add celery and carrot; cook for 1 minute. Remove from flame. Blend in flour well. Add pumpkin and then gradually add broth and seasonings. Return to flame; bring soup to a boil uncovered. Cover and simmer for 30 minutes. Purée all in a blender or Foley mill. To serve, turn on broiler. Pour soup into individual soup pots. Place 1 tablespoon of whipped cream on each and set under broiler for about 30 seconds. Cream will bubble and brown. Serve immediately. For a novel idea, serve in a scooped-out pumpkin, which is used as a tureen and brought to the table. Serves 6.

Fish broth makes a wonderful basic stock for fish chowders, bisques and sauces. When I was a child, my mother cooked this basic soup with fresh pike, sweet butter, sliced potatoes, onions and carrots—a most delicious one-course dinner.

Fish Broth

3- to 4-pounds fish, or fish bones,
   heads and scraps
6 cups water
2 onions sliced
2 stalks celery
1 carrot sliced
2 sprigs parsley

1 clove
3 tablespoons lemon juice
   or ¼ cup white wine
2 teaspoons salt
4 peppercorns
1 bayleaf

Place all into a soup pot, bring to a boil and skim off scum. Cover pot and simmer gently for 1½ hours. If fish is being used for a meal, remove it when it flakes easily. Strain broth through a fine strainer covered with triple thickness of cheesecloth. Discard all vegetables and bones. Fish broth can be used in fish sauces, bisques, bouillabaisse and aspics. Yield: 4 to 5 cups. Serves 6.

Store this in the freezer for that unexpected very important person.

Shrimp Bisque

2 tablespoons butter
1 shallot, chopped fine
   or 2 tablespoons minced onion
1 pound shrimp, cooked and diced
   fine (reserve 2 tablespoons)
2 tablespoons flour
2 cups chicken broth, heated with

1 cup fish stock
2 egg yolks
1 cup cream
2 tablespoons sherry
½ teaspoon salt
¼ teaspoon white pepper
1 tablespoon chopped parsley

1. Melt butter in soup pot. Sauté shallot for 1 minute and add shrimp, chopped fine. Stir in flour.

2. Pour combined broth and fish stock into mixture gradually. Cook until soup thickens slightly. Continue cooking over a low flame for about 5 minutes. Blend soup in electric blender for 1 minute or strain through Foley food mill. Return to pot.

3. Stir egg yolks well. Add cream to yolks very gradually.

4. Blend egg yolks and cream mixture into warm soup, stirring constantly. This will enrich and thicken soup. Season with wine, salt and pepper. Strain soup through a fine strainer.

5. At this point the soup can wait. When ready to serve bring soup to a boil and serve immediately. Garnish each bowl with a sprinkling of finely diced shrimp and chopped parsley. Serves 4.

SOUP QUESTIONS ANSWERED

Q *Must we use the exact ingredients and amounts you give in soup making?*
A Certainly not, use the general directions for soup and you can't go wrong. Go heavy on the meat and bones and light on the vegetables (vegetables color the soup) and seasoning. Experience and personal taste will eventually provide you with the best recipe.

Q *Is it necessary to spend three hours to cook soup?*
A Yes, it takes time for the flavor of meats, vegetables and bones to flavor water. Long simmering seems to do this best.

Q *The term broth, stock, bouillon, consommé are always used as though they are the same. Are they?*
A Broth, stock, bouillon are terms that may be used interchangeably. They all refer to the tasty liquid that results from cooking meats and vegetables together. Broth and bouillon mean soups served from the pot without further cooking. When the same broth or bouillon is used as the base for soups or sauces it is generally referred to as stock. Stock becomes a consommé when it is further enriched and generally clarified.

Q *How long can soups be kept in the refrigerator?*
A If soups are stored in clean containers, they should keep up to a week in the refrigerator. Be sure to leave a small amount of fat in the soup. When cool the fat will rise to the top and form a protective layer to guard against air. If you are in doubt about stored soup, simmer it for 20 minutes and taste it.

Q *Can all soups be frozen?*
A Yes, all soups freeze well. This is a tremendous help for the person who enjoys making large quantities. If freezer space is limited concentrate your stocks. Freeze them in plastic ice cube containers. Remove when frozen and package each cube individually or in plastic bags. When ready to serve, add enough boiling water to dilute frozen cube to desired strength. Poppy Cannon, who was a guest speaker at my cooking class, gave my students many helpful ideas, including this.

LESSON 3

The Sauce

Our constant yardstick for fine cooking is the great French cuisine. In the fine French restaurant or hotel, the saucier or head sauce chef is a most highly esteemed personage. It is no wonder; sauces play such an important role in every phase of cookery. Sauces may be gravies. They may be vegetable sauces. They may be pan sauces, salad dressings and dessert sauces. Interestingly enough (and this I learned as my experience increased) all sauces employ the same basic techniques. The more subtle sauces are no more complex than the simple ones. Techniques remain the same, ingredients change. Various herbs and wines will afford you tremendous variety in seasonings. You will find that creating your own combinations is great fun and not at all difficult.

Be aware of these primary facts:

Utensils are important for producing a fine sauce. You will need a heavy saucepan, a wooden spoon and the indispensable wire whisk. A heavy saucepan will prevent burning (sauces scorch easily). The wooden spoon is used for stirring while sauce is cooking. The whisk is used to blend in liquid and to remove lumps if they appear.

The best quality and the most flavorful ingredients should be used for sauces. The three ingredients most important to a sauce are butter, cream and good stock. (Stocks are discussed in Lesson 2.) Butter and cream add flavor and texture to both white and brown sauces. Use light cream if cream is part of the liquid used in the sauce. Use heavy cream if it is added at the end. This addition of heavy cream adds richness and a beautiful smooth texture. Very often a pat of butter is added to a brown sauce just before serving. Swirl the butter in the pan at the last minute and remove the pan from the heat. If the butter is just allowed to melt without stirring, it thickens the sauce slightly.

Several thickening agents for sauces are flour, cornstarch, potato starch, arrowroot and egg yolks. Flour produces an opaque sauce such as the white cream sauce, and American and German gravies. Cornstarch, potato starch and arrowroot thicken sauces to give a translucent appearance. These are the glaze type sauces that the French use to coat poultry as well as the fruit sauces they use for desserts. The Chinese use cornstarch as their one thickening agent. Many fine chefs prefer arrowroot flour for a last minute thickening. It is expensive but excellent for fast thickening because it leaves no flour taste.

All sauces are best when cooked down and concentrated somewhat. For this reason you will notice that the yield in each recipe is always less than the original amount of liquid added.

Since I cover only cooked sauces in this lesson, let us learn the various methods for cooking them.

1. *Roux method:* Melt butter in a heavy saucepan and add flour. Stir butter and flour (roux) over a low flame for a minute or two. Remove from heat and add warm liquid gradually. Warm liquid is preferable because it combines easily and quickly with the roux. Beat in liquid gradually at first, using wire whisk. When all the liquid is added, return the saucepan to the flame and cook over low heat till sauce thickens. Cook sauce for at least 5 minutes after it thickens to improve flavor and texture. Stir constantly with your wooden spoon at this point. If any lumps appear, use the whisk again or strain the sauce.

2. *Flour or cornstarch:* Work 2 tablespoons flour and ¼ cup cold water into a smooth loose paste. Stir into warm broth or pan gravy. Set on a low flame and continue stirring until gravy (or sauce) is thick; then simmer for another 5 minutes. Use the same method for potato starch and arrowroot flour. These flours blend easily with water. Approximately I tablespoon flour will thicken 1 cup of broth or sauce. For cornstarch, mix 4 tablespoons with ½ cup cold water. Pour into a

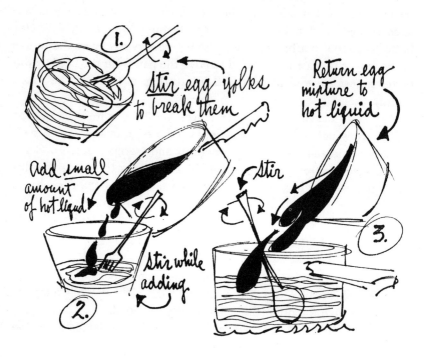

hot broth (or sauce) a little at a time, over very low heat. Stir madly with your whisk. When mixture starts boiling and desired consistency is reached, stop adding the solution. This procedure is used invariably for thickening Oriental dishes.

3. *Beurre Manié:* A quick method for thickening small amounts of sauce. Knead bits of butter and flour into tiny marbles. Use 1 tablespoon butter and 2 tablespoons flour for 1 cup liquid. Toss into warm stock or pan juices a few at a time, over low heat, until they melt smoothly. Continue stirring until sauce is thick and smooth.

4. *Egg Yolks:* If egg yolks are the only thickener, use 2 or 3 yolks for 1 cup of liquid. Stir egg yolks to break them up. Gradually add a small amount of hot liquid to the yolks, until yolks are warm and diluted sufficiently. Return egg mixture to the hot liquid in the saucepan. Stir on a low flame until mixture coats the spoon. If you cannot control the heat, use a double boiler. Sometimes an asbestos pad helps. Sauces thickened with egg yolks must be watched and heated just before serving.

Basic White Sauce

2 tablespoons butter	¼ teaspoon salt
2 tablespoons flour	⅛ teaspoon pepper
1¼ cups warm milk	(preferably white)

1. Melt butter in saucepan. Add flour and stir over low heat for two minutes. (This is a roux.) Take off heat.

2. Gradually stir in ½ cup milk. Pour in remaining milk. Add seasoning.

3. Return to heat and continue stirring with wooden spoon or whisk until mixture thickens and comes to a boil. Cook over very low heat for a few minutes, stirring constantly with spoon. Yield: I cup.

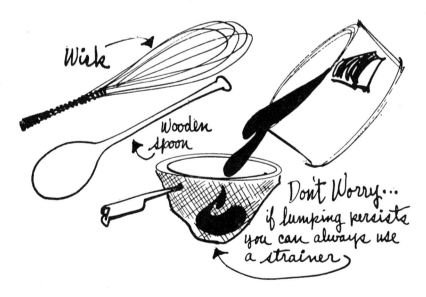

Whisk

Wooden spoon

Don't Worry...
if lumping persists
you can always use
a strainer

Cheese Sauce

Add 4 ounces sharp grated cheese to Basic White Sauce. Good over cooked vegetables or eggs.

Dill Sauce for Fish

Add 4 tablespoons fresh chopped dill and 1 tablespoon chopped parsley to 1 cup Basic White Sauce. Cook over low flame for 5 minutes, then add 2 tablespoons lemon juice.

Horseradish Sauce

Add ½ cup grated fresh horseradish to Basic White Sauce. Blend in 1 tablespoon lemon juice and ½ cup whipped cream. Heat and serve immediately. Try with cold beef.

Mushroom Sauce

Substitute ½ cup mushroom liquid for milk in Basic White Sauce or Rich Cream Sauce. Add 1 cup cooked sliced mushrooms.

~~~~~~~~

Rich Cream Sauce

2 tablespoons butter	¼ teaspoon salt
2 tablespoons flour	⅛ teaspoon pepper (white)
1¼ cup light cream	

Follows directions for Basic White Sauce. Yield: 1 cup.

~~~~~~~~

Mornay Sauce

2 tablespoons butter	1 egg yolk
2 tablespoons flour	¼ cup light cream
1¼ cups warm milk	2 tablespoons grated
¼ teaspoon salt	Parmesan cheese
⅛ teaspoon pepper	

Melt butter. Add flour and stir well. Cook roux for 2 minutes. Take off fire, add warm milk gradually; blend in salt and pepper. Set back on low flame and continue cooking until thick. Cook, stirring constantly for a few minutes. Stir egg yolk with cream. Add a small amount of hot sauce to yolk and cream. Blend this mixture and grated cheese with hot sauce in the saucepan. Cook over low heat till sauce is hot. Adjust seasoning and serve. Yield 1¼ cups.

Velouté Sauce

2 tablespoons butter
2 tablespoons flour

1¼ cups well-seasoned warm chicken broth

Melt butter. Add flour and stir well. Cook roux for 2 minutes on very low heat. Take off fire and add warm chicken broth gradually. Set back on low flame and continue cooking until thick. Cook slowly for 5 minutes stirring constantly. Adjust seasoning to taste. Yield: 1 cup.

Supreme Sauce

Add 3 or 4 tablespoons heavy cream to the Velouté Sauce—a supreme sauce to the last drop!

A brown sauce may be cooked according to the directions for white sauce with a few differences. Butter and flour (roux) must be cooked slowly for flour to turn brown. Care must be taken not to burn the flour. Meat drippings may be used instead of butter.

Simple Brown Sauce

2 tablespoons fat (meat drippings)
1 onion, diced fine
2 tablespoons flour

1½ cups warm beef stock
1 teaspoon tomato paste

1. Heat 2 tablespoons fat in a saucepan. Add onion to fat and brown it lightly. Blend in flour and stir briskly until the roux is brown.
2. Remove saucepan from flame. Add warm stock gradually. Blend in tomato paste and cook over very low heat. Stir until sauce is thickened.

3. Allow sauce to cook until it reduces to about 1 cup in quantity. Brown sauce differs here from white. It should not be stirred after it has thickened. Allow the sauce to simmer and concentrate. It will strengthen in flavor as it cooks and it will darken if it is not stirred too often.

4. Adjust the seasoning. Yield: 1 cup.

Creamy Brown Sauce

Add ½ cup heavy sweet cream to 2 cups Simple Brown Sauce. Excellent for sliced ham, chicken and veal.

Truffle Sauce

Add ½ cup Madeira wine to 2 cups Brown Sauce. Stir in 1 truffle, thinly sliced. Cook for 30 minutes until sauce is reduced to 1½ cups. Blend in 2 tablespoons Madeira wine and 1 tablespoon butter.

Rich Brown Sauce

4 tablespoons butter
1 onion diced
½ pound mushrooms or stems, sliced
1 clove garlic, cut in half
½ pound veal, diced
½ pound beef, diced
1 quart stock

1 tablespoon tomato paste
2 fresh tomatoes, diced
¼ teaspoon allspice
1 bay leaf
1 pinch sugar
6 tablespoons flour
1½ teaspoons salt
¼ teaspoon pepper

1. You will need 1 large skillet and a 2-quart saucepan. Heat butter in skillet. Sauté onion till almost brown, add mushrooms, garlic and meat. Brown all of this slowly.

2. In the meantime, heat stock, tomato paste, tomatoes, allspice, bay leaf and sugar in the saucepan. When meat mixture is browned add the flour and blend it in thoroughly. Cook until flour is lightly browned.

3. Remove skillet from flame and add heated stock gradually to mixture in skillet. When this mixture is well diluted, pour it back into saucepan. Return it to flame and cook until it thickens, stirring constantly. Season with salt and pepper.

4. Cover pan and cook for about 45 minutes. Strain sauce and use as needed. Yield: 3 cups.

Madeira Sauce

Add ¼ cup Madeira wine to 1 cup Rich Brown Sauce.

Quick Brown Sauce

2 tablespoons flour
4 tablespoons water
1 cup beef broth
1 teaspoon Bovril

1 teaspoon tomato paste
1 clove garlic
½ teaspoon dried mushroom powder
(optional)

Blend flour and water to make a smooth mixture (blender may be used). Place all ingredients in a saucepan and allow to thicken. Discard garlic. Yield: 1 cup.

Brown Mushroom Sauce

Sauté 1 small diced onion and ½ pound diced mushrooms until brown. Add onions and mushrooms to 1 cup Quick Brown Sauce. If desired add ¼ cup Madeira or Port Wine.

Ricky's Marinara Sauce

3 tablespoons olive oil
2 cloves garlic, cut in large slices
2¼ cups Italian plum tomatoes,
    mashed

½ teaspoon salt
¼ teaspoon pepper
¼ teaspoon oregano
1 teaspoon chopped parsley

Heat oil in skillet. Sauté garlic for 1 minute. Add tomatoes and cook for 5 minutes. Add seasonings and herbs. Use this sauce with Lobster Fra Diavolo or with pasta dishes. Yield: 2 cups.

Portugaise Sauce

2 tablespoons butter
1 shallot, finely diced
  or 2 tablespoons diced onion
1 teaspoon flour
¼ cup red or white wine
2 tomatoes, peeled, seeded
  and chopped

½ cup tomato purée
1 tablespoon chopped parsley
¼ teaspoon salt
⅛ teaspoon pepper
1 teaspoon sugar

Melt butter in saucepan. Sauté shallot for 30 seconds, blend in flour; lower flame and add wine. Cook to reduce liquid slightly. Add tomatoes; cook until soft. Blend in all other ingredients and bring to a boil. Excellent with baked fish.

Hollandaise Sauce

¼ pound butter, cut in 3 pieces
1 tablespoon lemon juice
½ teaspoon salt
¼ teaspoon white pepper

pinch cayenne
3 egg yolks
¼ cup heavy cream (optional)

1. Prepare a saucepan with one inch of warm water. Place an earthenware bowl in the pan (double boiler fashion) over low heat.
2. Place one piece of butter into the bowl with lemon juice, salt, pepper and cayenne. When butter is melted stir in egg yolks briskly.
3. When mixture is blended well, add second piece of butter, beating constantly with a wooden spoon.
4. When mixture starts to thicken add third piece of butter. Continue beating. Mixture should coat the spoon when it is thick. The entire beating time should take no more than 5 to 7 minutes.
5. If sauce seems too thick add cream. Heavy cream is a godsend in a case of curdling. Heavy cream or a teaspoon of boiling water will usually emulsify a mixture that starts curdling.

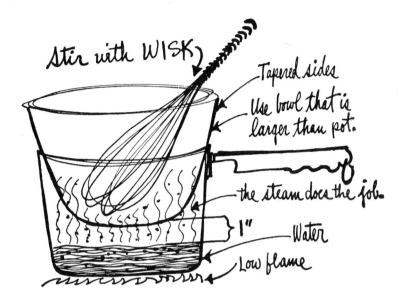

Stir with WISK

Tapered sides
Use bowl that is larger than pot.

the steam does the job.

1"

Water

Low flame

Teacher says:

Remove the psychological fear of Hollandaise. Remember it is only a simple blend of butter and egg yolks to make a creamy cooked sauce. Be aware that the mixture must never boil or you will end up with scrambled eggs.

Prepare the sauce in advance up to and including step 4. Remove bowl from saucepan of water. Continue beating until sauce is slightly cool. Now it can wait.

When ready to serve place bowl over warm water again. Do not permit water to boil hard.

Sauce may be made in the blender (follow blender directions) but you will still need that ever watchful eye when reheating. The blender method is great for cold Hollandaise or one of its variations like Maltaise (orange-flavored Hollandaise). When Poppy Cannon talked to my group about Hollandaise sauces, I arranged a lovely cold vegetable platter for her Maltaise Sauce. It consisted of crisp greens, baby carrots and tiny beets, arranged in groups around a bowl of sauce. Very appetizing for a first course or a cold vegetable.

~~~~~~~

Béarnaise Sauce

1 tablespoon minced shallots
  or onion
1 tablespoon chopped fresh tarragon
  (or 1 teaspoon dried tarragon)
1 tablespoon chopped fresh chervil
  (or 1 teaspoon dried chervil)
2 tablespoons white wine

2 tablespoons tarragon vinegar
¼ teaspoon salt
⅛ teaspoon freshly ground pepper
pinch cayenne
1 recipe Hollandaise Sauce
  (preceding recipe)

Simmer all the ingredients (except the Hollandaise Sauce) until moisture is reduced in half. Set aside to cool slightly. Prepare Hollandaise Sauce. Add cooled herb mixture to the sauce.

SAUCE QUESTIONS ANSWERED

Q *May I use margarine for a cream sauce?*
A I do not advise substitution of margarine here (unless for health reasons). The quality of sauces depends greatly on the fine flavor of butter.
Q *What can I do for a lumpy sauce?*
A Our precious wire whisk usually erases all lumps. If not, strain your sauce.
Q *Why are some sauces so unappetizing in appearance and floury in taste?*
A Sauce takes slow cooking, constant stirring and a certain amount of watchful care. If the roux is not carefully cooked or the sauce is not allowed to simmer gently after it has thickened, the flour may not be thoroughly cooked.
Q *Since sauce making does require time, can it be done in advance?*
A Yes, basic white and brown sauces may be cooked in bulk. Package it for the freezer in desirable quantities. White sauces may be stored in the refrigerator up to 2 days. Brown sauce may be kept in the refrigerator up to a week if a thin layer of fat protects the top.
Q *Very often in fine restaurants foods are coated with a sauce and browned to a lovely color. What type of sauce is this?*
A Sometimes this is a Mornay Sauce. Occasionally a Hollandaise Sauce is used. Very often a few tablespoons of whipped cream are

added to either the Mornay or Hollandaise sauce. This coating is delicious and makes a shiny bubbly surface when placed under the broiler for 30 seconds.

Q *When should wine be added to a sauce, during cooking or at the end?*

A Wine may be added at both times. When it is added during cooking its flavor does dissipate somewhat so that an added small amount is necessary at the end. As a rule wine is added at the finish of a white sauce; for a brown sauce it is generally cooked with the brown sauce.

Q *Shall I buy cooking wines for these sauces?*

A There should be *no* wine called *cooking* wine. Wine that is used in cooking should be pleasing to one's palate too. The flavor will come through. It is wise (for the budget) to remember that wine used during cooking does not have to be vintage or high quality wine. Use an average quality wine but make sure you like the taste. Wine added at the finish of cooking time, should be a fine quality wine.

Q *Why are some white sauces so lacking in flavor? What seasonings can be used to spark the flavor?*

A Milk and flour are bland so that white sauces can be tasteless if they are not seasoned properly. First taste sauce at the end of cooking to adjust salt and pepper. Worcestershire sauce, dry mustard, paprika, a pinch of cayenne are seasonings that add zest to white sauces. Recipes throughout the book use many seasonings, herbs and wines. Your experience will grow with every new dish.

LESSON 4

The Omelet

Of all the staple foods, the egg is above all my dearest friend. I should hate to be without it. There is no other one ingredient that can magically turn into a first course, an entrée or a dessert. The omelet makes one of the happiest and most successful of all cooking lessons.

Read these suggestions carefully before you engage yourself in omelet making.

1. Buy a heavy skillet with curved sides. An 8″ skillet is the most useful size. Use it only for omelets. You will find this your greatest help.

2. If possible, never wash inside of omelet pan. Wipe it with a cloth. This will be your insurance against sticking.

3. Occasionally a filling mixture will melt through on to the pan and cause a sticky substance. Sprinkle salt on the skillet and wipe smooth with paper toweling.

4. Be sure to heat your skillet slowly so that heat is evenly distributed. I sometimes place my skillet on a low flame a good 10 minutes before I am ready to start my omelets. The skillet should be hot enough to sizzle butter without browning it.

5. This omelet recipe is a simple one but it is the dexterity in handling that will make a perfect omelet.

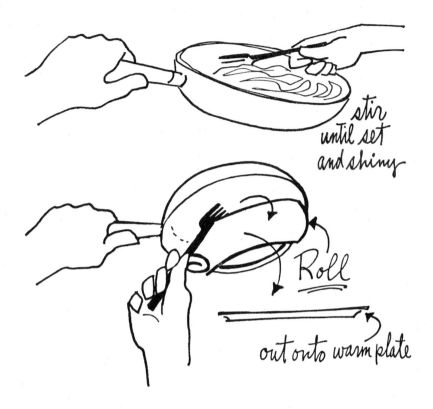

stir until set and shiny

Roll

out onto warm plate

6. Remember, if you prepare a 2-egg omelet in a six-inch skillet you will have a fluffier, higher omelet than if you prepare the same 2-egg omelet in a 10-inch skillet. Do not make omelets with more than 3 or 4 eggs.

7. Do not use a beater. Break eggs and stir with a fork just enough to combine yolks and whites.

8. The final taste will depend on the quality of your eggs and the swiftness of preparation. The omelet should be soft and delicate.

9. It is possible to serve 4 omelets family style. Make each omelet and place on a large ovenproof platter. Keep heated in a 250° F. oven. When all four are finished place under broiler for 30 seconds.

10. A breakfast omelet may be "just eggs." The lunch and dinner omelets are heartier when filled. The dessert omelets make good breakfast and luncheon dishes as well as desserts.

Basic Omelet

2 or 3 eggs
¼ teaspoon salt

1 teaspoon water
1 teaspoon butter

1. Heat pan slowly. Test pan by dropping ½ teaspoon butter into pan. If butter sizzles immediately without browning, then the pan is ready. If butter blackens, then pan is too hot. Lower flame or remove pan from flame for a minute.

2. When pan is ready, stir water and salt into eggs just enough to combine yolks and whites.

3. Drop a teaspoon of butter into pan. Holding the handle of skillet with your left hand pour eggs into pan. Continue to stir eggs in pan with right hand, while tilting pan with left. This allows all the moisture to run to the sides. You will notice that in a few seconds, the egg is set and shiny. Stop stirring!

4. Place desired filling or sauce down the center. Cook for 1 minute. Roll omelet off the pan to a warm dish.

5. Eggs should be eaten moist and soft so that your omelet literally takes no more than 2 minutes to cook. If you have a rebel who insists on dry eggs, fill and roll up in the pan. Cook the omelet for another minute. If he insists on a brown omelet, pop it under the broiler for ½ minute. The 2-egg omelet yields a dinner serving for one person. A 3-egg omelet may serve 2.

Herb Omelet

Chop very fine 1 tablespoon each of fresh chives, parsley and chervil. Stir herbs into eggs and proceed as in cooking directions. Use only herbs whose flavors you enjoy. If only the dried variety are available then use ½ teaspoon of each, but spark the flavor with 2 tablespoons chopped fresh spinach. Yield: 1 omelet.

Cheese Omelet

Cook omelet as directed and when omelet is set, sprinkle 2 tablespoons of grated cheese down the center. Allow it to melt slightly. Fold and serve. A combination of cheddar and Gruyere cheese is excellent. Before serving try sprinkling a tablespoon of freshly grated Parmesan over top of omelet and place it under the broiler for ½ minute. Yield: 1 omelet.

Ham Omelet

Just before eggs set completely sprinkle ¼ cup finely chopped ham over omelet. Fold and serve. Yield: 1 omelet.

Country Omelet

Dice finely 1 small onion, ½ green pepper, 1 stalk celery, 1 small tomato and 2 tablespoons smoked meat (ham, salami or sausage).

Before eggs are completely set, sprinkle mixture of the above over the omelet. Allow it to cook for at least a minute or two. Fold over and serve. Yield: 2 omelets.

Country Omelet Encore

Dice finely 1 scallion, 1 small green pepper, 1 tablespoon parsley, ¼ cup ham. Add these ingredients to eggs in the bowl and then pour mixture into omelet pan. Continue as for regular omelet. Yield: 2 omelets.

~~~~~~~~

Spanish Omelet

2 tablespoons butter	2 tablespoons tomato sauce
2 onions, chopped	1 tablespoon chopped parsley
8 mushrooms, sliced	1 tablespoon flour
1 stalk celery diced	½ teaspoon salt
½ green pepper, diced	⅛ teaspoon sugar
1 fresh tomato, diced	¼ teaspoon pepper

In a saucepan, sauté chopped onion in 1 tablespoon butter until brown. Add mushrooms, celery, green pepper, tomato, tomato sauce and parsley. Cover and cook for 3 minutes. Remove pan from flame, sprinkle flour over vegetables and blend. Add seasonings and cook on low flame while stirring. Adjust seasoning. Place part of this sauce down center of omelet when eggs set in skillet. Serve omelet topped with remainder of sauce. Yield: 2 omelets.

Mushroom Omelet

Sauté 1 finely diced onion in 1 tablespoon butter until brown. Add 1 cup of sliced mushrooms. Sauté for 2 minutes or cover pan and steam mushrooms. Remove from flame and sprinkle 1 teaspoon of flour over mushrooms. Blend together; add 2 tablespoons of milk and set pan on flame to continue cooking for a few minutes until mixture thickens. Season with salt, pepper, ¼ teaspoon paprika, ½ teaspoon Bovril. Use as filling for omelet. Yield: 1 omelet.

Mushroom Omelet Supreme

Proceed as above but omit flour. Add 4 tablespoons heavy sweet cream and 2 tablespoons sherry to sautéed mushrooms. Cook liquid down until almost completely absorbed. Fill omelet with this mixture for a fine treat. Yield: 1 omelet.

Chicken Liver Omelet

Cut 4 chicken livers into 2 or 3 pieces each. Sprinkle chicken livers with 1 teaspoon soy sauce and 1 teaspoon Worcestershire sauce. Sauté 1 chopped onion in 1 tablespoon butter until brown. Add livers and stir with wooden spoon until livers are brown on the outside but slightly pink inside. Proceed as with other omelets. Place livers down center, fold and serve. Yield: 1 omelet.

Cream Cheese Omelet

Soften 1½ ounces of cream cheese with 1 tablespoon chopped chives and mix with beaten eggs. Stir briskly and pour into skillet. When set, cover tightly and cook for 2 or 3 minutes. Fold and serve. This makes a drier fluffy omelet. Yield: 1 omelet.

My Favorite Omelet

Stir 1 tablespoon each of chopped chives and parsley into ¼ cup sour cream at room temperature. Prepare regular omelet. Just before folding place sour cream mixture down center. Roll on to serving dish. Garnish with a necklace of red caviar around omelet and a crisp full sprig of watercress.

Dessert Omelet

Prepare regular omelet, fill with your favorite jam or fresh berries. Fold and place on serving platter. Sprinkle with powdered sugar. Flame with brandy if desired.

Dessert Cream Cheese Omelet ★ ★ ★

Soften 1½ ounces of cream cheese and stir into regular omelet mixture. Stir briskly and pour into skillet. When set, cover for 3 minutes. Place fresh berries or your favorite jam down center and fold omelet. Slip on to heated plate. Sprinkle all over with powdered sugar. Warm kirsch (cherry brandy) in a small pan. Put a flame to it and pour over omelet.

OMELET QUESTIONS ANSWERED

Q *How do you measure a skillet?*
A I measure it across the bottom so that I know the final size of the omelet or pancake. An eight-inch skillet measures 8″ across the bottom of pan.
Q *According to the French, omelets should be moist but I like them dry. Is there a happy compromise?*
A Yes, I think so. If the omelet is made properly, it is a delicate soft dish not necessarily wet. For more dryness, place omelet under broiler for 30 seconds.
Q *Wouldn't a rotary beater make the eggs fluffier?*
A No, beating the eggs too much makes them heavy and watery.
Q *May I use milk instead of water for the omelet?*
A You may. Water supplies the moisture needed for tenderness; I prefer it to milk.
Q *How is the fluffy omelet made?*
A The fluffy omelet is more like a soufflé. At least 3 or 4 eggs are separated. Yolks are beaten with a tablespoon of milk and ½ teaspoon salt. Whites are beaten stiff (but not dry) and folded into yolks. Start omelet in a hot buttered skillet but finish cooking in a 400° F. oven for about 6 or 7 minutes.

LESSON 5

The Soufflé

It is hard to understand why the soufflé has built up such a reputation of "Don't try me—I'll be a flop." On the contrary, it is not as temperamental as the rumors imply. The egg, which we've already extolled in our last few lessons, takes on a real importance with the soufflé. The egg is the thing. Become well acquainted with it through the soufflé because so many phases in cooking and baking depend on the egg.

1. Eggs should be fresh and of good quality.

2. Eggs should be room temperature. They are more easily separated when cold but beat up to more volume when warm.

3. Egg whites do beat fluffier when done by hand but I stop at 5 egg whites. Any amount more than five is easier to do with the electric mixer.

4. For soufflé, beat egg whites until they just hold a peak. Stop immediately! The white will still be moist and not as dry as you would beat them for a meringue.

5. Egg whites keep their volume when *folded* by hand into a mixture. They should never be beaten in, even at low speed in the electric mixer. To fold, move your spatula around the side of the bowl from left to right, clockwise, coming underneath mixture in bowl and then over mixture. This movement repeated blends the egg whites in gently.

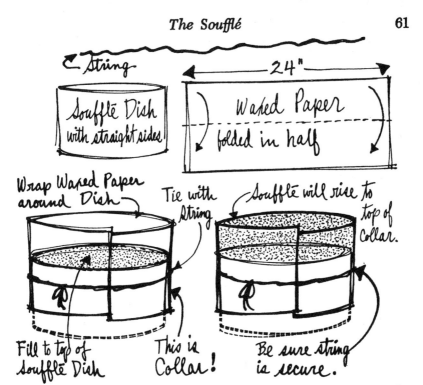

It is best to fold in half the beaten egg whites at a time. Fold the first half in thoroughly; fold the second half in more gently, leaving an occasional white spot.

6. An extra egg white should always be added for lightness.

7. Soufflés are composed approximately of 1 cup cream sauce and 1 cup bulk (vegetable, meat, dessert flavoring, etc.) 4 eggs and 1 extra egg white.

8. The soufflé may be baked in any casserole but the classic soufflé dish is round with perfectly straight sides. Soufflés will rise higher if they are not baked in too large a dish. The proportions given are for a 1-quart soufflé.

9. For a 1-quart soufflé dish, cut a piece of waxed paper 24 inches long. Fold it in half and set it around the outside of your soufflé dish like a collar. Tie it with a string.

10. When using a soufflé dish with a collar, the soufflé mixture should reach to the top of the dish before baking. It will then rise along wax paper sides to make a high crown.

11. If you are using a regular casserole dish, fill it ¾ full and it will rise in a mound above the dish.

12. Soufflés sometimes fall! It doesn't matter, they always taste delicious.

Cheese Soufflé

3 tablespoons butter	¼ teaspoon pepper
3 tablespoons flour	¼ teaspoon dry mustard
1 cup milk	pinch cayenne
1 cup grated sharp cheddar cheese	4 eggs, separated
2 tablespoons Parmesan cheese	1 extra egg white
½ teaspoon salt	

Preheat oven to 375° F. Tie collar around a greased 1-quart soufflé dish. Melt butter in saucepan; add flour to make a roux. Take off flame and add milk gradually. When completely blended return saucepan to flame. Bring mixture to a boil, stirring constantly. When sauce is thickened remove from flame. Add cheeses and all seasonings. Cool slightly. Beat egg yolks with a whisk till light in color. Add to cream mixture. Beat 5 egg whites stiff but not dry. Fold one-half of egg whites into cream mixture until quite well blended. Fold in second half lightly; it is permissible to see a few white globs here and there. Pour into a buttered soufflé dish and bake for 30 minutes at 375° F. Set temperature up to 400° F. for 5 minutes more if you like it very crusty and slightly dry. Serves 4.

Western-Style Soufflé

3 tablespoons butter	¼ teaspoon monosodium glutamate
2 onions, diced	¼ teaspoon soy sauce
2 stalks celery, diced	½ teaspoon salt
1 green pepper, diced	¼ teaspoon pepper
½ cup ham, diced	4 eggs
3 tablespoons flour	1 extra egg white
1 cup milk	

Preheat oven to 375° F. Grease a 1-quart soufflé dish. Melt 1 tablespoon butter in a saucepan and sauté onions until brown. Add celery, green pepper and ham. Cook for 1 minute. Add remainder of butter. Melt it and stir in flour. Lower flame, add milk gradually. Bring mixture to a boil. When thick, remove from flame, add all seasonings and cool slightly. Beat egg yolks with a whisk, till light in color. Add yolks to cream mixture. Beat egg whites stiff but not dry. Fold ½ of whites into cream mixture until blended and then second half. Bake at 375° F. for 35 minutes. Serves 4.

~~~~~~

This lobster soufflé is my version of the one served at Maxim's in Paris. It is an elegant dinner entrée, especially if whole Maine lobster is used. It is ideal and unusual as a hot appetizer or luncheon main course served in individual shells or ramekins.

Lobster Soufflé ★ ★ ★

TO PREPARE SAUCE:

4 tablespoons butter
4 tablespoons flour
1 cup milk
½ cup fish broth

¼ cup sherry
1 teaspoon salt
¼ teaspoon white pepper

Melt butter in saucepan. Stir in flour well. Cook for 1 minute. Remove from flame and gradually add milk, then broth, wine and seasonings. Return to flame and allow sauce to thicken. Cook for 5 minutes stirring constantly, then cool. Yield: 1½ cups.

TO PREPARE LOBSTER MIXTURE:

3 tablespoons butter
½ pound mushrooms, sliced
3 tablespoons cognac
6 lobster tails,
   cooked and cut in chunks
   (4 1-pound lobsters may be used)

1½ cups sauce for soufflé
½ cup heavy sweet cream
¼ teaspoon salt, dash pepper,
   pinch cayenne
3 egg yolks
4 egg whites

1. Melt butter in a skillet. Sauté mushrooms till brown. Pour cognac over mushrooms and flame. Add lobster meat, 1 cup of reserved sauce and heavy cream. Adjust seasoning and simmer for 3 minutes. Spoon into individual dishes or lobster shells. Set aside.

2. Twenty minutes before serving time, set oven at 375° F. Beat yolks until light in color. Combine with remaining ½ cup sauce. Beat egg whites stiff but not dry. Fold into egg mixture. Spread a layer of this mixture to completely cover lobster. Bake for 15 minutes. Serves 4 dinner portions or 12 to 14 appetizer portions.

‹⁓⁓⁓⁓⁓›

My men students who enjoy ruling the kitchen on Sunday mornings use this next recipe for a switch from pancakes and scrambled eggs. It can be placed in the oven to bake while the table is set, coffee is brewing, toast is burning and the family is coralled. No cream sauce used in this one; it all depends on the eggs.

Breakfast Soufflé

¼ pound ham cut in strips
¼ pound Swiss or cheddar cheese,
   cut in strips
6 eggs separated

½ teaspoon salt
¼ teaspoon pepper
⅛ teaspoon dry mustard

    Set oven at 400° F. Grease a 1-quart casserole or soufflé dish. Line the bottom of dish with strips of ham and cheese. Reserve some for the top. Beat egg yolks with a whisk until light in color. Add seasonings. Beat whites until stiff but not dry. Fold one half of whites in beaten yolks, then second half. Do not blend too thoroughly. Pour into buttered dish. Top with remainder of cheese and ham. Bake at 400° F. for 25 minutes. Serves 4.

DESSERT SOUFFLÉS

    Dessert soufflés are sensational for company dinners and wonderful fun for the family, provided that neither group is too large. Most 4-egg recipes serve 4, but sometimes we stretch it to 5. If I'm serving 6, I simply enlarge the recipe by a half as much and make a six- or seven-egg soufflé. Taking liberties seems to matter little; an extra egg can be thrown in for more volume.

    Prepare the cream sauce in advance. Have eggs separated and ready to be beaten. If all ingredients are neatly set out, the last-minute blending and beating accounts for about 3 minutes. Your guests will not miss you for that short time; they'll be anticipating some very special thing.

    For family preparation, I usually do the last-minute beating and folding while the main course is being served around. In this way our dessert soufflé is cooking while we are enjoying dinner. I don't mind because I'm always last to start eating anyway; besides there are times when the joy of cooking is more fun than dinner itself.

Chocolate Soufflé

1 teaspoon butter	1 cup milk
1 tablespoon sugar for soufflé dish	4 egg yolks
4 tablespoons sugar	4 ounces semi-sweet chocolate,
4 tablespoons flour	melted
⅛ teaspoon salt	6 egg whites

1. Butter and sugar a 1-quart soufflé dish; tie a wax paper collar around it. Preheat oven to 375° F.

2. Put sugar, flour and salt in a heavy saucepan. Add milk gradually to make a smooth mixture.

3. Put mixture on low flame to cook. Bring to a boil, stirring constantly. When sauce thickens remove it from flame.

4. Beat egg yolks with a whisk till light in color. Add sauce to yolks gradually and stir briskly.

5. Add melted chocolate to this mixture. The last steps can be done well in advance.

6. Forty minutes before serving time, beat 6 egg whites until stiff but not dry. Fold one-half of whites into chocolate mixture. Finish by folding in remainder of whites (don't hesitate to leave a few white globs).

7. Pour mixture into soufflé dish and bake for 35 minutes if you like a dry soufflé, 30 minutes for a slightly moist soufflé and 25 minutes for a moist soufflé. Serve with whipped cream or the following Rum Sauce. Serves 4.

RUM SAUCE

2 egg yolks	2 tablespoons rum
¼ cup confectioners sugar	¼ cup sweet cream, whipped
1 teaspoon vanilla	

Beat yolks till light in color. Add sugar gradually. Blend in flavorings. Fold in whipped cream.

~~~~~~~

Grand Marnier Soufflé ★ ★ ★

1 teaspoon butter	1 cup milk
1 tablespoon sugar for soufflé dish	5 egg yolks in a large bowl
4 tablespoons sugar	¼ cup Grand Marnier
4 tablespoons flour	finely grated rind of an orange
⅛ teaspoon salt	6 egg whites

1. Grease and sugar a 1-quart soufflé dish. Tie a collar of folded wax paper around it. Preheat oven to 400° F.

2. Mix sugar, flour and salt in a heavy saucepan. Gradually add milk to make a smooth mixture.

3. Set pan on a low flame and bring to a boil, stirring constantly.

4. When mixture thickens, remove from flame. Beat egg yolks with a whisk (in a large bowl). Add hot sauce to egg yolks a little at a time.

5. Stir Grand Marnier and grated orange rind in hot cream sauce. Allow to cool.

6. Forty minutes before serving, beat egg whites stiff, but not dry. Fold in ½ egg whites lightly but thoroughly; fold in the remainder so that occasional white puffs are seen. Bake for 25 to 30 minutes. Serve with the following Sauce au Marrons. Serves 4 to 5.

SAUCE AU MARRONS

1 teaspoon flour	6 marrons in syrup (⅓ cup)
2 tablespoons sugar	1 tablespoon cognac
2 egg yolks	1 cup unsweetened whipped cream
1 cup milk	

Blend flour, sugar and egg yolks in a heavy saucepan. Stir in milk gradually. Set over low flame and cook until mixture coats spoon. Set aside, uncovered, and cool. Occasionally stir it to prevent a film from forming. When mixture is cool, fold in marrons, cognac and whipped cream. Chill thoroughly.

Use a flat oven-proof platter

One spring my husband and I stopped at Amboise to travel the Château area along the Loire River. We arrived at our charming inn to be welcomed by a busy host and hostess. After we had settled, we learned that our visit was perfectly timed. On that very day, Monsieur and Madame Gibaudan had invited the town dignitaries and friends for a champagne christening, celebrating the opening of their newly designed dining room, glass enclosed with a full view of the Loire. That evening we had the specialty for dessert, Soufflé Meringué au Grand Marnier. My questioning brought forth the following recipe—fast and delicious, different because it's practically all egg whites and no custard.

Soufflé Meringué au Grand Marnier

2 egg yolks	4 tablespoons sugar
Butter and sugar for soufflé dish	pinch salt
1 teaspoon grated orange rind	1 tablespoon Grand Marnier
1 teaspoon flour	8 pineapple bits
7 egg whites	2 maraschino cherries, cut in half
	3 tablespoons Grand Marnier

1. Preheat oven at 450° F.

2. Prepare a flat oval oven platter. Butter it and sprinkle with 1 tablespoon sugar.

3. Beat egg yolks till light in color add rind and flour. Set aside.

4. Beat egg whites with salt till frothy. Add sugar gradually till whites are stiff as meringue.

5. Pour egg yolks into whites and fold them gently.

6. Heap meringue on platter in a large mound. Bake for 7 minutes.

7. Remove from oven. Place pineapple and cherries around soufflé. Warm Grand Marnier and ignite. Pour on to fruits and soufflé. Serve at once. Yield: 4 servings.

Note: As a substitute for Grand Marnier use 3 parts Cointreau with 1 part cognac.

SOUFFLÉ QUESTIONS ANSWERED

Q *Can a soufflé be prepared in advance?*
A Many people do prepare it in advance just before guests are due. Pour the batter into a casserole or soufflé dish. Cover it until time to pop it into the oven. The texture and final height of soufflé is slightly different if this method is used. Although I complete all advance preparations, I prefer to beat and combine the egg whites just before baking.

Q *How can soufflés be made for 12 people?*
A Enlarge soufflé recipe to 6 or 7 eggs and other ingredients accordingly. Bake 2 soufflés in 1½ quart dishes. Soufflés made larger than that do not bake properly.

Q *If dinner is detained what can one do with a soufflé in the oven?*
A Soufflés must never be made unless guests are ready and waiting. However, if timing has been miscalculated lower the oven to 350° F. Do not open oven. A tolerance of 10 or 15 minutes can be counted on by reducing the heat.

Q *What do you do with leftover egg yolks?*
A Egg yolks have many uses. Poach egg yolks till hard cooked and use as a garnish on salad.

Use egg yolks for thickening soups and sauces.

Many cooky recipes call for yolks only.

Toss an extra egg yolk into pancake batter.

Egg yolks are excellent in frosting and butter cream.

Q *How do you store egg yolks?*
A If covered well, egg yolks keep in the refrigerator for 2 or 3 days.

If they seem to harden in your refrigerator, cover with cool water and store.

Egg yolks may be frozen. Package them in quantities that you will be most likely to use.

LESSON 6

The Pancake, Crepe and Blintz

When we were little children, the morning fried egg in our house was called the "Pfankuchen." This was sort of a simplification of the French pancake. It was thin, flat and fried on both sides. No flour was used; sometimes a little milk was added. Many years later I discovered that the thin egg pancake could be much improved if a small amount of flour was added to make a batter. The fabulous crepe or "pfankuchen" batter has been a staple food in my house for many years now. Thanks to the French, German, and Scandinavian cuisine, the number of variations for these thin wonders are endless. At first it may seem like work to turn over such fragile pancakes but ease in handling comes with practice. Their versatility is so great that you will have dozens of exciting recipes for breakfast, luncheon, appetizer and dessert dishes. Your enthusiasm will mount with each delicious morsel.

Helpful facts on pancake-making.

1. If you own an electric blender, use it but take just a minute to thoroughly mix batter. Do not overbeat. Without a blender you are wise to beat it by hand and strain it to remove lumps.

2. Allow batter to stand at room temperature for at least 2 hours before using. (I confess that with the blender I have made and served

breakfast pancakes inside of fifteen minutes.) The batter, however, does improve with age. Keep batter in refrigerator up to 4 days.

3. Use a good heavyweight skillet that heats and fries evenly. Choose the size appropriate for the recipe. Usually a 5" or 6" skillet is used for breakfast or dessert pancakes, an 8" skillet for appetizer or luncheon dishes and a 10" skillet for a large apple pancake.

4. Butter the pan with every pancake.

5. Use the same amount of batter for each one to make pancakes uniform. Usually about 2 tablespoons makes a 6" pancake. The less batter the thinner the pancake.

6. Pour batter into pan and tilt pan to roll batter over the surface. The pancake becomes dry on the top side in less than a minute. Slide a narrow spatula under the pancake and turn it.

Don't worry

Repair any holes by adding small amount of batter.

THE PANCAKE

Pancake Batter I

3 eggs	1 teaspoon sugar
¾ cup flour	1 cup milk
⅛ teaspoon salt	2 tablespoons melted butter

1. Beat eggs lightly; add dry ingredients alternately with milk. Add melted butter last.

2. If you own a blender, use it for pancake batters. If not you may have to strain the batter.

3. When time permits allow the batter to stand at least 2 hours before using. The batter seems to make more tender pancakes if it is made one or two days in advance. It keeps well for 4 days in the refrigerator. Makes 20-24 pancakes.

Teacher says:

Pancake Batter I can be used for everything from breakfast pancakes to Crepes Suzette. It is easy to handle in the pan and it stores very well. Most often I make it in double quantity and use it through the week for breakfast pancakes, apple pancake, for one of the different dessert pancakes or even as a base for a soufflé recipe.

~~~~~~~~~

Pancake Batter II

2 eggs
2 egg yolks
1 cup flour
¼ teaspoon salt

1¼ cups milk
1 teaspoon grated orange rind
1 tablespoon Cointreau
2 tablespoons melted butter

1. Beat eggs lightly, add dry ingredients alternately with milk. Add orange rind, Cointreau and butter last.
2. Use blender if available or strain to remove any lumps.
3. Allow batter to rest for 1 or 2 hours before using. This batter also tenderizes with age and may be kept up to 4 days in the refrigerator. Makes 20-22 pancakes.

Teacher says:

Pancake Batter II has the orange flavor and is perfect for Crepes Suzette as well as other dessert pancakes. Try both batters and make your own choice.

TO MAKE PANCAKES

1. Have batter ready. Line the top of your counter with paper toweling.
2. Heat skillet slowly over medium heat. Skillet is ready when a bit of butter sizzles immediately upon touching pan. Use 1 teaspoon butter for each pancake.
3. Melt butter on skillet. Pour in 2 tablespoons of batter. Holding the handle of pan, roll batter around the pan so that it just covers the entire bottom of pan and dries almost immediately. If there seems to be too much wet batter on the pan, tilt pan over bowl of batter and pour back excess.

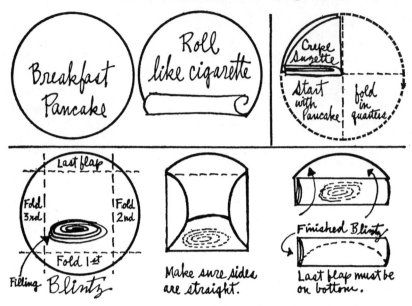

4. When pancake is delicately browned on the underside, turn it over and brown on the other side. Holding the handle of the skillet, quickly turn it over on to absorbent paper. Pancake should fall out.

5. Repeat, making up to the number you wish. Leftover batter may be stored in refrigerator and used another time.

Pancakes for Breakfast

Make pancakes. Fill each one with jam and roll up into tight long rolls. Another morning, sprinkle cinnamon and sugar over pancakes and roll up. If you wish to make them in advance prepare as many as needed. Place on a well buttered baking pan. Bake for 5 minutes at 400° F. just before time to serve. Prepare at least 3 pancakes for each.

THE CREPE

Crepes Fromage

4 ounces Swiss cheese, grated
4 ounces sharp cheddar cheese, grated
4 tablespoons Parmesan cheese, grated
2 tablespoons chopped parsley
1 tablespoon chopped chives

1 teaspoon Worcestershire sauce
⅛ teaspoon freshly ground pepper
12 crepes, 6″ in diameter
4 tablespoons Parmesan cheese and 2 tablespoons butter, crumbled together, for topping

Mix cheeses and seasonings well. Place a full tablespoon on each crepe and roll up tight. Place on a buttered baking sheet. Sprinkle with Parmesan and butter topping. Bake at 400° F. for 10 minutes.

~~~~~~~~

Every version of this sea food delicacy is slightly different. The most popular one refers to a rolled crepe with a wonderful creamy filling, a topping of sauce, and a quick broil.

Crepes Délices

8 crepes made from Pancake Batter I
5 tablespoons butter
1 shallot, diced fine
  or 2 tablespoons minced onion
4 mushrooms, diced fine
6 tablespoons flour
1 cup milk
½ cup chicken broth or fish stock
½ cup cream
¼ teaspoon dry mustard

1 teaspoon salt
½ teaspoon white pepper
1 tablespoon cognac
2 cups combined sea food
  (any mixture of crabmeat,
  lobster, shrimp, scallops)
2 egg yolks
½ cup whipped cream
2 tablespoons Parmesan cheese
2 tablespoons sherry wine

1. Make 8 crepes. Cover well and set aside until ready to fill.

2. Prepare a cream sauce: Melt 2 tablespoons butter in a saucepan. Sauté shallot and mushrooms for 2 minutes. Add remainder of butter. Blend in flour and stir well. Remove from flame and add milk, broth and cream a little at a time. Season with mustard, salt, pepper and cognac. Return to flame and allow sauce to thicken. Cook for 2 or 3 minutes. Remove from flame and cool slightly.

3. Blend sea food with 1½ cups sauce. (Set aside remaining ½ cup of sauce.) Taste and adjust seasoning. Divide mixture between 8 crepes by placing 2 or 3 tablespoons of it along center of each crepe and roll up. Place crepes on a buttered baking pan or set on individual oven dishes (one for hors d'oeuvre portion, two for luncheon or dinner main course). Bake for 10 minutes at 400° F.

4. Stir egg yolks well and slowly add ½ cup cream sauce to yolks. Fold in whipped cream, cheese and sherry. Mask each crepe with reserved sauce. Place under broiler until sauce bubbles and browns (about 1 minute). Serves 4 for main course.

~~~~~~~~~~

Each year I invite gourmet guest lecturers to demonstrate to my classes. This has been a source of great interest to my students, who are always eager for new ideas. We have been round the world of cooking with Grace Chu, Alvin Kerr, Paula Peck, Edith Lattimer, Poppy Cannon and Elaine Ross. The writers, teachers and students in the field share tremendous enthusiasm for each other and for their subject. Friendships seem to spark in minutes when a love for cooking is the common interest. Elaine Ross (one of my first guests) and I became friends from the moment we started talking recipes. Since the crepe is one of my favorites, I was delighted when Elaine suggested Layered Pirog for her demonstration. Her newest book, Small Meals for Company, *includes the Pirog that she did for us.*

~~~~~~~~~~

Layered Pirog

½ cup bulghour
4 hard-cooked eggs
2 large onions
4 tablespoons butter
½ pound mushrooms
1 cup dill, stems removed
   (loosely packed)

5 cups minced chicken
salt, pepper
12 8-inch crepes, fried on one side
4 tablespoons butter, melted
1 lightly beaten egg
3 tablespoons fine, dry breadcrumbs
1 pint sour cream

Filling:

1. Cook bulghour in salted water and drain.

2. Chop eggs fairly fine.

3. Peel and mince the onions. Sauté in 2 tablespoons butter until tender and pale gold.

4. Slice the mushrooms and sauté in 2 tablespoons butter for 5 minutes.

5. Chop the dill.

6. Mix all these ingredients with the chicken. Season with salt and pepper to taste.

To layer the crepes:

1. Butter a 9″ spring form.

2. Place 1 crepe, unfried side down, on the bottom of the spring form.

3. Cut 3 crepes in half and place them around the sides of the form, unfried side out.

4. Dribble some of the melted butter on the crepe, scatter some of the filling on it and cover with another crepe. Repeat until filling, butter and crepes are used up, reserving one crepe for the top.

5. Before you put on the top crepe, tuck in the tops of the crepes lining the sides of the form to make a neat finish. Brush the top with a portion of the beaten egg and sprinkle with bread crumbs. (All this preparation may be done in advance.)

6. Three-quarters of an hour before serving, preheat oven to 450° F. Twenty-five minutes before serving time, place form in oven and bake until piping hot.

7. Remove rim of spring form and place on a platter. Serve with bowl of sour cream separately. Serves 8.

Cheese Pancakes Orange

Prepare 12 pancakes (Batter I or II). Place 1 tablespoon cottage cheese and 1 teaspoon good peach jam in each pancake. Roll them up and set aside. When ready to serve, melt 2 tablespoons butter in a hot skillet. Add 1 cup orange juice and cook for 1 minute. Heat pancakes in juice. Serve immediately. (Of course warmed cognac or Cointreau may always be sprinkled over heated pancakes.) Serves 4.

I've had the pleasure of watching Arnold Reuben's chef make the famous Reuben's pancake, but don't think for a minute that you can duplicate it. The flames fly so high that you would chance burning your house. The grease spatters so far that no pancake would be worth the clean-up. Second best is not bad, so try it this way.

Apple Pancake ★ ★ ★

Prepare Pancake Batter I. Pare and slice a McIntosh apple very thin. Heat a 10-inch skillet and turn on your broiler. Drop 2 table-spoons of butter into the skillet. It should sizzle immediately. Pour in 3 tablespoons batter to just cover bottom. Place thin slices of apples all over pancake. Pour 1 tablespoon of batter over apples. Sprinkle with 1 tablespoon sugar and ⅛ teaspoon cinnamon. Wait for pancake to dry and set all over. Set skillet under broiler (allow handle to hang out of oven) until pancake puffs. Serve immediately. Yield: 1 serving.

Teacher says:

It is not easy to serve Apple Pancakes to guests all at one time. This is somewhat like preparing the omelet. Each serving must be made fresh. Two skillets may be used or each pancake could be transferred to an oven platter for final broiling.

~~~~~~~~~~

Maple Pancake

Pancake Batter I or II
4 tablespoons sugar combined with
  1 teaspoon cinnamon

2 tablespoons butter
½ cup maple syrup
4 tablespoons cognac

Make 16 pancakes. Stack crepes with sugar and cinnamon between. Pile 8 pancakes on each stack. Melt 2 tablespoons butter in a large skillet. Add ½ cup maple syrup. Heat this mixture to a boil and place crepes in hot syrup. Warm 4 tablespoons cognac. Add to skillet over pancakes and ignite. Serve pancakes by cutting each stack in half. Serves 4.

~~~~~~~~~~

Lingonberry Pancakes

Make 12 pancakes using Batter I or II. Place 1 tablespoon lingonberries in each pancake and roll up. Sprinkle with sugar. Heat a skillet with 1 tablespoon butter. Sauté pancakes in skillet for 1 minute. Warm ¼ cup kirsch, ignite it and pour over pancakes. This should be enough kirsch for 12 pancakes, but if you like more, go to it! Serves 4.

~~~~~~~~~~

Crepes Suzette

1. Blend together 1 stick sweet butter (¼ pound), ¼ cup sugar, 2 tablespoons orange juice, and thin sliced rind of 1 orange and 1 lemon.

2. Have ready 1 cup orange juice, shaker of confectioners' sugar, Cointreau or other orange liqueur, Grand Marnier and cognac.

3. Prepare 12 crepes (Batter II).

4. Heat crepe suzette pan or a large skillet. For every 3 crepes (1 serving), use 2 tablespoons orange butter mixture. Pour in 3 or 4 tablespoons orange juice and heat. Immerse crepes in hot juice. Fold each crepe in half then half again.

5. Sprinkle with confectioners' sugar, Cointreau and Grand Marnier.

6. Pour in cognac, flame and serve immediately. If skillet is large enough you may be able to prepare 2 servings at one time.

Teacher says:

The above service is fashioned after restaurant procedure. For easier home service, heat orange butter mixture, orange juice and Cointreau in a large skillet. Immerse crepes in hot juice. Sprinkle them with confectioners' sugar and Grand Marnier. Lastly flame the crepes with cognac.

In a Paris restaurant my husband and I were seated by chance just in front of the glass-enclosed kitchen. We couldn't have had better seats. All through dinner the chef came out and we conversed in my poor French and his poor English. After an exquisite dinner and much friendly chatting, he offered to prepare a special dessert. It turned out to be a crepe filled with ice cream and served with hot chocolate sauce. My recipe was inspired by that evening in Paris.

Frozen Cream Crepes ★ ★ ★

4 macaroons
2 tablespoons sherry

1 cup sweetened whipped cream
12 crepes

Soak macaroons in sherry until soft and add whipped cream. Place 2 tablespoons of mixture in the middle of each crepe, being careful not to come to either side. Roll the crepes and freeze them on a tray. Package them after they are frozen. Do not keep for longer than 1 month, and do not defrost before using—immersing them in hot sauce will bring the crepes to proper temperature. Serves 6.

SAUCE

1 tablespoon butter   4 tablespoons Kirsch, rum or cognac
1 package frozen strawberries
  thawed

Heat butter in a large skillet and add strawberries. When hot, add crepes, turning each one to heat both sides. Warm Kirsch or other liquor, ignite and pour over crepes. Serve immediately. It is wise to do no more than 4 crepes at a time so as not to crowd skillet. The crepes must be hot and the cream remain frozen. After a heavy dinner, one crepe probably will do for each serving, otherwise prepare 2 for each.

THE BLINTZ

The blintz is just a variation of the crepe; its main difference lies in the folding and frying. Although I am offering you another batter recipe, any one of the others may be used.

Blintzes freeze well before frying. Wrap them securely after they are filled and folded. Fry them frozen, on a low flame, allowing at least 15 to 20 minutes to defrost in the skillet.

Blintzes

BATTER

4 eggs   ⅔ cup milk
1 cup all purpose flour   ⅓ cup water
½ teaspoon salt   2 teaspoons melted butter
2 teaspoons sugar

1. If an electric blender is available, blend all together except butter or mix by electric beater or by hand. If there are any lumps remaining, strain mixture. Add melted butter at the finish.

2. Heat a 6-inch skillet until a bit of butter sizzles when added.

3. Pour about 2 tablespoons of batter into the pan. Immediately roll pan around so that batter spreads evenly. If there is too much wet batter in pan, pour it back into bowl.

4. When underside is brown and top is dry, turn it out on to absorbent paper. Different from crepes, blintzes are fried on *one* side.

5. Repeat process until all batter is used.

6. It is not necessary to grease pan each time. Makes 20 to 24.

TO PREPARE BLINTZES

Place one heaping tablespoon of filling (see three recipes which follow) on to cooked side of pancake, at end closest to you. Turn horizontal end closest to you over the filling. Bring vertical ends over on either side. Roll up the delicious package. Fry in butter until brown.

Blintzes freeze very well, uncooked. Fry while still frozen, but give them more time to heat.

Cheese Blintzes

½ pound cottage cheese
½ pound farmer cheese
4 ounces cream cheese

1 teaspoon sugar
1 egg yolk
pinch of salt

Beat all together until smooth. Add flavorings to suit individual taste. Makes filling for 20 blintzes. Fill and fry as directed in first blintz recipe.

The cheese blintz is the one popularly known. As is the case with recipes that are commonly used and handed from one generation to the next, many variations are possible. The one given is mine and certainly may be changed to suit your taste. Just remember that cottage cheese is quite watery and should not be used alone.

Meat Blintzes ★ ★ ★

3 onions diced fine
1 teaspoon butter or oil
2 pounds ground chuck steak

¼ teaspoon paprika
salt and pepper
2 tablespoons flour

Heat skillet, add onions. When onions start browning, add butter or oil. When onions are brown, add meat and stir with a large fork until meat is brown and separates. Season to taste. Remove from flame and blend in flour. Cool before using. Makes filling for 24 blintzes. Fill and fry as directed in first blintz recipe.

Meat blintzes are not generally known but they are favored in our house. I use them as a main course for dinner, served with a hot vegetable and tossed salad as a pleasant change of menu. A bowl of sour cream is passed around with all types of blintzes.

~~~~~~~~

Fruit Blintzes

½ cup sugar
2 teaspoons cornstarch

2 cups fresh berries
   or sliced fresh fruit
2 teaspoons lemon juice

Blend sugar and cornstarch together. Stir all ingredients together lightly. Makes filling for 12 blintzes. Fill and fry as directed in first blintz recipe.

PANCAKE QUESTIONS ANSWERED

Q *How can I freeze crepes?*
A Crepes may be frozen in stacks if waxed paper separates each one. I like to make crepes fresh, but if this is impossible, freezing is second best. Crepes Délices and other filled crepes freeze very well. As long as they are cooked right from the freezer, not defrosted first, they do not suffer in flavor.
Q *Many Italian dishes seem to use a large pancake. Can any pancake batter be used?*
A Yes, very often a canneloni (meat filled pasta) is made with a thin pancake, not a true pasta. In most cases the homemade crepe is so much better than the store bought pastas.
Q *What is the best method for defrosting and cooking frozen blintzes and filled crepes?*
A *Do not* defrost them! Fry the blintzes slowly allowing them to thaw while they cook. Any filled crepe or blintz, frozen or fresh, may be browned in a hot oven, provided it is masked first with butter or sauce. However, my own preference is for browning in butter on top of the stove.
Q *Do you recommend crepes as a company dish?*
A I certainly do. They are one of the most versatile and popular of dishes.
Q *Can I prepare crepes ahead without freezing?*
A Yes, make them early in the day, but be sure to cover them well, so they won't dry out.

LESSON 7

The Fish

It is unfortunate that the American palate has no great taste for fish, since our rivers, lakes and oceans supply such an abundance. Perhaps most people think of fish as dry and tasteless, but handled properly from the time it is caught to the time it is cooked, fish is a gourmet specialty. No food cooks faster than broiled or my fast-bake fish. No turning is required for fish. A simple dressing of butter, lemon juice and parsley is delicious and classically correct for all fish. Most people fail with fish because they cook it too long. Fish is delicate in texture. It is completely cooked when it loses its translucence and flakes easily when touched by a fork.

Buying fish:

If possible buy fish fresh, not frozen. Allow ½ pound per person if fish is boned (filet or steak). Allow 1 pound per person if the fish is whole. Fish cooked with bones and head is always tastier, but this will depend on the recipe. Today, fish is usually cleaned at the store so that all you need to do is wash and dry it. Sprinkle lemon juice on it and store it in the refrigerator, tightly covered. Use fish as quickly as possible; it may be refrigerated for 24 hours. Do not buy or use fish that has a strong odor. Fish should smell sweet. If you are using frozen fish, thaw it in the refrigerator until it is soft enough to handle.

The five principal methods for cooking fish are:

1. *Poaching:* This is perhaps the least-used method but it insures a moist and flavorful fish. Poaching means to simmer in a small amount of seasoned water or stock. Poached fish may be eaten hot or cold. It may be used for salads and aspics. The resulting fish broth may be used for fish sauce or a soup.

Depending on the thickness of the fish, poached fish can cook from 6 minutes (filet) to 20 minutes (whole fish).

2. *Broiling:* Whole small fish as well as filets and steaks may be broiled. Fish may be dredged in flour or bread crumbs if you like a crusty surface. Always preheat pan under broiler. Melt a liberal amount of butter in pan and place fish on hot buttered pan. It is very important to baste fish with butter or oil during cooking time. Most fish (filets or split whole fish) are completely broiled in 5 to 8 minutes at 3 inches from broiler heat. Fish is cooked if it flakes easily when gently poked with a fork.

3. My *Fast-Baking Method:* For those who overcook fish when broiling it, quick baking is an excellent alternate method. The oven should be very hot (450° F.). Preheat pan and melt butter on it. If no other dressing is made for the fish, baste it during cooking with butter or oil. For a pleasant change baste your fish with white wine.

Filets bake almost as fast with this method as in broiling. Whole fish and steaks require more time; allow approximately 10 minutes to a pound.

4. *Sautéing:* This method is excellent for small whole fish. A heavyweight skillet is required so that fish browns evenly without sticking. A combination of oil and butter is best for sautéing; butter alone burns too rapidly. Be sure to preheat skillet until fat sizzles. Always dredge fish in flour or in a combination of flour and bread crumbs. This is a good protection for the delicate fish and also a tasty coating.

5. *Deep-frying:* Recommended only for small-boned fish, filets or sea food. It is accomplished best by good equipment and proper thermostat.

This lesson includes fish recipes that demonstrate the various methods of fish cookery. Each may be used for a luncheon or dinner, as first course or as main dish.

Poached Halibut, Lemon Herb Sauce

1 slice halibut, 1½ to 2 pounds
2 cups water
¼ cup white wine
2 tablespoons lemon juice
1 stalk celery
1 small onion studded with a clove
1 sprig parsley
½ teaspoon salt

¼ teaspoon white pepper
1 tablespoon butter
2 tablespoons flour
½ cup cream (or milk)
2 tablespoons lemon juice
1 tablespoon chopped parsley
1 tablespoon chopped chives
1 tablespoon chopped dill

1. Place halibut in a shallow saucepan (with cover). Add water, white wine, lemon juice, celery, onion, parsley, salt and pepper. Bring to a boil. Cover and simmer for 15 minutes. Remove halibut carefully to a serving platter or oven dish. With a slotted spoon remove and discard vegetables from fish broth.

2. Cook down fish broth to about half its quantity.

3. In the meantime knead butter and flour together with your fingers. When broth is reduced, lower flame and add "beurre manié" bit by bit until it blends with sauce.

4. When sauce is thickened, add cream, lemon juice and herbs. Pour sauce on to halibut and serve. Serves 4.

Broiled Salmon Steak

4 tablespoons butter
2 tablespoons lemon juice
½ teaspoon salt

¼ teaspoon pepper
4 slices salmon steak
   (2 to 3 pounds total)

Preheat broiler. Soften 3 tablespoons butter and gradually work in lemon juice, salt and pepper. Heat a shallow baking pan and grease it with 1 tablespoon butter. Place salmon steaks on greased baking pan. Brush surface with some softened butter mixture. Broil 4 inches from the heat for 10 to 12 minutes for steaks 1-inch thick. Continue basting fish with softened butter. Fish is cooked when it looks opaque and flakes easily when touched with a fork. Serves 4.

Quick Baked Filet of Sole

4 slices filet of sole	½ teaspoon salt
4 tablespoons bread crumbs	¼ teaspoon pepper
4 tablespoons butter, softened	¼ teaspoon paprika
2 tablespoons lemon juice	1 tablespoon chopped parsley

Preheat oven to 450° F. Set fish on a preheated greased flat baking dish (jelly roll pan is good); sprinkle all over with bread crumbs. Mix softened butter with lemon juice, seasonings and parsley. Spread over the fish. Bake fish for 5 to 7 minutes. If not brown enough for your taste, set it under the broiler for 1 minute. Serves 4.

Quick Baked Fish Steaks and Whole Fish

Bake fish steak, such as halibut and salmon, using the method above. For steaks cut ¾″ thick, bake approximately 12 minutes, then broil 2 minutes to brown. Smaller bluefish, red snapper and striped bass may be split, boned and baked by this method. Larger fish may be stuffed and baked a little slower as in the next recipes.

Stuffed Fish

2- to 3-pound bluefish	1 egg
or striped bass, boned	¾ teaspoon salt
½ teaspoon salt	¼ teaspoon pepper
juice of a lemon	¼ teaspoon paprika
4 large onions diced	½ teaspoon sage and marjoram mixed
4 tablespoons butter	1 tablespoon chopped parsley
6 mushrooms, diced fine	1 tablespoon chopped chives
½ cup bread crumbs	½ cup white wine

1. Wash and dry fish. Salt inside and out, rub lemon on skin. Sprinkle inside with lemon juice. With a sharp knife, score fish across top to mark portions. Set fish aside.
2. To make stuffing: Heat a skillet and start to brown onions on the dry hot skillet. Onions will brown faster this way, especially when you are doing so many. Stir onions if they are browning too

rapidly. Add 1 tablespoon of butter and mix in with mushrooms. Cook for 1 minute. Remove from stove.

3. Add bread crumbs, egg, seasonings and herbs. Another tablespoon of butter may be added to stuffing. Pile stuffing into cavity of fish and close with toothpicks.

4. Heat remaining 2 tablespoons of butter in a baking dish in the oven at 375° F. When butter melts place fish on hot baking dish. Bake for 35 minutes. Baste with wine and drippings while baking. Portugaise sause (see index for recipe) may be spooned around fish. Serves 4 to 6.

Rolled Filets with Shrimp ★ ★ ★

4 tablespoons butter
1 clove garlic crushed
1 onion, minced
⅓ green pepper, minced
10 cooked shrimp
 (8 diced fine, 2 cut in half)

¼ cup bread crumbs
1 tablespoon parsley and chives
¼ teaspoon salt
⅛ teaspoon pepper
4 filets (flounder or sole)

1. Melt 2 tablespoons butter in a skillet. Add garlic and onion. Sauté until lightly browned. Add green pepper, 8 diced shrimp, crumbs, herbs and seasonings. Remove from flame.

2. Place 2 tablespoons of mixture on boned side of each filet. Roll up filet to enclose stuffing.

3. Heat an oven dish with 2 tablespoons butter in a 350° F. oven.

4. When butter is melted, roll the filets in the butter and place them flap side down, close together (they won't need tying). If there is additional filling, poke it into open sides of fish rolls.

5. Bake at 350° F. for 25 minutes. Before serving top with any one of the cream sauces or Hollandaise Sauce (see index). Garnish with ½ shrimp on each filet. Serves 4.

Teacher says:

My recipes call for fresh herbs. If they are not available, use ½ to 1 teaspoon dried herbs for 1 tablespoon fresh.

The shrimp in this recipe may be replaced with ½ pound cooked fresh flaked salmon.

All preparations may be done beforehand, up to baking.

This recipe has tremendous appeal. Don't hesitate to use it for guests; it is unconditionally recommended.

On our first trip to Paris, my husband and I enjoyed our first dinner in the restaurant of the railroad station in the eastern part of the city. Since Relais Paris D'Est was highly recommended, we were not as surprised as we might have been to find such elegant classic cuisine and service in a busy terminal. Our introduction to Paris food began with a first course of trout, caught fresh from the tank in full view of the restaurant patrons. Although trout pools are not always accessible, it is not difficult to reconstruct this recipe with quick-frozen trout. La Truite en Chemise awakens such fond memories that merely cooking it is reliving a traveling experience.

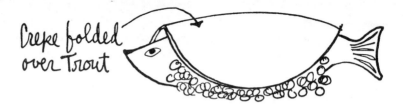

Crepe folded over Trout

La Truite en Chemise (Trout in a Folder)

2 tablespoons butter
½ pound mushrooms, minced
¼ teaspoon salt
⅛ teaspoon pepper
1 tablespoon flour
⅓ cup cream
4 brook trout (¾ pound each) boned

juice of a lemon
½ cup flour seasoned with
  ½ teaspoon salt and
  ⅛ teaspoon pepper
4 to 6 tablespoons butter or oil
  or combination
4 crepes, 8-inch
  (see index for recipe)

1. Melt butter in a hot skillet. Sauté mushrooms until brown. Salt and pepper.

2. Sprinkle flour over mushrooms; stir well and blend in cream. Continue cooking until thickened. Set aside to cool.

3. Wash and dry trout. Sprinkle lemon juice in cavity. Dredge in seasoned flour.

4. Prepare a large baking pan to hold the four fish. Set out 4 crepes on pan. Preheat oven to 350° F.

5. Heat skillet with 2 tablespoons oil and 2 tablespoons butter. Brown trout in skillet. When trout is brown on both sides remove trout.

Place fish on front half of crepe. Spread a little mushroom mixture in the cavity of fish and also on top of the fish. Bring other half of crepe over to cover top mushroom mixture. The crepe is rolled around the trout so that the head and tail show. Do the same with each trout.

6. Bake trout for 20 minutes in a 350° F. oven.

Serve with parsley dipped lemon wedges and, of course, a very good white wine. Serves 4.

Many of the most delicate fish dishes are made on a base of raw ground fish. These take shape as individual balls, large ring molds or puddings. Subtly flavored, they combine well with sea-food garnishes. The next two recipes are delicious both hot and cold, at luncheon or dinner.

Fish Mousse Ring with Shrimp Sauce

1 tablespoon butter
1 tablespoon flour
½ cup milk
2 eggs separated
½ teaspoon salt
¼ teaspoon white pepper

⅛ teaspoon paprika
1 pound halibut or haddock,
   ground raw
1 tablespoon oil
1 cup heavy cream, whipped

1. Heat butter in a saucepan, blend in flour. Remove from flame. Stir in milk gradually. Return to flame and cook until thick, stirring constantly. Remove from flame.

2. Beat egg yolks and stir into cream mixture a bit at a time. Season with salt, pepper, paprika. Add ground fish and allow to cool.

3. Set oven at 375° F.

4. Grease 1½-quart ring mold (lightly with oil) and prepare a large pan of hot water, large enough for ring mold to set in.

5. Beat egg whites with a pinch of salt until stiff.

6. Fold whipped cream into fish mixture then fold in beaten egg whites.

7. Pour mixture into greased ring mold. Place mold in a pan of hot water and bake for 45 minutes.

8. Remove from oven; allow it to rest 1 or 2 minutes (it will fall slightly, never mind). Release sides of mold with a sharp knife. Place large heated platter on mold and turn over. Fill cavity with Shrimp Sauce. Serves 6.

SHRIMP SAUCE

3 tablespoons butter
1 clove garlic, crushed
1 pound shrimp, cleaned raw
  (whole or diced)
2 tablespoons flour
½ cup chicken broth
½ cup milk or cream

2 egg yolks
½ teaspoon salt
¼ teaspoon pepper
1 tablespoon mixed herbs
  (parsley, chives, dill)
1 tablespoon lemon juice

Heat skillet. Melt 3 tablespoons butter and add garlic. Sauté shrimp with garlic until shrimp are pink and firm. This takes no more than 2 minutes. Stir in flour and blend well. Remove from flame and add liquids gradually. Set back on flame. Bring sauce to a boil slowly until thickened. Remove from flame. Add beaten egg yolks by blending a little hot sauce into egg yolks first, then stir all together. Season with salt, pepper, herbs and lemon juice. Reheat on a slow flame. When hot, serve immediately. If sauce is overcooked egg yolks will curdle.

Teacher says:

The mousse is not tricky to unmold. However, if a large chunk sticks to the mold take it out and patch the ring. Garnish the top with halves of shrimp or strips of pimento, a good cover up.

The fish mousse may be baked in the ring mold, a casserole or individual custard cups. It makes a wonderful cold salad for appetizer or luncheon. For a cold ring, fill the cavity with one of the dunks, a tomato cocktail sauce, or seasoned sour cream. Fancy it up with deviled eggs, shrimp and olives. Good enough for a party!

Prepare the shrimp sauce while fish mousse is baking. If you are pressed for time, don't fret. The fish mousse is fine even if it cooks a little longer.

Shrimp may be sliced in half, lengthwise or diced fine for the sauce. They may be left whole if you prefer.

This Shrimp Sauce recipe provides a quick main course for dinner.

~~~~~~~~~~

This sole, salmon and spinach ring is delightful to eat and lovely to look at. Try it at least once if only for the sheer pleasure of turning it out!

Pour mixture over the fish →

Use two quart Ring Mold →

Allow ends of fish to hang over edges of pan..

(after filling with mixture, fold fish ends over.

Sole Laurentian ★ ★ ★

3 tablespoons butter
1 shallot, finely chopped
5 tablespoons flour
1 cup milk
1 teaspoon salt
½ teaspoon pepper
4 eggs separated
4 slices filet of sole

1 pound fresh salmon, ground raw
½ teaspoon paprika
¼ teaspoon chervil
1 package frozen chopped spinach cooked and drained
½ teaspoon nutmeg
½ cup bread crumbs browned in 2 tablespoons butter

1. Prepare a well-oiled 2-quart ring mold and a big pan to hold it.

2. Melt butter in a saucepan. Sauté shallot (or onion) until golden. Blend in flour and stir well. Remove from flame, add milk gradually. Set back to cook slowly until sauce thickens. Add salt and pepper; set aside.

3. Beat egg yolks and blend in a small amount of cream sauce, finally add remaining sauce. Allow to cool.

4. Line the mold with the filets, evenly spaced. Allow tips to hang out over mold. Preheat oven to 375° F.

5. Place salmon, paprika and chervil in one bowl and spinach and nutmeg in another bowl. Divide the cream sauce evenly between the two. Taste and adjust seasoning.

6. Beat egg whites stiff but not dry. Again divide half the beaten whites between both salmon and spinach. Fold into mixtures.

7. Spread spinach mixture onto filets in ring mold to make the first layer.

8. Spread salmon mixture over spinach for the next layer. Fold in the tips of the filets. Bake mold in pan of hot water for 45 minutes. Unmold and fill cavity with lobster sauce supreme or any creamed sea-food. Cavity may also be filled with a Mushroom Sauce (see index).

LOBSTER SAUCE SUPREME

2 tablespoons butter
1 shallot, minced
4 lobster tails, defrosted raw
  and diced
2 tablespoons flour

1½ cups heavy cream
½ teaspoon salt
¼ teaspoon pepper
½ cup sherry

Melt butter in skillet. Sauté shallot and lobster. When lobster turns opaque white, add flour. Stir well. Lower flame; add cream and seasonings. Taste and adjust salt. Allow sauce to cook down slightly (about 3 minutes) then blend in wine. Serve.

━━━ ∿∿∿ ━━━

Compare the traditional Gefulte Fish with the Fish Mousse or quenelles (fish balls) which are poached. The Fish Mousse and quenelles are French in origin, the Gefulte Fish, Russian Jewish. In the former, the flavor is very delicate, in the latter, it is sharper with the pronounced flavor of onion. Fortunately we do not have to make a choice; we can cook both. Each in its own way is excellent.

Thanks to a fond remembrance of a bustling kitchen, I can somewhat reconstruct "Mother's" Gefulte Fish (no reference to a trade name here). Everybody's mother seems to make the best fish, and mine was no exception. Students tell me repeatedly that they have had such fabulous success with this recipe that in the future, I suspect, daughter's Gefulte Fish may become mother's favorite!

Gefulte Fish

FOR THE POT

3 onions, sliced
3 carrots, sliced
1 tablespoon salt
¼ teaspoon pepper

bones and heads of fish
  (1 carp head)
4 cups water

FOR THE FISH

3 onions
¾ cup water
5 pounds white fish and pike,
  ground (save bones and head)
4 eggs

½ cup matzo meal or cracker meal
1½ tablespoons salt
½ teaspoon pepper
1 teaspoon sugar

1. Prepare a 6- to 8-quart enamel pot with a close-fitting cover. (If possible, have a rack that fits it.) Add all ingredients for the pot. Boil for ten minutes.

2. While fish broth is boiling grate or grind 3 onions. If you have a blender cut the onions into small chunks and place in the blender with ¾ cup of water.

3. Put ground fish in the large bowl of the electric mixer. Beat in ground onions and water, one egg at a time, matzo meal and seasonings. Beat for 3 to 5 minutes until mixture is pasty.

4. With 2 large tablespoons, first dipped in water, form mixture into large oval shape in the spoon. Move fish from spoon to spoon to shape the oval. Place fish on rack in slowly boiling broth. Place fish next to one another. If it is necessary to make several layers, boil first layer until all fish is firm (5 minutes) then proceed to the next layer. Cover pot and cook for 2 hours.

5. Allow fish to cool before removing to platter. Strain broth to remove all bones. Garnish each portion of fish with a slice of carrot and pour broth over fish. Yield: 20 to 24 pieces.

Teacher says:

It is obvious that methods have modernized since mother's time. The blender and electric mixer are great helpers and so, I confess, is my fish dealer. He grinds the fish; no tedious chopping necessary.

Gefulte fish improves with time. It may be refrigerated up to 10 days; delicious served cold as well as hot.

For a broth that surely jells, use a carp head. If broth does not jell after 24 hours in refrigerator, boil it again and reduce the quantity.

SHELLFISH

Method for Cooking Shrimp and Lobster

There is not *one* method, but several.

Shrimp may be cooked in their shells. The shell adds flavor to the shrimp and the broth (if you are planning to use it). Wash shrimp well, place in a saucepan with water to cover, salt (1 tablespoon to 1 quart of water) 4 peppercorns, 1 stalk celery, sprig parsley, 1 bay leaf, ¼ cup lemon juice, vinegar or wine. Bring water to a boil. Shrimp are finished 2 minutes after water boils. Keep it at a simmer. Sea food toughens when it is boiled too hard.

Shrimp may be cleaned raw, then cooked as above. As soon as water comes to a boil, turn off flame. Wait 1 minute and shrimp should be finished. Turn cooked shrimp immediately on to ice cubes. Cool them rapidly.

Lobster tails may be cooked in the same manner. Allow 1 minute per ounce of weight, plus 1 minute more for each tail. If tails are frozen use the same method. Time your lobster from the moment the water starts boiling.

For whole live lobsters it is best to boil up broth first and then immerse lobsters. Cook lobsters by the same timing. Generally small lobsters take 15 to 20 minutes, larger, from 25 to 30 minutes.

Teacher says:

Shellfish, especially shrimp, have become very popular in this country. Lobsters must be bought alive; clams and oysters in the shell should be tightly closed. Shellfish such as shrimp and lobster can be bought cooked but unless you have an exceptional fish dealer, it will probably be overcooked. Be sure he has kept it on a bed of ice.

As soon as raw seafood enters my kitchen, it is washed and generously sprinkled with lemon juice. Neither fish nor seafood ever seem to get too much. If seafood is to be used later in the day rather than immediately (which is preferable) I cover it with the lemon rind before refrigerating it.

Lobster and shrimp appear frequently on my week-end shopping list. As an hors d'oeuvre with drinks, a quick effortless family dinner, and to serve drop-in guests, shellfish are superb.

Wine and Garlic Shrimp

2 tablespoons butter
2 cloves garlic, crushed
1 pound shrimp, cleaned raw
2 tablespoons lemon juice
¼ teaspoon salt

¼ teaspoon pepper
½ cup sherry wine
1 tablespoon chopped parsley
  and chives

Melt butter in skillet (or in the blazer pan of chafing dish directly over flame). When butter is sizzling, add garlic and shrimp. Sprinkle lemon juice and salt and pepper over shrimp. Stir occasionally, allowing shrimp to cook rapidly. When shrimp are pink and opaque, pour in wine and herbs. Bring to a boil and serve on toast points or as a pick up for an appetizer. Good for a buffet table, kept hot over a flame. Serves 2 to 3.

Sea-food Newburg

2 tablespoons butter	2 egg yolks
2 cups mixed sea-food (cooked lobster, crabmeat, shrimp, scallops)	½ teaspoon salt
1 tablespoon flour	¼ teaspoon pepper
1¼ cups cream	¼ teaspoon paprika
¼ cup dry sherry	1 tablespoon cognac

Melt butter in a heavy saucepan or blazer of chafing dish and heat sea-food. Stir in flour and gradually add 1 cup cream (reserve ¼ cup). Stir constantly until sauce is thickened. Add sherry and cook for a few minutes (3 to 5 minutes). Stir ¼ cup cream into egg yolks and blend well. Add this mixture to the sea-food and stir all together. Add seasonings and cognac, constantly stirring and keeping flame very low. Serve immediately on toast points. Serves 4.

Teacher says:

Newburg is excellent on fluffy rice. It is a delicate sauce, rich but always correct for luncheons and light suppers.

If the sea food is chopped fine, this becomes a most delicious sauce combined with fish rings.

After the egg yolks are added the sauce must not boil hard, lest it curdle.

Lobster Newburg is perhaps the most classic of all chafing dish recipes. Rightly so, because it is easily prepared on an alcohol or sterno flame. Whether it is lobster or sea-food Newburg, start the cooking directly over flame. After adding the egg yolks always place the Newburg over the bottom pan filled with hot water.

It is quite dramatic to do your cooking in front of your guests. They will enjoy it and you will be the star of the evening.

~~~~~~~~~

Sea food lends itself to chafing dish cookery. It can quickly be heated with sauces or vegetables to make an endless number of combinations. One of these small creations came to me from an innkeeper in New Hampshire. Mrs. Freeman Bates, a fine New England cook and, according to my youngsters, the best white-bread baker up and down the eastern coast, is the donor of Shrimp Wiggle.

~~~~~~~~~

Shrimp Wiggle

1 tablespoon butter
1 small onion, chopped
1 cup tomatoes
  (canned, well drained)
1 cup cooked rice
1 pound cooked shrimp

½ teaspoon salt
¼ teaspoon pepper
¼ teaspoon sugar
1 cup heavy cream
1 tablespoon chopped fresh parsley

Melt butter in saucepan or blazer of chafing dish over direct heat. Sauté onion until translucent. Add tomato, rice and shrimp. Season. Heat to the boiling point. Add cream slowly and blend well. Serve as soon as the mixture is hot. Sprinkle chopped parsley on top.

Baked Stuffed Shrimp,
page 285

Two-Minute Shrimp,
page 26

Five-Minute Shrimp,
page 27

Imperial Crab Baltimore,
page 25

Melon Crabmeat Bowl,
page 277

Lobster Soufflé,
page 63

Sea-Food Kebab,
page 270

Mr. Ricky Torella, a local restaurateur, and one of my recent guest lecturers, is the fastest and neatest professional chef that I have ever seen. His love for cooking is positively contagious and, although he works at it constantly, he seems never to be weary of it. This is enthusiasm!

Lobster Fra Diavolo

3 or 4 tablespoons olive oil	2 cups Ricky's Marinara Sauce
2 lobsters, split, claws and body	(see index)
cut into large chunks	⅔ cup clam juice
2 cloves garlic	½ teaspoon salt
4 clams, cleaned and shelled	¼ teaspoon pepper
4 raw shrimp, shelled and deveined	½ teaspoon oregano
2 tablespoons white wine	1 teaspoon chopped fresh parsley
	pinch crushed red pepper

1. Heat olive oil in skillet. When hot, add chunks of lobster flesh side down. Add garlic, cut in large pieces, to be removed later. Sauté for 1 minute. Turn lobster over. Cook for 1 minute. Pour off oil and garlic.

2. Add clams and shrimp. Pour wine over all and allow it to cook down 1 minute.

3. Add marinara sauce, clam juice and seasonings. Cover and cook for 10 minutes. Lobster should look white and puffy. Sauce should have thickened slightly. Serve immediately. Serves 2.

Baked Whole Clams

Clams en Coquille

See index for recipes.

FISH QUESTIONS ANSWERED

Q *Which fresh fish makes the best salads?*
A Cod, haddock, halibut and salmon are all delicious for salad. Use each alone or in combinations.

Q *Can the Fish Mousse or Gefulte Fish be frozen?*
A They can and have been, but I feel that their flavor and texture suffer through freezing.
Q *How can one recognize a fresh fish?*
A Fresh fish has shiny scales and is firm to the touch. The eyes are bright and the gills very pink.
Q *How long is it safe to keep fish?*
A A great deal depends on how fresh it is. It will be finest in flavor if cooked immediately. Most fish can be kept refrigerated for at least one day.
Q *What are the best fish recipes to cook in my chafing dish for company service?*
A The poached fish, shrimp or lobster recipes in this lesson can be completely cooked in a chafing dish or at least kept warm in one. Seafood dishes are great company fare.
Q *Have you any suggestions for using leftover cooked fish?*
A Leftover cooked fish makes an excellent hot or cold appetizer. Heat "en coquille" topped with buttered bread crumbs or serve cold with Rémoulade sauce (see index) or good mayonnaise.
Q *After every fishing trip my wife and I are burdened with more fish than my family can eat. What is the best method for keeping fresh fish?*
A Clean fish immediately and freeze as quickly as possible. For the best freeze, place fish in a pan of water and freeze it so that it is encased in a block of ice. Remove from pan when frozen and wrap very well. Do not keep more than 2 months.

LESSON 8
The Bird

Chicken is abundant all year around and generally economical. Its texture and flavor allow for much flexibility in the use of herbs, spices, sauces and wines.

The general quality of poultry marketed today is good. However fresh-killed poultry has the finest flavor of all. Do look for it and buy it when available. Often, deliveries are made to neighborhood stores and even to the home by local farms. Some high-quality meat stores carry fresh-killed poultry.

Selecting the bird

For broiling, choose a plump small bird. They weigh between 1½ to 2½ pounds and show very little fat.

An all-purpose bird weighs from 2 to 3½ pounds. It is perfect for sautéing, frying and quick braising.

For roasting, select chicken weighing from 3 to 5 pounds. It is usually heavier breasted and well fatted. When fresh poultry is available it is sometimes possible to get a larger roaster. These are very succulent and practical for serving more than 4. The capon, a specially bred chicken, falls into this category too.

For soups, stews and fricassees, a fowl is usually best. Fowls are tough birds and need long slow cooking but they are very flavorful.

Preparing the bird

Wash freshly-killed poultry in cold water (never soak it): dry well. Sprinkle salt and lemon juice in cavity and on the outside. Refrigerate, loosely covered, for one or two days. Fresh-killed poultry should be stored for about a day before using (its flavor improves).

Thaw frozen poultry in the refrigerator. Cook it within a day after it is defrosted because poultry deteriorates in flavor. Never refreeze poultry. This poultry may be seasoned with salt and lemon juice too.

Poultry bought in parts for sautéing, braising or frying, may be washed, dried, seasoned and coated with flour or bread crumbs. Place in the refrigerator until ready to use. Use within 24 hours.

The chicken recipes given in this chapter are those which my students selected as their favorites.

THE CHICKEN

Roast Chicken Tarragon

1 roasting chicken, 4 to 5 pounds	1 tablespoon fresh parsley chopped
juice of a lemon	4 tablespoons butter
1 teaspoon salt	1 sprig fresh tarragon
½ teaspoon pepper	½ cup white wine
1 teaspoon fresh tarragon, chopped fine or ½ teaspoon dried	

1. Wash chicken thoroughly with cold water, inside and out. Remove any pinfeathers. Dry chicken well. Sprinkle lemon juice over chicken and rub inside of cavity with lemon. Salt chicken with about ½ teaspoon salt. Chicken may be prepared this way and allowed to rest 12 to 24 hours in refrigerator, especially if it is fresh killed.

2. Set oven at 350° F. and prepare an open roasting pan or shallow casserole.

3. Make a paste of ½ teaspoon salt, pepper, tarragon, parsley and 4 tablespoons butter or fat.

4. Rub outside of chicken with 2 tablespoons of this mixture. Put 1 tablespoon of mixture into cavity of chicken with sprig of tarragon.

5. Truss chicken by folding wing tips back under bird. Set white string under back, bring both ends of string between wings and sides of bird, cross string under tail end and up to tie legs in a knot.

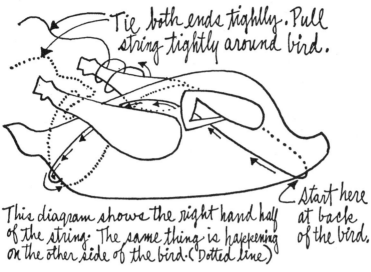

Tie *both ends tightly*. Pull string tightly around bird.

Start here at back of the bird.

This diagram shows the right hand half of the string. The same thing is happening on the other side of the bird. (Dotted line)

6. Set chicken in roasting pan. Bake at 350° F. for 1 hour and 15 minutes.

7. During roasting, baste with remainder of butter and white wine. Serves 4 to 5.

Note: If a sauce or gravy is desirable, heat 1 cup chicken broth (thicken if you wish with 1 tablespoon flour or cornstarch). When chicken is removed from pan, blend hot chicken broth with pan juices.

━━━━━━━

The next recipe combines the sauté method with baking. A variety of crusts may be used; the choice is personal. Save crushed crumbs from the bottom of corn flakes and other cereal boxes. These are flavorful additions for coatings.

Baked Crusty Chicken

1 roasting chicken, 4 pounds, cut in eighths
juice of a lemon
½ teaspoon salt
½ cup bread crumbs
½ cup flour
½ teaspoon salt
¼ teaspoon pepper
½ teaspoon paprika
1 tablespoon fresh chopped parsley
1 teaspoon sweet basil
2 tablespoons oil
2 tablespoons butter

1. Wash chicken with cold water, clean thoroughly and dry. Sprinkle lemon juice and salt over all parts of chicken.

2. Combine all other dry ingredients and dredge chicken in mixture. Reserve remainder.

3. If there is time, allow chicken to rest in refrigerator. When ready to cook, dredge chicken again in reserved crumbs.

4. Heat a skillet with 1 tablespoon oil and 1 tablespoon butter. Prepare a large shallow baking pan. Preheat oven to 350° F. Sauté pieces of chicken in hot fat just to brown on both sides. Use more oil and butter as needed. Transfer to baking dish and bake for 45 minutes at 350° F. Serves 4.

Teacher says:

Here are six different methods:

1. *For a heavier crust:* Dip chicken in crumbs, then in 2 eggs beaten with ¼ cup water, and in crumbs again.

2. *An even simpler method:* Dip each piece of chicken in oil and melted butter, then in crumb mixture, and on to baking pan. No sautéing. Compare flavors for *your* preference.

3. Soak chicken in sweet cream then dip in crumb mixture and sauté.

4. Sauté chicken as directed. Return pieces of chicken to skillet, add 1 cup white wine cover and braise for 30 minutes.

5. Add 12 sliced mushrooms and ½ cup Madeira wine for a sensational change.

6. For baked chicken with a different flavor, use a can of pitted bing cherries. Drain cherries and reserve 1 cup of juice. Thicken juice by cooking it with a mixture of 1 tablespoon cornstarch plus 2 tablespoons water. When juice is boiling and thickened take it off flame. Add cherries and 2 tablespoons brandy for flavor. Pour cherry sauce on to chicken 5 minutes before serving.

Marinades for Chicken

See index for recipe.

People around Great Neck have been feasting on this unusual combination. It is on our list of "top ten" dinner-party favorites.

Chicken with Grapes and Pignoli

1 4-pound roasting chicken, cut in eighths
1 cup white wine
1 teaspoon salt
¼ teaspoon pepper
¼ teaspoon rosemary
¼ teaspoon savory
2 cloves garlic, crushed

4 tablespoons olive oil or melted butter
4 ounces pignoli (pine nuts) ground
½ cup bread crumbs
½ teaspoon salt
¼ teaspoon paprika
1 cup seedless grapes

Wash chicken in cold water, clean thoroughly and dry well. Soak chicken for 1 to 2 hours in wine, salt, pepper, rosemary, savory and garlic, turning once. Grease a baking pan well with olive oil or butter. Combine ground nuts with bread crumbs salt and paprika. Roll each piece of chicken in this seasoned mixture. Press nuts and crumbs onto chicken to coat it well. Reserve the wine marinade. Preheat oven to 350° F. Place chicken on to greased baking sheet. Drizzle with oil or butter. Bake for 45 minutes uncovered. Pour wine marinade over chicken, add grapes to pan and bake for 5 minutes longer. If chicken is not brown enough, set oven up to 400° F. or place 4 inches under broiler for 2 minutes. Serves 4.

Serve with risotto, spinach, escarole salad and tart dressing; call the dinner Italian. Choosing a dinner menu becomes harder when so many fine recipes are within our scope. It is exciting to know that in our range of knowledge and food availability, we could easily do a different chicken recipe once a week throughout the year. Try that as your resolution for next year!

~~~~~~~~

Arroz Con Pollo

2 tablespoons olive oil
1 4-pound roasting chicken,
  cut in eighths
1 cup rice
1 onion, diced fine
1 green chile pepper, diced fine
2 large ripe tomatoes, diced
  or 1 cup drained canned tomatoes

½ teaspoon chili powder
1 teaspoon salt
½ teaspoon pepper
1 clove garlic, crushed
¼ teaspoon saffron dissolved in
2 cups boiling water

Prepare a large casserole or roasting pan with tight-fitting cover. Set oven at 350° F. In a skillet heat olive oil and brown pieces of chicken. When chicken is brown on all sides transfer to the casserole. In the same skillet, brown rice. Turn rice into casserole with chicken. Add all other ingredients. Cover and bake at 350° F. for 40 minutes. Uncover, blend ingredients lightly, taste, and adjust seasoning. If moisture is not absorbed bake for another 15 minutes uncovered. Serves 4.

Note: If green chile pepper is not available use sweet green pepper. Seasoning is often a matter of personal taste. If you care for this dish on the spicier side, add more chili powder and a pinch of red pepper.

Layered Pirog

See index for recipe.

~~~~~~~

Coq au Vin Rouge

2 roasting chickens 3 to 4 pounds
   each, cut in eighths
juice of a lemon
1½ teaspoons salt
½ cup flour
½ cup bread crumbs
½ teaspoon salt
¼ teaspoon pepper
¼ teaspoon paprika
1 tablespoon chopped fresh tarragon
   or ½ teaspoon dried
2 onions, diced

2 tablespoons oil
2 tablespoons butter
1½ cups red wine (Beaujolais
   or other dry red wine)
1 cup beef, veal or chicken stock
1 teaspoon tomato paste
1 teaspoon Bovril
1 tablespoon flour
1 clove garlic, crushed
1 pound cooked white onions
1 can baby carrots

Wash chickens with cold water, dry and sprinkle with lemon juice and salt. Combine flour, crumbs, salt, pepper, paprika and tarragon. Dredge chicken parts in the dry mixture and coat them lightly. Line the bottom of a shallow baking dish with diced onion. It is preferable to use a casserole you can bring to the table. Set oven at 375° F. Heat skillet with oil and butter adding more if needed. Brown chicken, piece by piece, and transfer to baking dish. Place chicken close together on bed of onions, if necessary in layers. Bake uncovered at 375° F. for 20 minutes. Lower temperature to 325° F. Pour wine over all and cover. Continue baking for 20 minutes. Blend the stock, tomato paste, Bovril, flour and garlic by shaking them in a covered jar. Pour on to chicken. Continue to bake for another half hour. Baste chicken and adjust seasoning if necessary. More wine may be added if desired. Uncover the casserole 10 minutes before serving. Add onions and carrots to the chicken and allow to heat thoroughly. Serve with plenty of crusty bread and salad. Serves 8.

Coq au Vin Blanc

Just change from red to white wine!

Paella

1 medium lobster or 2 lobster tails	2 onions, diced
1 pound shrimp	1 green pepper, diced
1 dozen clams (Little Neck)	1 hot Spanish sausage (chorizo)
juice of a lemon	sliced
½ cup olive oil	1 tablespoon capers
1 clove of garlic, crushed	2 large ripe tomatoes, diced
1 teaspoon salt	or 1 cup canned tomatoes
½ teaspoon freshly ground	3 cups boiling water, in which
black pepper	½ teaspoon saffron is dissolved
1 roasting chicken (2 to 3 pounds)	1 package frozen peas
cut in eighths	3 pimentoes, sliced
1½ cups converted rice	

1. Cut lobster into chunks. Shell and devein shrimp. Wash clams. After cleaning shellfish always sprinkle a little lemon juice over it. Set aside.

2. Make a paste of 2 tablespoons olive oil, 2 tablespoons lemon juice, garlic, salt and pepper. Rub this all over pieces of chicken. Set oven at 350° F.

3. Heat skillet with 2 tablespoons oil. Brown chicken on both sides and remove to casserole. Add oil as needed.

4. When chicken is all browned, add 2 tablespoon oil to skillet. Brown rice and onion together, stirring constantly.

5. Turn rice and onion into casserole with chicken. Add green pepper, sausage, capers, tomatoes and water with saffron. Cover and bake for 20 minutes.

6. Uncover casserole, turn rice and chicken to blend them and bake for another 15 minutes.

7. Add clams, lobster, shrimp and peas. Cover casserole and bake for 10 minutes or until clam shells open. (If they are small they should open rapidly).

8. Serve this dish from the casserole and garnish it with slices of pimento. Serves 6.

Chicken Breasts Riviera

See index for recipe.

Chicken with Almonds

3 breasts of chicken, halved
4 cups cold water
1 teaspoon salt
1 onion

1 carrot
1 sprig parsley
1 leek
1 stalk celery

Place chicken in saucepan. Cover with water, seasonings and vegetables. Bring to a boil. Simmer for 45 minutes. Remove from flame. Cool in stock. When chicken is cool, remove bone and cover chicken well to keep it moist. Reserve stock for the sauce.

SAUCE

3 tablespoons butter
1 shallot, diced fine
  or 2 tablespoons minced onion
12 mushrooms, sliced
4 tablespoons flour
1½ cups chicken broth
½ cup milk or cream

¼ teaspoon dry mustard
1 teaspoon Worcestershire sauce
½ teaspoon monosodium glutamate
1 teaspoon salt
¼ teaspoon white pepper
2 tablespoons sherry wine
½ cup toasted slivered almonds

Melt 1 tablespoon butter in a heavy saucepan. Sauté shallot and mushrooms until lightly browned. Add 2 tablespoons of butter to pan, allowing it to melt. Blend in flour thoroughly. Remove pan from flame and add chicken broth (made from the breasts of chicken) and milk gradually. Set back on to flame. Bring sauce to a boil, stirring constantly. Blend in all seasonings except almonds. Heat chicken breasts in sauce and serve immediately, covered with almonds. Serves 4 to 6.

Teacher says:

For a luncheon or light supper, figure one-half breast per person. For dinner, figure almost one breast of chicken per person. When using the whole chicken, figure 1 pound of poultry per person.

A creamed chicken recipe with rice pilaff is always a good choice for luncheon or dinner. For elegant service use the boned whole breasts as described; for buffet service slice the breasts in bite-size pieces and keep warm in a chafing dish. For family style, use the entire chicken cut in parts. The flavor is more robust when the whole chicken is used.

Sliced pimento and chopped chives provide added color as a garnish.

The entire recipe may be prepared a day ahead. Whenever a cream sauce dish is made in advance, allow it to cool uncovered, stirring it occasionally. If covered when hot, the vapor breaks down the consistency of the sauce. When ready to use, heat chicken in sauce uncovered over a slow flame or a pan of hot water (chafing dish). Serve it as soon as chicken is piping hot.

Rock Cornish Hens

See index for recipe.

~~~~~~~~

Chicken Birds ★ ★ ★

4 chicken breasts, boned (breasts of 2 chickens, cut in half)
2 chicken livers, raw
2 shallots, chopped fine or 4 tablespoons minced onion
1 tablespoon chopped parsley
1 teaspoon chives
½ teaspoon tarragon

¼ cup toasted bread crumbs
¼ teaspoon salt
⅛ teaspoon pepper
6 tablespoons butter
8 mushroom caps
2 tablespoons flour
1 cup chicken broth
½ cup sweet cream

1. Pound chicken to flatten slightly.

2. Put liver and shallots through Foley food mill or fine sieve. Mix this raw liver purée with herbs, bread crumbs, salt and pepper.

3. Divide mixture by placing a spoonful in the center of each chicken breast. Place ½ tablespoon of butter on each and roll up securely, tying with a string.

4. In a heavy saucepan melt 2 tablespoons butter. Brown mushroom caps and set aside on a dish. Add chicken to same pan and brown on all sides. Remove to dish with mushrooms.

5. Add remaining butter to pan. When melted, blend in flour smoothly. Remove from flame and gradually add broth.

6. Return to flame and bring sauce to a boil. When mixture is thickened add sweet cream.

7. Place chicken and mushrooms in sauce. Cook covered over low heat for 30 minutes. Serve with fluffy white rice. Serves 4.

Teacher says:

The chicken birds freeze well in the sauce. They may be prepared in bulk and frozen well in advance for a party.

This dish may be kept warm in a chafing dish for buffet service.

As a change from rice, serve spinach noodles with the Chicken Birds. Tossed salad, hot crusty rolls and white wine complete a perfect dinner menu for you.

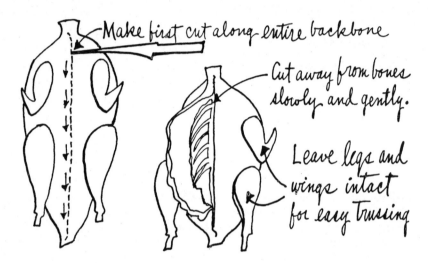

Make first cut along entire backbone
- Cut away from bones slowly and gently.

Leave legs and wings intact for easy trussing

How to Bone Chicken

Boned poultry is intriguing when it is being sliced and served. If you are enthusiastic about your cooking lessons, you will want the challenge of boning the bird yourself. Partially freeze the chicken. It will be easier to handle. Using a small sharp knife, hold the bird with its back up and cut down the center of the skin over the backbone. From here on the job is all yours. Work carefully, cutting away the meat of the chicken very close to the bone and trying not to tear the skin. For the bones that extend towards the joints and the tiny bones, scrape alongside the bone lightly. Very often the bone will slip out without use of the knife, breaking at the joint.

I prefer to leave wings and legs intact so that the chicken retains its natural shape when sewn together. Each serving may be a slice of boned chicken and a wing or leg. First-time guests will gasp with surprise and enjoy a real treat.

Stuffed Boned Chicken

1 whole 4 pound chicken, partially frozen	1 tablespoon chopped fresh herbs (parsley, tarragon, chervil)
2 tablespoons butter or chicken fat	1 egg
2 onions, finely diced	½ teaspoon salt
½ pound mushrooms, finely diced	¼ teaspoon pepper
1 pound ground beef or veal (or combination)	2 tablespoons butter softened or chicken fat
½ cup bread crumbs	½ teaspoon salt
	½ teaspoon paprika

1. Bone chicken or ask your butcher to do it. Leave bones in the wings and legs.

2. Reserve chicken bones, neck and gizzard to make broth for the sauce.

3. Melt butter in a heated skillet. Sauté onion until brown. Add mushrooms. Stir and cook for 2 minutes. If there is not enough room in the skillet remove mushrooms and onions to a side dish. Then brown the ground meat in the skillet. Separate the bits of meat with a fork while browning.

4. Remove from flame when meat is browned; add mushrooms, onions, bread crumbs, herbs, egg, ½ teaspoon salt, ¼ teaspoon pepper.

5. Prepare a roasting pan with a rack. Set oven at 325° F.

6. Place chicken flat on a board, skin side down. From one end, with a large needle and dental floss, start sewing the back together half way. When you have made enough of a pocket, place stuffing in chicken and finish sewing down the back.

7. Blend butter, salt and paprika.

8. Rub butter mixture all over chicken. Tie chicken legs together.

9. Place chicken on rack and roast for 1½ hours. Baste with the sauce below. For the last 10 minutes, set oven up to 400° F. to brown. Serve garnished with crisp watercress. Serves 4.

SAUCE

2 cups seasoned broth (made from chicken bones and giblets)	¼ cup Madeira wine
2 teaspoons Bovril	1 tablespoon cornstarch or arrowroot diluted in 2 tablespoons water

Bring all ingredients to a boil. Baste chicken as specified with this sauce. When serving pour sauce over chicken to glaze it.

THE DUCK

For many years, duck was forgotten in the average American home. In Long Island we have rediscovered our native bird and given it a proper place on the home menu. It can be delicious and crisp, a welcome change from other poultry.

~~~~~~

Roast Crisp Duck ★ ★ ★

4- or 5-pound duck	1 apple, unpeeled,
1 teaspoon salt	¼" cut off both ends
¼ cup lemon juice	1 onion
1 orange, unpeeled,	1 cup orange juice
¼" cut off both ends	1 orange, sliced

1. Wash duck with cold water. Dry it well. Salt inside and out. Sprinkle lemon juice in cavity and rub skin with lemon juice too. If duck is fresh killed, refrigerate it for 1 or 2 days.

2. Place orange, apple and onion in cavity of duck. These will be removed after roasting and discarded. Preheat oven to 350° F.

3. Truss bird by bringing cord under back and around sides of breasts, under tail, and then tie around legs. Place duck on a rack in an open roasting pan and cook for 1 hour.

4. Set oven up to 400° F. and roast 30-60 minutes more. During this time, turn bird for even browning and baste with orange juice.

5. Remove duck from oven and drain all fat from pan. Save brown drippings and 2 tablespoons fat for your sauce.

6. Duck may be kept in oven while you cook the sauce.

7. If you own a rotisserie by all means use it. This is an excellent method for duck. Allow about one hour on high heat. Entire cooking time for oven roasting should be 2 to 2½ hours.

8. For family style service, cut duck into eighths 30 minutes before dinner. Place duck and orange slices on an ovenproof platter. Coat all with sauce. Before serving, broil for 1 minute, 4 inches below flame. Yield: 2 to 3 servings.

SAUCE

Rind of 1 orange, coarsely grated	4 tablespoons currant jelly
1 cup water	2 tablespoons lemon juice
2 tablespoons duck fat	½ cup duck broth or drippings*
3 tablespoons brown sugar	4 tablespoons cornstarch
1 cup orange juice	4 tablespoons water

Simmer rind and water for 5 minutes. Add duck fat with brown sugar, orange juice, jelly, lemon juice and duck broth. Simmer all gently for 2 to 3 minutes. Blend cornstarch with water in a cup. Add the cornstarch mixture slowly; if you obtain the desired thickness before you have used it all, stop.

* If you have not used giblets to prepare broth, hold roasted duck over sauce to allow cavity juices to run down into sauce. This fortifies the duck flavor of the sauce.

Teacher says:

Do not prick duck! It remains more crisp without pricking.

There is much waste in duck. For adult portions and healthy appetites, even a 6-pound duck will serve no more than 3 good-sized portions.

Don't make the sad mistake that one of my students did. She was determined to have a change for Thanksgiving so she roasted *one* duck instead of turkey. In telling me this woeful tale, she described her guests' sorry looks of hunger as they rapidly cleaned the duck platter. Lucky for them, she baked plenty of cake! !

Chinese Barbecue Marinade,
page 263

Wine Marinade,
page 263

Spicy Marinade,
page 263

Three good marinades for duck.

Rolled Boned Duck

Bastes for Duck

See index for recipes.

THE TURKEY

Thanksgiving is *the* day of the year for our family. I think I enjoy it most of all—every minute of the 2½ days which I spend on preparation and actual cooking. As the season approaches, I begin my hunt for something new in appetizers, soups and vegetables. The traditional turkey remains on the menu, but one never knows what the stuffing will be. After many years of trying various ones, a recurring favorite is the Ritz cracker recipe (for meat and small birds as well as turkey). It originated with one of my neighbors, Clyta Birman, a truly fine cook. As you can see from the menu of the Hillman's latest Thanksgiving dinner, the turkey isn't all we stuff that Thursday!

THANKSGIVING MENU

Sole Laurentian   Crabmeat Rémoulade (served cold)
Black Mushroom Soup
Celery   Olives
Roast Stuffed Turkey   Acorn Squash   Onions in Casserole
Fresh Cranberry Mold   Easy Rolls
1961 Bernkasteler Riesling
Rum Chestnut Pie   Peach Chanteclair
Coffee   Brandy   Liqueurs

Roast Stuffed Turkey

Depend on a good butcher to supply you with a young plump turkey. Clean and wash bird with cold water. Dry inside and out. Salt inside lightly and sprinkle the juice of a lemon into the cavity. Refrigerate until ready to stuff. Lightly spoon stuffing into neck cavity, using enough so that poultry will look plump when served. Sew or skewer neck skin to the back of the bird. Fill the abdominal cavity with remaining stuffing. Sew the skin together with dental floss or skewer the skin together and lace with a heavy string. Twist wing tips under the back to hold them in place. Tie legs together securely.

Prepare a mixture of ¼ pound melted butter (or other fat), 1 teaspoon salt, ½ teaspoon pepper, and 1 teaspoon paprika. Rub ¼ of mixture over the entire surface of turkey. Place stuffed bird on a rack in a dry roasting pan. Dip a double square of cheesecloth in the remaining fat mixture and cover the bird loosely. Roast uncovered in a slow oven (300° F. to 325° F.).

If turkey is not too large it may be roasted breast side down to start and then turned. If it is too large leave the turkey on its back. Turkey may be basted with melted fat or broth. How to time the cooking:

Timing a turkey can be a problem because sometimes a *young* large bird cooks much faster than the time charts indicate. A 12- to 16-pound turkey with stuffing roasts in approximately 5 hours. A 16 to 20-pound turkey with stuffing roasts in approximately 6 to 7 hours. For the most scientific timing use a thermometer. Insert a meat thermometer into skin between 1st and 2nd ribs of turkey so that bulb end rests in the center of stuffing. Turkey is finished when thermometer registers 165° F. Doneness of meat may also be judged by the ease with which the drumstick moves up and down; also if the thigh meat feels soft to touch and if juices run out clear when the second joint is pierced with a long tined fork.

Allow 20 minutes rest period after cooking time for easier carving.

TO PREPARE GRAVY:

Cook at least 1 quart of broth the day before roasting a turkey. Use giblets and extra chicken parts if necessary. Make a generous amount of broth (see index for chicken broth) so that you will have enough for basting as well as gravy. To do away with as many last-minute chores as possible, I suggest thickening the broth (with flour or cornstarch— see index for sauces) a day ahead. Two hours before turkey is finished, baste it with *hot* thickened broth. This will produce a delicious gravy because it will absorb the flavors and brown color of the pan drippings.

RITZ CRACKER STUFFING

½ cup sautéed onion
1 box (large) Ritz crackers,
  finely crushed
2 eggs, beaten
½ cup diced celery
1 large carrot grated

1 tablespoon chopped parsley
½ pound cooked chestnuts
  or pistachio nuts
1 cup cold water
salt and pepper to taste

Blend onions into crushed crackers. Add the 2 beaten eggs and all other ingredients. Stuff turkey lightly and roast immediately.

Teacher says:

If you are preparing a bread stuffing figure ¾ cup of stuffing per pound of turkey. For a 12-pound turkey use approximately 16 slices of bread.

It is recommended that you prepare and measure your ingredients for stuffing ahead of time, but never combine the wet and dry ingredients until the last minute. Stuff turkey and roast immediately.

For a fluffy stuffing fill the cavity lightly. As the juices are absorbed during the roasting time, the stuffing will expand.

Freezing is not recommended for stuffings.

POULTRY QUESTIONS ANSWERED

Q *Is it necessary to truss poultry?*
A Yes, the legs and wings should be held close to the body. This will keep the breast moist. If a chicken or other poultry is not trussed, the legs will be forced out by the heat. The poultry will be difficult to turn and will not look so lovely when it is served.

Q *I read about food poisoning from stuffings. How can we avoid this?*
A Stuffing ingredients may be prepared ahead of time but mix them and stuff the bird just before roasting it. Remove leftover stuffing from bird after serving time. Always stuff a bird loosely so that stuffing can be eaten at first sitting if possible. An extra quantity of stuffing may be heated in a baking dish. The reason for these precautions is that stuffing provides a perfect medium for the growth of bacteria.

Q *How can broiled chicken be completely cooked without being dry?*
A Be careful not to select a scrawny bird. Broil chicken flesh side up first, at least 4 inches from the flame. It takes approximately 20 minutes on one side and 15 on the other. Constant basting with oil, butter, wine or broth will insure moistness. Serve it immediately after it is cooked; broiled chicken dries if it waits to be served.

Q *Which poultry recipes can be prepared in advance?*
A All the recipes except the whole roast chicken recipes can be partially cooked in advance. The chicken dishes that require moist cooking improve in flavor when reheated. In Arroz con Pollo, be careful not to overlook the chicken. In Paella, cook the rice with chicken in advance, but add the sea food just before dinner time.

LESSON 9

The Meat Course

We in the United States are great meat eaters and I hear around me a constant cry for more variety. Variety may be accomplished not only by the use of different meat (beef, veal, lamb and pork) but also by the methods of cooking. It does not always occur to the average cook that steak can be sautéed or pan-broiled as well as broiled; that the ordinary meat ball can be sautéed, broiled or stewed. Each method of cooking requires a slight change of seasoning which in turn lends interest to the same meats.

Principal methods of cooking meats are by dry heat and by moist heat.

1. *Roasting:* Dry heat cooking in an oven, uncovered and without added water. Covering or adding water produces vapor; this gives the meat a steamed texture; it is *not* roasting. It has been proven in many laboratory tests that a constant low temperature results in less shrinkage and loss of juices. A low oven temperature keeps the meat juicy and cooks it more uniformly. Allow roasts to set at least 20 minutes before serving. Open the door of the oven. Turn off the heat. The roast will be more easily sliced. Roasting is used for tender large cuts of beef, lamb, veal or pork.

113

The beef roasts most used besides prime ribs of beef are silver tip, top sirloin, eye round, sometimes a center cut of cross rib (shoulder steak), and chuck. For lamb, the leg, the rack (ribs) and the saddle make the best cuts. Shoulder may be used too. Veal roasts are usually made from the leg or saddle. Pork roasts most used are the leg (fresh ham) and the loin or rib cut. The shoulder is sometimes boned for a roast.

2. *Broiling,* the method by which meats are cooked by dry direct heat or over hot coals. Broiling temperature may be controlled by regulating the distance of the broiler pan from the source of heat. Broiling is more successful for thick tender cuts of steaks and lamb chops. (Pork and veal chops may be broiled but unless this is done expertly they tend to dry since they need longer cooking. Sautéeing and braising are preferable for these meats.)

3. *Pan-broiling,* the method by which tender meats are cooked on a hot heavy skillet without fat or water. Pan-broiling may be used for the same tender meats used for broiling. Pan-broiling is more successful for thinner steaks and chops (½″ or under) than is broiling.

4. *Sautéing and frying,* the methods by which meat is cooked in a small or large amount of fat (respectively). Sautéing is a favorite method of mine and can be a great boon for the busy cook. It is a tremendous help in the advance preparation of many excellent meat dishes which can then be reheated in the oven just before serving. The opportunities to introduce new seasonings and wines are boundless when sautéing beef, veal, pork or lamb.

5. *Braising,* moist-heat cooking, by which meat is browned and then allowed to simmer with a small amount of juice in a covered pot. Braising is used for less tender cuts of beef and small cuts of veal, lamb and pork.

6. *Stewing,* the method by which meats are cooked in a covered pot with much liquid. Stewing includes beefs for potting, less tender cuts of veal and pork. Smoked meats are often cooked this way.

BEEF

Steak and potatoes are family fare. Given a totally new look, the planked steak becomes party fare as well. Each semester my first group of lessons starts with the planked steak. Although I've taught this many times, each new group is as enthusiastic as the last. I enjoy teaching the wonderfully useful technique of the decorating bag—new

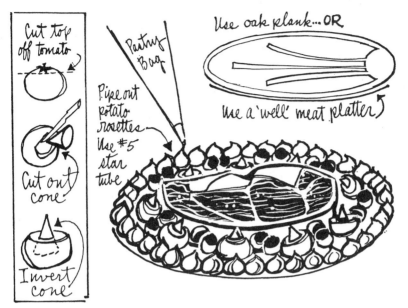

students are always impatient to try their hand at piping potato rosettes around the steak. When the garnishes of tomato, stuffed mushrooms and crisp parsley are finally tucked in place, the gestures and whispers usually indicate spontaneous approval.

The Planked Steak

1 sirloin steak, 1½ inches thick (4 pounds)

1 tablespoon Worcestershire sauce
2 tablespoons soy sauce

POTATO BORDER

6 medium potatoes
4 tablespoons butter

¼ cup hot milk

STUFFED MUSHROOMS

12 large whole mushrooms (stems only to be chopped fine)
3 onions, diced (1 pound)
2 tablespoons butter
½ cup fine bread crumbs

½ teaspoon salt
¼ teaspoon pepper
¼ teaspoon paprika
1 tablespoon chopped parsley

TOMATO GARNISH

6 tomatoes
3 tablespoons Parmesan or cheddar cheese

1 tablespoon chopped parsley
salt and pepper

1. Marinate steak in Worcestershire and soy sauces at room temperature for 2 hours, or even the previous night—the longer the more flavorsome.

2. An hour or so before the meal, peel potatoes, cook in boiling salted water until tender. Drain and dry for a few minutes over fire. Whip potatoes with 4 tablespoons of butter and enough hot milk to moisten lightly.

3. While potatoes are boiling, prepare the stuffing for the mushrooms. Sauté diced onions in a *dry*, heated skillet. When onions start turning brown, add 1 tablespoon of butter. Add the chopped stems of mushrooms. Cover for 2 minutes until mushrooms are slightly cooked. Uncover and add bread crumbs and a lump of butter. Season with salt, pepper, paprika, and chopped parsley. Stir well and stuff mushroom caps.

4. Cut off slice of tomato near stem end. With a small sharp knife, cut into tomato around the side to remove the center of tomato in one cone shape. Sprinkle the cavity with salt, pepper, parsley and cheese. Dot with butter if desired. Replace cone of tomato with point up. Place mushrooms and tomatoes on greased baking sheet. Bake for 20 minutes before broiling steak in a 350° F. oven.

5. Fill pastry bag half full with whipped potatoes while still warm and pipe decoratively around the edge of plank. This may be kept warm in the oven or on top of the stove in a warm area.

6. Use a broiling pan with a rack. Broil steak 10 minutes on one side, about 3 to 4 inches from flame, at highest degree. Turn steak and transfer to heated plank. Broil for 3 minutes.

7. Surround steak with tomatoes and mushrooms. Broil for about 5 minutes or at least until potatoes are pleasantly browned. Serves 4 to 6 depending on appetites.

8. To serve: Place plank on an asbestos sheet or stainless steel tray. Remove portions of potatoes and mushrooms garnish to warmed dinner plates. Then slice steak ½-inch thick for individual portions. With one large steak you can generally take care of both the well done and rare steak eaters. Invariably, the ends will be crisper and better done than the center. Yield: 4-6 servings.

Use of Pastry Bag

Buy a large bag. This may be used for large as well as small quantities.

To fill bag, hold bottom end in left hand. Fold top over hand forming cuff. Fill opening with potato or any desired filling. Holding upright, unfold bag, twist top tightly until filling shows through tube opening. To pipe potatoes, hold twisted top of bag; use pressure from right hand, and very gradually, continue to press out a fancy border all around the edge of plank.

If this is a new experience, practice by using white shortening on back of any baking dish. The shortening can be re-used for other cooking.

Teacher says:

Advance Preparations: Mushrooms and tomatoes may be prepared as much as a day in advance, and refrigerated ready to bake. Potatoes can be piped on to plank in the morning and allowed to rest until ready to use. Do not refrigerate. Potatoes may be heated on plank when mushrooms and tomatoes are baking. The only last-minute preparation is the broiling of the steak. To avoid raw purple look in center of steak, set steak 1½ inches or thicker in a 250° oven for one hour before broiling.

Broiling Instructions: Meat should always be room temperature. Thick cuts of meat, 1 to 2 inches, are best for broiling. However, if you must broil thinner cuts, bring broiling pan as close to flame as possible. Butter the surface of the steak for added flavor and brownness.

> *1½-inch steaks:* If preheated in oven, place broiler pan
> *2″ from flame* and shorten broiling time 3 minutes on
> each side; if not preheated, 3″ to 4″ from flame.

Planking: Seasoning new plank: Coat plank with salad oil and heat in 200° F. oven for 2 hours. Remove and wipe excess oil. Store for future use. Never expose plank to direct flame. Plank must always be covered with food or aluminum foil. Plank may be heated in warm oven. An 18-inch plank is my preference.

Wash plank lightly. Do not use abrasives. A stainless steel or other oven platter may be used. A plank is useful because it may be carved on. When not in use as a plank it may be used as a carving board.

Think of how many ways you can use this recipe! The plank can be used for any broiled meats. If carving and serving worry you, try planking individual steaks. You may even glorify the hamburger. For sheer elegance, plank filet mignon. The stuffed mushroom is delicious as a hot hors d'oeuvre, a first course, or as a vegetable. Remember to use the stuffing recipe for poultry or fish. For poultry, livers and a touch of rosemary may be added. For fish, use added whole mushrooms as well as the stems, and plenty of fresh parsley.

~~~~~~~~

This is one of the most popular steaks served in the better restaurants in France. Strangely enough, the coarsely-cracked pepper produces a flavor which is more aromatic than truly pungent. Although generally done in the skillet, as I give it below, Steak au Poivre may also be grilled over charcoal.

Steak au Poivre

4 filet, shell, club or chicken steaks	½ cup Port wine
8 to 12 black peppercorns, coarsely cracked	4 tablespoons rich beef broth
4 to 8 tablespoons butter or combination of butter and oil	4 slices French bread, browned in butter

Trim steaks of excess fat. Press pepper into both sides of the steaks. Heat a large skillet. Add 2 tablespoons butter. Over a high flame, sear steaks on both sides. Pour in wine and cook for 2 minutes. Remove steaks to a preheated platter. Add broth to wine in skillet. Allow sauce to reduce slightly. Lower flame and add butter, bit by bit, stirring well. Sauce will become shiny. Immediately pour over steaks and serve hot over butter fried French bread croutons. Serves 4.

~~~~~~~~

The quickest cooking method is the Chinese stir and fry, mostly used for Cantonese dishes. Flank steak thinly sliced and quickly seared is as tender as its superior, the filet. Watch the seconds in timing, because overcooking toughens the fibers of the meat. When the Chinese bok choy is not available use Chinese cabbage.

Beef and Bok Choy

1 pound flank steak, sliced thin against the grain	¼ cup chicken stock
2 tablespoons oil	1 tablespoon sherry
1 teaspoon salt	1 teaspoon soy sauce
3 slices fresh ginger root	½ teaspoon monosodium glutamate
1 bunch bok choy sliced (use only white part)	⅛ teaspoon pepper
	1 tablespoon cornstarch mixed with 2 tablespoons water

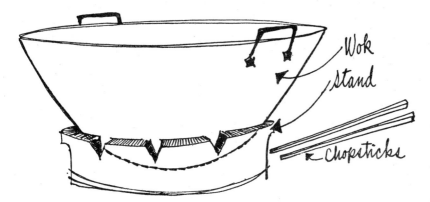

1. If entire flank steak was bought cut 4 strips with the grain. Use 2 strips for this recipe. Freeze the other 2 for use at a later date. As a matter of fact it is easier to slice meat thin when it is partially frozen because it is firm. Cut each strip into thin slices (⅛").

2. Heat a large skillet. Add 2 tablespoons oil and ½ teaspoon salt. When oil smokes throw in 3 slices ginger.

3. When ginger is brown add bok choy. Stir fiercely with 2 spoons (or better still chopsticks). (This is the quick stir and fry.)

4. Add ¼ cup chicken stock and cover. Cook for 1 minute. Remove all to a side platter (vegetables and juice). Ginger root may be discarded now if you do not care to eat it.

5. Add 1 tablespoon oil to the skillet and ½ teaspoon salt. When oil is smoky add meat, 1 tablespoon sherry, 1 teaspoon soy. Stir and fry until meat is browned. If oil is very hot, meat should be browned in 30 seconds.

6. Stir in cooked bok choy; season with ½ teaspoon monosodium glutamate and ⅛ teaspoon pepper. Thicken with cornstarch and water mixture. Heat for 10 seconds. Serve with Steamed Rice (see index). Serves 4.

Teacher says:

Beef and Bok Choy is traditionally cooked in a Chinese wok.

Believe it or not; this takes 4 minutes to cook. I've included time for you to read the recipe step by step.

Preparation is important. Slice meat and vegetables in advance. Be sure to slice both meat and vegetables against the grain. In a stir-and-fry dish, if meat is sliced, vegetables are sliced; if meat is minced, vegetables are minced.

Set out meat and other ingredients on a tray ready to be cooked. Now proceed to cook following the directions carefully. I have repeated all the amounts so you need follow only the directions.

See Index for other Chinese dishes. Look for Beef Curry with Onions, Sweet and Sour Spareribs, Chinese Marinades.

~~~~~~~~~~

The famous Beef Stroganoff, another quick-sautéed dish is not far afield from the stir-and-fry method. Preparation is as important here as it is in Chinese dishes. Be daring, mix Chinese-style rice with Russian-style Stroganoff.

Beef Stroganoff

2 pounds steak, cut in ⅛″ strips	½ pound mushrooms, sliced
2 tablespoons lemon juice	2 tablespoons flour
1 teaspoon Worcestershire sauce	½ cup beef broth
½ teaspoon salt	1 teaspoon tomato paste
¼ teaspoon pepper	1 cup sour cream
2 tablespoons butter	12 pimento stuffed olives
2 onions diced	

Season beef with lemon juice, Worcestershire, salt and pepper. Allow to stand at room temperature for 2 hours. Heat a skillet with 1 tablespoon butter. Sauté onion until brown and then add mushrooms. Transfer onions and mushrooms to a side dish. Heat skillet with remaining tablespoon of butter. Brown meat over a high flame, stirring briskly. Allow meat to remain slightly rare; browning should take no more than 2 minutes. Stir onions and mushrooms into meat. Lower flame, sprinkle flour all over meat and blend it in well. Pour broth over meat; add tomato paste and stir all together. Blend in sour cream thoroughly. Bring to a simmer and serve immediately with fluffy rice. Garnish with stuffed olives. Serves 4.

Teacher says:

This recipe is at its very best when filet of beef is used. If this seems too extravagant use sirloin, cross rib, chuck steak or round. Too often, Stroganoff is made with the tougher cuts and allowed to cook until tender, becoming a sort of stew. For a true Stroganoff, the meat should be a tender cut.

As a matter of fact try this for a perfect quick dinner. If the meat is tender, cooking time should be no more than 10 to 15 minutes; 5 minutes for preparation (dicing and cutting), and the remainder of time for the sautéing.

With onion and mushroom sautéed in advance, cooking may be completed in the chafing dish, at the table. Cook meat in the blazer pan directly over the flame.

There are not many ways for successfully using leftover roast beef in a hot dish. Rare roast beef can be sliced for Stroganoff, making another meal for another day.

———————

There are times through the year when a gala occasion calls for an equally gala roast. Filet Wellington is my choice for those very special times. The tender filet, blanketed in mushroom purée and puff pastry, makes a sensational and dramatic main course.

Filet Wellington ★ ★ ★

Buy a whole filet (4½ to 5½ pounds) and store it in refrigerator for 2 to 3 days.

Advance Preparation: Make puff pastry (use pie pastry if you wish) and *make the following stuffing:*

2 tablespoons butter	2 tablespoons cream
2 shallots, minced	2 tablespoons Madeira or Port wine
or 2 tablespoons minced onion	1 tablespoon parsley chopped
1½ pounds mushrooms, minced	½ teaspoon salt
1 tablespoon flour	⅛ teaspoon pepper

Melt butter in hot skillet and then sauté shallots with mushrooms. When mushrooms turn brown and moisture is cooked away, stir flour into them. Lower flame and add cream, wine, parsley and seasonings. Cook 2 minutes to thicken. Set aside to cool. Refrigerate if it is to be kept overnight.

On the morning of the dinner:

Allow filet to stand at room temperature. Sprinkle it with 2 tablespoons soy and 2 tablespoons Worcestershire sauces. Roll out ½ recipe of puff pastry into a rectangle 16″ by 9″. Pastry should be a little longer than filet and just over twice as wide. Place rolled out dough on to a jelly roll pan and refrigerate.

2 to 3 hours before dinner:

Preheat oven to 400° F.

Spread 3 tablespoons butter or olive oil all over the filet. Roast for 30 minutes. Take out of oven and set aside to cool. Reserve juice in pan for sauce.

45 minutes before serving: Take pastry and mushroom dressing out of refrigerator. Spread mushroom mixture down the center of pastry. Place filet top side down on mushrooms. Fold dough over to enclose meat completely. Turn filet over on to clean jelly roll pan so that the seam of dough is on the bottom. Make criss-cross design over top with a sharp knife. Brush with beaten egg yolk and water.

Bake for 400° F. for 35 minutes.

Serve with Wine Sauce au Perigord. Serves 8 to 10.

WINE SAUCE AU PERIGORD

2 tablespoons pâté (goose liver or chicken liver)	1 tablespoon cornstarch or arrowroot
1 small truffle minced	2 tablespoons water
½ cup port wine	1½ cups beef broth
	Reserved juices of filet

Blend pâté, truffles and wine together. Mix cornstarch and water in a cup. Cook beef broth with reserved juices of filet for 3 to 5 minutes. Blend all ingredients, stirring constantly until sauce thickens.

Serve filet on a large oval platter, garnished with watercress. Spoon sauce over each slice of filet as it is served. Slices should be at least ½″ thick. This recipe is illustrated in color.

The sandwich meat loaf makes good eating for a simple family dinner, excellent sandwiches for teen-age parties and summer barbecues.

Sandwich Meat Loaf

2 pounds ground chuck	3 frankfurters
1 grated onion	¼ cup prepared mustard (Dijon or Dusseldorf)
2 raw potatoes grated	1 teaspoon ginger
2 eggs	2 cans (New England style) baked beans
1 teaspoon salt	
½ teaspoon pepper	

1. Set oven at 350° F. Prepare a 13″ by 9″ baking pan.
2. Blend together the meat, onion, potatoes, eggs, salt and pepper.

Place mixture on a large sheet of waxed paper. Spread mixture out to form a rectangle the length of baking pan to be used.

3. Place frankfurters along the length of the beef and roll to enclose frankfurters. If three frankfurters are too long, cut off frankfurters to fit. Use waxed paper to help mold meat into a long roll.

4. Lifting the meat with the waxed paper, place it in the baking pan. Spread meat with a mixture of mustard and ginger.

5. Bake for 1 hour, then add baked beans to the pan and complete the baking. Total baking time should be about 1 hour 10 minutes for medium rare, 1 hour 30 minutes for well done. This loaf slices perfectly to fit a hamburger bun.

Teacher says:

The softener for the meat loaf in this case is the raw potato. It may well be that you prefer bread as in Swedish Meat Balls, page 125.

Mustard and ginger are used a good deal by the Scandinavians. Try this seasoning on a silver tip roast beef or chuck pot roast, if only for the appetizing aroma.

For the barbecue this meat roll can be broiled in one piece if watched carefully for even cooking. Or it may be cut in 1" slices and broiled for sandwiches. To do this, partially freeze the meat loaf so that you will find slicing it very easy.

Frosty days invite cooking with steam. More time indoors allows more time for Dutch oven cooking; cold weather arouses the appetites for stews and heavier sauces.

Tenderloin en Brochette

Eggplant Florentine

Meat Pastries

Meat Blintzes

See index for recipes.

Since stews are best cooked slow and long, many tough economical cuts of meats can be used. Wines play a major part here because they not only enhance flavors but also act as tenderizers. Boeuf Bourguignon is only one example of a beef stew. Follow the same method for a pot roast, with or without wine.

Boeuf Bourguignon

2 pounds chuck or rump of beef	2 cloves garlic, crushed
3 tablespoons flour	bay leaf, 2 cloves, parsley sprig
1 teaspoon salt	(all tied in a cheesecloth bag)
½ teaspoon pepper	1 cup red wine (Burgundy)
¼ teaspoon paprika	½ pound mushrooms sliced
2 large onions, diced fine	1 tablespoon chopped parsley
4 slices bacon, cut in small pieces	
(optional)	

Dredge meat in flour mixed with salt, pepper and paprika. Preheat oven to 425° F. Place meat in a casserole on a bed of onions, reserving some onions to be placed on top of meat. Brown meat, uncovered in 425° F. oven. This should take about 15 minutes. When meat is well browned, stir it and add bacon if desired. Add garlic, bay leaf, cloves and parsley. Lower oven to 350° F. Cover and bake for 1 hour. Add 1 cup red wine, mushrooms and bake for 1 hour more. If more sauce is desired add 1 cup more wine, hot broth or hot water. Taste and adjust seasoning. Test meat with a fork for tenderness. Sometimes this stew takes longer cooking depending on the quality of the meat. When ready to dine sprinkle fresh parsley over the meat and serve with boiled new potatoes or buttered noodles. Serves 4 to 5.

Teacher says:

Neck of lamb is economical and delicious for a winter stew. Use the same method as above, employing either white or red wine. An addition of 1 cup canned tomatoes (instead of or with mushrooms), four or five small potatoes and four carrots makes this a complete dinner. You will need 1 cup broth to provide more gravy. With lamb it may be necessary to skim off fat. The easiest way to accomplish this is to cool the gravy to harden the fat which is then discarded.

Of course, like soups, stews are better tasting each time they are reheated. If you prepare a stew in advance you'll have no trouble skimming off the fat. It will taste better the second day.

Selecting recipes for ground meat stews could be endless, but surely these are the ones that every cook should have. Each has its very own flavor; each is a weekday meat yet makes wonderful party fare. The dishes freeze well in their sauces and are favorites for the hors d'oeuvres hot buffet.

Swedish Meat Balls

1 pound ground veal or pork	½ cup sautéed onions
1 pound ground beef	1 teaspoon salt
3 slices stale white bread, soaked in ½ cup milk	½ teaspoon pepper
	½ teaspoon freshly ground nutmeg
2 eggs, slightly beaten	2 tablespoons butter

Combine meat with bread, eggs, onions and seasonings. Use your hand to blend it lightly but well. Dipping your hands in cold water form small balls. They are tastier and more delicate when made small. Heat skillet and melt 2 tablespoons butter. Brown the meatballs on all sides and transfer to a saucepan or oven casserole. Prepare the following sauce.

SAUCE

3 tablespoons butter	1 teaspoon tomato paste
1 large clove garlic	1 teaspoon Bovril
4 tablespoons flour	1 cup sour cream
2 cups consommé or beef broth	

In the skillet used for browning meat, add 3 tablespoons butter. When butter is melted and sizzling, add crushed garlic. Blend flour in well over flame. Remove from flame and gradually add consommé, paste and Bovril. Set over a low flame and allow sauce to come to a boil, stirring constantly. When sauce is thickened, turn off flame. Stir a tablespoon of hot sauce into sour cream. When it is blended well add another and then another until sour cream is thoroughly blended with at least one cup of hot sauce. Pour all into skillet and stir well. Heat on low flame for 1 minute. Pour over meat balls and turn meat balls in sauce. Heat meat balls uncovered over a low flame for 20 minutes, or bake in casserole in a 350° F. oven for 20 minutes. Serve with buttered noodles or plain boiled white rice. Serves 6.

Teacher says:

In adding the sour cream you will notice that, like egg yolks, it must be blended with hot sauces first; if not it curdles. If the sour cream is not blended thoroughly with the hot sauce, you may see white specks. Ignore them; your taste buds will not know the difference.

Nutmeg may be a brand new seasoning experience for you. Use less than suggested the first time. Always use small amounts of new herbs and spices when first trying them.

The job of sautéing these tiny meat balls can be tiresome. If you are preparing a double recipe, brown them in a flat greased baking pan (jelly roll pan) for 10 minutes at 450° F. Turn them once or twice. To make neat-looking meat balls grease the palms of your hands with a little oil.

These meat balls are just as good without the sauce. They can be served from the blazer of a chafing dish with or without sauce for a hot hors d'oeuvres. For a big party their preparation can be completed days or weeks in advance. Refrigeration is fine for a few days, longer than that use your freezer.

Remember that this meat mixture is fine as a meat loaf. The bread gives the meat a soft texture and extends the quantity. If necessary, substitute water for milk. The sautéed onion adds more flavor than would raw onion. Many recipes call for sautéed mushrooms too. The combination of sautéed onion and mushroom enhances any meat recipe. If available use them!

Since stuffed cabbage is made all over town, it is truly amazing that there are constant requests for the recipe. Each recipe differs slightly but I always find that it is a great help to have at least one set of good proportions. The individual cook should taste and season, adjusting the amount of sugar, tomatoes, ginger, etc.

Stuffed Cabbage

1 large green-leaved cabbage

FOR THE MEAT:

2 pounds ground beef
¼ cup converted rice
  or 1 cup cooked rice
½ cup sautéed onion
2 eggs

¼ teaspoon monosodium glutomate
½ tablespoon crushed garlic
  or ¼ teaspoon garlic powder
1 teaspoon salt
¼ teaspoon pepper

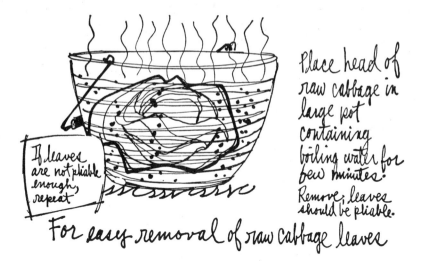

Place head of raw cabbage in large pot containing boiling water for few minutes. Remove; leaves should be pliable.

If leaves are not pliable enough, repeat.

For easy removal of raw cabbage leaves

FOR THE POT:

3 onions diced
any leftover cabbage cut in shreds
4 cups tomatoes (or #3 can)
1 8-ounce can tomato sauce)
3 tablespoons lemon juice
¼ cup wine (if available) sweet or dry

2 tablespoons brown sugar
8 gingersnaps
½ cup water
1½ teaspoons salt
¼ cup raisins (optional)

1. Cut off slice from bottom of cabbage. Cut out as much core as possible. Wash cabbage well.

2. Boil a large potful of water. Immerse cabbage in water and allow it to boil for a few minutes. As soon as leaves start to wilt slightly, take cabbage out, drain and remove outer leaves or as many as are already wilted. You may have to repeat this until a good many outer leaves fall off easily in one piece. Be careful not to tear them.

3. Drain leaves on paper toweling.

4. Blend all the ingredients for the meat in one bowl.

5. On each leaf of cabbage place 1 tablespoon of meat on the end closest to you. Bring cabbage end over meat. Fold both vertical sides over towards center and roll up the package. Finish all the cabbage rolls until meat is completely used.

6. Use a 5- or 6-quart dutch oven or oven casserole. Line the bot-

tom with diced onion and cabbage shreds (leftover cabbage not used for rolls).

7. Place cabbage rolls in neat layers. Cover with all the remaining ingredients for the pot. Cook for 2 hours over a low flame, tightly covered. This may be baked in the oven at 350° F. for 2 hours. Serves 6.

Teacher says:

For hors d'oeuvres or buffet use, cut the cabbage leaves in half and fill them with half the amount of meat. These will make small rolls.

For the children in the house who don't care for cabbage, form some of the meat into balls and drop them on the top.

For a completely different flavoring, use 3 cups beef broth instead of tomatoes and tomato sauce.

When gingersnaps are not in the cupboard use 1 teaspoon ginger powder. The snaps also provide a thickening for the sauce so in their absence you may want to thicken sauce with a mixture of 2 tablespoons cornstarch and 4 tablespoons water.

Seasoning in a sweet sour sauce such as this depends a great deal on the cook. The proportions of lemon juice to sugar and salt may vary depending on the cabbage. Taste!

Italian Meat Sauce

2 tablespoons olive oil	1 4-ounce can tomato paste
1 onion diced	1 teaspoon salt
2 cloves garlic crushed	½ teaspoon pepper
1 pound ground beef	⅛ teaspoon red pepper
½ green pepper, diced	½ teaspoon allspice
½ pound mushrooms, diced	½ teaspoon oregano
1 tablespoon chopped parsley	1 teaspoon basil
1 #3 can tomatoes (Italian style)	1 bay leaf
1 8-ounce can tomato sauce	1 teaspoon sugar

In a 5- to 6-quart heavy Dutch oven or saucepan, heat olive oil and sauté onions with garlic lightly. Add meat. Brown meat stirring with a wooden spoon to break it up into small pieces. Add green pepper and mushrooms to meat. Cook for 2 minutes. Stir in all other ingredients. Cover and cook for 2 hours over low heat. Taste and adjust the seasoning. Serves 4 to 6—enough to cover 1 pound spaghetti.

Teacher says:

Whole Italian sausages may be added to the sauce and served with it.

For a hot flavor, cut up hot Italian sausage into sauce.

Use this sauce for lasagne. It is very good served over veal and topped with Mozzarella and Parmesan cheeses (Veal Parmigiana).

The same tomato sauce may be made without meat and used in combination with vegetables, pasta and meats.

The sauce is simple to make in double quantity and frozen in amounts packaged for future use.

If meat balls are used instead of meat sauce, prepare the meat balls by sautéing them in oil. When brown turn them into the sauce and cook for 2 hours.

Barbecued Hamburger

See index for recipe.

VEAL

Veal, cut Italian style, cooks in minutes and many interesting recipes can be created around it. Buy veal that looks pale pink and free of tissues. Next to beef, veal is always a safe choice for guests, for it is universally enjoyed. Any one of the veal recipes is a fine choice for a dinner party.

Butterfly Veal Parmesan

See index for recipe.

～～～～～

Veal in Marsala

½ cup bread crumbs   2 pounds veal, cut Italian style
½ cup flour   4 tablespoons oil
1 teaspoon salt   4 tablespoons butter
⅛ teaspoon pepper   ½ pound sliced fresh mushrooms
⅛ teaspoon paprika   1 cup dry Marsala wine
¼ teaspoon oregano

1. On a large sheet of waxed paper blend crumbs, flour, seasonings and oregano all together. Dredge veal in this dry mixture.

2. Heat large skillet with 1 tablespoon oil. Add 1 tablespoon butter. When butter is melted sauté meat until brown on both sides (1 minute on each side).

3. Tranfer meat to a flat baking pan as it browns. Use more oil and butter to finish browning, reserving some butter for mushrooms.

4. When all the meat is browned, melt remainder of butter in skillet and sauté mushrooms over a high flame for one minute.

5. Pour wine on to mushrooms. Cook for thirty seconds. Pour wine and mushrooms over meat.

6. Bake for fifteen minutes at 350° F. Serve immediately. Serves 6.

Teacher says:

If you prefer a heavier coating on veal, dredge veal many hours in advance. Reserve leftover crumb and flour mixture. Before browning, dredge veal in this mixture once more. This is a very fine company meat, because the first five preparations may be done many hours in advance.

Veal may be completely cooked in the skillet. Brown veal quickly on both sides, lower flame and cook for three to four minutes. Set aside to complete all the meat. At the end set veal slices into skillet with wine and mushrooms. Reheat for a minute and serve.

Veal, sliced Italian style, usually yields seven slices to a pound. If you desire it thinner you may want to pound it.

This becomes Veal Saltimbocca alla Romana if a slice of prosciutto ham and a fresh sage leaf are fastened with a toothpick to every piece of veal, as I discovered at several of the best restaurants in Rome. Dried sage available here is not a good substitute. If you don't grow sage in the garden, use basil or rosemary.

〜〜〜〜〜

Veal aux Provinces ★ ★ ★

1 cup of crumb and flour mixture (as in Veal in Marsala)	3 tablespoons oil
2 pounds veal, cut Italian style	3 tablespoons butter

Prepare veal by dredging it in crumb mixture. If time permits allow meat to rest and dredge again before sautéeing. Heat one tablespoon oil in a large skillet. Add one tablespoon butter and proceed to brown veal in hot fat. Add oil and butter as needed for browning. As each slice is browned, transfer it to a flat baking dish large enough to hold all the meat without crowding. When the meat is all browned prepare the following sauce.

SAUCE

½ cup Sherry or Madeira wine	2 tablespoons flour
1 cup brown stock	3 tablespoons water
1 teaspoon tomato paste	½ cup heavy cream

Pour wine into the same skillet that meat was browned in (do not wash it), cook it down for one minute. Add brown stock and tomato paste. Make a smooth paste of flour and water. Turn off flame and add thickening to the sauce in skillet. Turn on flame and allow sauce to come to a boil and thicken, stirring constantly. Add sweet cream and blend in thoroughly. (All of this may be done in advance.) Pour half of sauce over the veal to mask it. Bake 10 minutes at 400° F. Reserve the remainder of sauce to be passed around at serving time. Serve around a pyramid of buttered rice. Accompany it with a tossed salad, crusty rolls and your dinner is set. Serves 6.

Note: For brown stock, use beef broth or consommé. A stock made with chicken or veal would be excellent. An added teaspoon of Bovril may be used for brown color and flavor.

〜〜〜〜〜

Last year a reporter from the New York Herald Tribune *covering the Bermuda Yacht races was amazed to find Veal Cordon Bleu on an entrant's menu. He tracked it down to one of my prize students, Murray Hirsh, whose plan for eating during the races seemed to re-*

quire a fine, well-equipped kitchen rather than the tight squeeze of a ship's galley. He used the recipe which follows. In earlier veal recipes, we used a light bread-crumb-and-flour coating. For Veal Cordon Bleu it is desirable to have a heavier breading since it is necessary to seal the ham and cheese between two slices of veal. For this reason we employ eggs in conjunction with the dry mixture. When a heavier crust is desired, dip meat first in dry mixture, then eggs and water, then dry mixture again.

Veal Cordon Bleu

12 slices veal, Italian style
   (1¾ pounds)
½ teaspoon salt
¼ teaspoon pepper
6 slices Swiss cheese
6 slices prosciutto or boiled ham

1 cup mixed crumbs and flour
   seasoned (see Veal in Marsala,
   page 130)
2 eggs beaten with 4 tablespoons
   cold water
½ teaspoon salt
4 tablespoons oil
2 tablespoons butter

Advance Preparation: Two to twelve hours prior to cooking, pound veal to flatten. Season with salt and pepper. Place one slice each of cheese and ham on six slices of veal. Cover each with remaining six slices of veal. Do not allow any cheese or ham to show through veal. Dredge each veal sandwich in crumb mixture, reserving leftover mixture. This can be set in refrigerator overnight or in the freezer for two hours. It is easier to work with when it is very cold or even partially frozen.

When ready to cook, set out leftover crumb mixture. Stir eggs, water and salt together in a pie plate. Preheat oven to 375° F. Heat skillet with two tablespoons oil and one tablespoon butter. Dip very firm, cold veal first in crumbs, then egg, then crumbs again. Place in hot fat and brown on both sides for about two minutes on each side. Transfer to a flat baking pan. Brown all the veal, using more oil and butter as needed. Bake for ten minutes at 375°.

Serve with the following sauce. For dinner parties, all preparation except for actual baking may be finished in advance. Sauce may be cooked in advance too. If for some reason serving is delayed, lower the temperature of oven and baste with a small amount of the sauce. Serves 6.

SAUCE

1 cup chicken or beef stock	½ cup Marsala or Madeira wine
1 teaspoon Bovril	1 tablespoon cornstarch
1 teaspoon tomato paste	2 tablespoons water

Combine stock, Bovril, tomato paste and wine in a saucepan, bring to boil. Blend cornstarch and water. Lower flame under sauce. Add cornstarch, stirring constantly, and allow to thicken.

~~~~~~~

It is true that we do not have as consistently good quality veal as we do beef, nevertheless, there are occasions when veal is featured in the meat market. Good veal is usually a pale pink; avoid the darker meats. The leg and saddle of veal are most expensive but hardly necessary for this roast which is well flavored and stuffed with a large assortment of vegetables. My choice is breast of veal. If you prefer the shoulder, it may be boned too with a pocket prepared for the stuffing.

Roast Breast of Veal — Fresh Vegetable Stuffing

FOR STUFFING:

2 tablespoons butter	2 tomatoes, diced
3 onions, diced	1 tablespoon chopped parsley
½ pound mushrooms, diced	4 cups toasted bread cubes
4 stalks celery, diced	or seasoned stuffing bread cubes
1 carrot, grated	1 teaspoon salt
½ eggplant, diced (unpeeled)	½ teaspoon pepper

Melt butter in skillet. Sauté onions in butter. Then brown the mushrooms. When onion and mushrooms are brown, add the other vegetables and sauté for a few minutes. Remove from stove. Add all the other ingredients. Season and cool.

PREPARING AND ROASTING:

1 breast of veal with pocket for stuffing (4-5 pounds)	1 cup white wine
	2 cups consommé
1 teaspoon salt	1 teaspoon Bovril
½ teaspoon pepper	¼ cup tomato purée
½ teaspoon paprika	2 tablespoons flour
2 tablespoons flour	4 tablespoons water
2 onions, diced	½ cup Madeira wine

1. Season the veal with salt, pepper, paprika. Then dust all over with flour. Set oven at 400° F.

2. Fill the pocket with cool prepared vegetable stuffing. Skewer or sew up the opening.

3. Lay veal on a bed of diced onion in an open roasting pan. Place into the oven at 400° F. Roast uncovered for 30 minutes.

4. Lower oven to 350° F. and baste veal with 1 cup of white wine. Cover and continue cooking for 1 hour.

5. Prepare a mixture of 2 cups consommé, 1 teaspoon Bovril, ¼ cup tomato purée, 2 tablespoons flour mixed with 4 tablespoons water, and ½ cup Madeira wine. Add this mixture to the veal for the last half hour of roasting.

6. Veal should be timed about 30 minutes to a pound. Most veal roasts, stuffed, should bake 2½ to 3 hours. The veal and gravy improves with slow longer cooking. Serves 6.

Teacher says:

Veal is a lean, mild flavored meat. Used as a roast, it must be basted with wine, broth or a tomato base sauce.

Herbs lend a fine fragrance to veal dishes of all kinds. Try marjoram, rosemary, basil, savory or oregano in various recipes and at different times. Experiment with one herb at a time; each herb will change the flavor slightly. With every change you will be educating yourself to the differences of herb flavors.

PORK

Pork chops need to be cooked to thorough doneness and for this reason are so often cooked into thorough dryness. The following recipes avert this disaster by combining pork with a good sauce or wine. The pork is thus thoroughly cooked while the sauce gives it flavor and moistness. Everyone can enjoy this rich meat in tranquility.

Pork Chops in Tomato-Orange Sauce

8 pork chops
½ cup bread crumbs and flour
   mixture (as in Veal Marsala)
½ teaspoon sage or oregano
2 cups tomato sauce

1 cup orange juice
1 tablespoon brown sugar
2 tablespoons honey
1 tablespoon oil

Dredge pork chops in crumb mixture with sage or oregano (whichever you prefer). Set oven at 350° F. Combine tomato sauce, orange juice, brown sugar and honey. Heat skillet with 1 tablespoon oil. Brown chops in skillet. When browned on both sides transfer to a large shallow baking pan or casserole (from oven to table). Pour sauce over pork chops and bake for 1 hour 15 minutes at 350° F. Serve directly from baking dish or set a mound of rice in the center of a platter surrounded by chops. Serves 4.

A cook is greatly dependent on the butcher who can be part teacher and part supplier. The young bride would be wise to deal with one good butcher who can be called upon to answer questions and offer suggestions. With the advent of our supermarket system, this is not easily done today. My good fortune has always brought me in touch with butchers who were willing to share their knowledge. My neighbor and butcher, Carl Blumenschein, is one of those rare people who inherited from his family a love and skill for his business. Each meat package is wrapped with personal pride. His suggestions have always been happily received by me.

One summer's day many years ago, he boned and rolled an entire rack of pork (rib end to loin) and suggested we barbecue it. Barbecued or roasted indoors, this pork roll is succulent to the last drop. Pork must be eaten well done. Use a meat thermometer if necessary but be careful not to overcook.

Pork Roll

loin of pork (5 to 6 pounds before boning)	½ teaspoon pepper
1 teaspoon salt	2 to 3 cloves garlic

Have butcher bone and tie pork. Salt and pepper the pork. Preheat oven to 350° F. Make small incisions in top fat of pork. Insert slivers of garlic. Roast pork, uncovered on a rack in a 350° F. oven. Time it at 35 minutes to a pound. Serves 6.

This is a perfect meat for a cold meat platter. What a sandwich treat! Gravy may be made in the usual manner but I serve it unadorned with new potatoes, sweet potatoes or rice. Don't forget the applesauce or some other form of fruit.

Chinese Roast Pork (Barbecued)
Chinese Spareribs (Barbecued)
Sweet and Sour Spareribs
See index for recipes.

~~~~~~~~~

Pork Chops Vermouth

8 pork chops
½ cup seasoned crumb mixture
1 tablespoon oil
1 clove garlic
¼ cup sweet vermouth

⅓ cup chicken broth
1 teaspoon soy sauce
1 tablespoon cornstarch
2 tablespoons water
¼ pound snow peas

Dredge chops in crumb mixture. Heat a large skillet with oil. Place garlic in skillet and sauté until brown on both sides. When browning, do not crowd pan. Remove chops to a side dish until all are completed. Remove garlic and discard. Place all chops in the skillet. Pour on vermouth and cook down for a few seconds. Add broth and soy sauce. Cover and cook for 35 minutes. Blend cornstarch and water. Uncover skillet, toss snow peas around chops, cover and cook 1 minute. Uncover, remove chops to a serving platter. Lower flame, blend cornstarch mixture gradually into the broth and snow peas until the mixture takes on the proper thickness as it boils. Pour sauce and snow peas over chops. Serve immediately with rice. Serves 4.

LAMB

The Sunday roast has been and still remains the traditional dinner in many households. As the next recipe demonstrates, it need not be a rib roast or leg of lamb all the time. Rib lamb chops, prepared to form a crown, can came to the table decorated with gay paper frills. Ask your butcher to tie the crown for you. He will also trim the meat along the bone and grind it. The next step is yours.

~~~~~~~~~

Crown of Lamb

1 tablespoon oil or butter
1 clove garlic, crushed
2 onions, diced
ground lamb scraped from ribs
½ cup bread crumbs
⅛ teaspoon mixed herbs
    (rosemary, sage, thyme)

1 tablespoon fresh chopped parsley
½ teaspoon salt
½ teaspoon pepper
rack of lamb, at least 16 ribs,
    tied into a crown
1 teaspoon salt
½ teaspoon rosemary

1. Heat a skillet. Add oil or butter and sauté garlic and onion.

2. When onions are brown add ground meat, separating bits of meat with a fork as it browns.

3. When meat is browned, strain off excess fat. Blend meat with crumbs, herbs, salt and pepper. Cool slightly. Preheat oven to 325° F.

4. Salt rack of lamb lightly on top, bottom and sides. Sprinkle with rosemary.

5. Fill the cavity in the crown, lightly pressing the meat mixture in. Protect the meat stuffing with a sheet of aluminum foil. Also cover each tip of bone with foil.

6. Place crown of lamb on a metal rack in an open roasting pan. Roast for 2 hours at 325° F. (medium).

7. If meat is not brown enough, remove foil from stuffing 10 minutes before end of cooking time. Set oven up to 400° for 10 minutes. For well-done lamb (which we do not recommend) roast the crown for 2½ hours.

Barbecued Double Baby Lamb Chops

Shish Kebab

See index for recipes.

MEAT QUESTIONS ANSWERED

Q *Timing presents the biggest problems in roasting and broiling. What is the solution?*

A Timing charts may be used but they are mainly helpful for checking total cooking time. The best check for large cuts of meat is to use a meat thermometer. For steaks and smaller cuts make a small incision near the bone and observe the color.

Q *If slow cooking is so much superior to searing and high temperatures why do you use a hot oven for Filet Wellington?*

A There are always exceptions. The filet must be seared quickly, first to produce a fast brownness over the entire surface (for flavor) and secondly to keep the meat rare and juicy. The meat must be rare to withstand the high temperature that the pastry requires in the second step of baking.

Q *Do you use tenderizers?*
A No, I do not. At present the tenderizers being marketed change the natural flavor of the meat. I prefer to use marinades (see index for Barbecue lesson) for tenderizing.

Q *Which cooked meats freeze well?*
A Meats that are moist and have a fair quantity of sauce freeze very well. This includes all stews and meats with sauces.

Q *Please explain the different cuts of steak suggested.*
A Filet steak refers to the filet mignon, the small round section on one side of the porterhouse steak. The club steak is simply a name for a packaged trimmed rib steak. This is a much richer meat than the filet and is also very tender and delicious.

Various names for beef cuts are used in local super markets. These are some of the most common ones. The Delmonico is first cut porterhouse steak. T-bone steak is the porterhouse which includes the Delmonico and the filet (mignon). When the Delmonico portion of the porterhouse is sold separately, it is called a *shell steak*.

Chuck steak is sold with many labels. The small marquise shape filet above the bone is sold as "chicken steak." The center of the chuck is called "King steak" (see Barbecue Lesson for more information).

Many terms are manufactured by the individual butcher or supermarket. They do not indicate the actual cut of meat. For your own comprehension, observe the different cuts and become familiar with their appearance, so that you will know their comparative uses.

LESSON 10

The Vegetable and the Grain

Vegetables can glamorize a meal with their variety of colors, textures and presentations. If your family neglects them, perhaps vegetables come to the table overcooked and dull in color. Good selection is important too. Vegetables should be bought crisp and bright in color, preferably neither dehydrated nor prepackaged. Choose a shop that takes proper care of its produce. On occasion the use of canned or frozen vegetables is perfectly fine but for the most part buy fresh vegetables in season. Daily newspapers which keep you informed of weekly produce should be your greatest aid in planning menus. At times when certain main courses cry out for a particular vegetable out of season, by all means make use of our modern conveniences and the abundance of frozen products.

There are many successful methods for cooking vegetables. You may want to try them all for different occasions.

Boiling may be used for almost all vegetables. Use as little water as possible. Salt the water lightly using ¼ teaspoon to 1 cup of water. Green vegetables stay greener if they are cooked uncovered; white vegetables stay whiter if they are cooked tightly covered.

Steaming is an excellent method for delicate vegetables, such as spinach. Very little or no water is used (only water that clings to the leaves). Steaming also includes pressure cooking which may be used for all vegetables. Warning: Unless the timing is precise, vegetables are in danger of becoming too mushy.

Sautéing produces one of the most flavorful vegetables. Vegetables must be cut in small dice or lengths and in uniformity. The French and the Chinese use this method for cooking vegetables. Occasionally a small amount of liquid is added. The pot is covered for 2 to 3 minutes for those vegetables that take longer cooking (broccoli for instance). These vegetables have a more crunchy texture than vegetables that are boiled or steamed.

Baking may be used for almost any vegetable. Potatoes, squash, tomatoes can be baked in their skins uncovered. Covered casseroles are excellent dishes for cooking combinations of vegetables. For instance, couple frying peppers with zucchini; combine celery and carrots; layer eggplant, onion and tomato; combine mushroom and potatoes (the only combination to stay away from is peas and carrots)! These same combinations may be cooked in covered saucepans on the stove.

Because plant life is so delicate, a watchful eye is a primary requisite! Set your timer if necessary. Whether you are boiling, steaming, sautéing or baking, be sure to test for doneness. Timing varies greatly with each vegetable and each size. Pierce vegetable with a fork or taste a snip after given time elapses. Every family enjoys its vegetables at a different degree of softness or firmness. Attempt to educate your diners towards crunchier vegetables and a willingness to try all varieties.

THE ARTICHOKE

Buy artichokes that are very green without too many brown spots. Scrub them well with cold water and a stiff brush. If there are many brown spots, scrape them off very lightly.

Artichokes seem formidable to most people because of their appearance. They are actually very simple to prepare. First trim the base of the artichoke so that it stands straight. Cut off ¼" across the top to remove prickles; also trim the ends of the leaves if you can spare the time. This is not necessary; it is done mainly for appearance. The leaves may be spread apart and the "choke" (hairy portion attached to

the bottom or heart) removed before or after cooking. Soak artichokes in cold water with a tablespoon of lemon juice for about 30 minutes.

Unusual as it may seem, artichokes (plain boiled) are usually a favorite with children. They enjoy the ritual of eating them. For a family of four cook 2 artichokes. Place one at either side of the table to be shared by 2. A dish of clarified butter (see index) is placed next to each serving. Instruct the family to pull off each leaf, dip it into butter and then eat soft meaty portion, discarding the base of the tough leaf. (Have a bowl handy for discarding leaves.) When the bottom is reached, gently scrape off the fuzzy portion with a spoon. The prize of the artichoke is the heart below it.

Boiled Artichoke

Water to cover artichokes
1 teaspoon salt

1 tablespoon lemon juice
4 artichokes, cleaned

Use a pot large enough to cook the 4 artichokes, standing straight. Boil water with salt and lemon juice. Place artichokes in boiling water and cook uncovered for 30 minutes (or more depending on size). Pull off a leaf to test for doneness. Artichokes may be cooked in pressure cooker for 18 to 20 minutes. Serve with a dish of clarified butter and more lemon, if desired.

Artichokes à la Greque

See index for recipe.

~~~~~~~~~

Hearts of Artichokes in Mornay Sauce ★ ★ ★

Water to cover artichokes
1 teaspoon salt
1 tablespoon lemon juice
4 artichokes, cleaned
2 tablespoons butter

1 small tin liver paté
   (about 2 ounces)
1 cup Mornay Sauce
   (see index for recipe)

1. Use a pot large enough to hold 4 artichokes upright. Boil water with salt and lemon juice.

2. Place artichokes in boiling water and cook uncovered for 30 minutes (or more depending on size). Pull off a leaf to test for doneness. Artichokes may be cooked in pressure cooker for 18 to 20 minutes.

3. When finished, drain artichokes and pull off all outer leaves (cook this at an appropriate time so your family can eat the leaves). Clean the choke off the hearts by scraping it gently off with a spoon.

4. Butter a flat baking pan. Place artichoke hearts on the pan. Place 1 teaspoon of pâté on each heart. Preheat oven to 350° F. Cover the entire heart with Mornay Sauce.

5. Bake in a 350° F. oven for 10 minutes. Set under the broiler for 30 seconds just before serving.

~~~~~~~~~

The cold artichoke is constantly seen on the antipasto tray in Italy. Cold or hot, try this one we tasted in a tiny Italian village.

Artichokes Acquapendente

4 artichokes
1 teaspoon salt
juice of a lemon
2 tablespoons butter
2 tablespoons grated
   Parmesan cheese

3 anchovy filets, mashed
1 tablespoon chopped parsley
¼ teaspoon oregano
1 teaspoon salt
½ teaspoon pepper
olive oil

Scrub artichokes with a stiff brush. Cut one-half inch off the top and a slice off the stem. Each leaf may be trimmed if you care to take the time. Open the leaves so that you can clean out the choke at the bottom of the center. Cover artichokes with water, salt and juice of a lemon while you prepare the following stuffing: Blend together the butter, Parmesan, anchovies, parsley, oregano and salt and pepper. Drain off artichokes. Fill the centers with the stuffing, also the spaces between the leaves. Place the artichokes in a saucepan with water to half cover them. Sprinkle a few drops of olive oil over all. Cover tight and cook for 40 minutes. Eat hot or cold. Serves 4.

Artichoke Hearts Surprise

2 packages frozen artichoke hearts	1 package frozen chopped broccoli
1 tablespoon lemon juice	1 onion, diced
1 tablespoon butter	1 cup Cream Sauce
¼ teaspoon salt	(see index for recipe)
½ teaspoon pepper	2 tablespoons Parmesan cheese

Prepare a 1-quart shallow casserole. Preheat oven to 375° F. Cook artichoke hearts (not quite done). Drain, season with lemon juice, butter, salt and pepper. Place in casserole. Cook broccoli with onion. When finished, drain and put into blender or through Foley food mill. Combine broccoli with cream sauce and cheese. Taste and correct seasoning (seasoning will depend on your cream sauce). Spread broccoli purée completely over artichoke hearts. Bake for 10 minutes at 375° F. Serves 6.

This unusual vegetable combination can be completely set up the day before. Place it in the oven 10 minutes before serving. If it comes directly from refrigerator, add 5 minutes.

ASPARAGUS

Buy asparagus as soon as they appear in early spring. These are usually the California variety; they are not sandy and excellent in flavor. Buy them very green with the tip ends tightly closed. Break off the tough end of the asparagus by snapping it with your hand. It will break at just the right spot. Do not cut it unless you must have uniformity of size. Wash asparagus well and gently scrape off some of the outer leaves. If asparagus are sandy the stalks may have to be lightly peeled.

Steam asparagus on a rack with a small amount of salted water and cover tightly. Better still stand the asparagus in the lower part of a double boiler. Add boiling salted water to cover ⅔ up the length of the stalks. Cook uncovered for about 10 minutes. Cover with the upper portion of the double boiler and cook for another 5 minutes or until just tender. ½ to ¾ pound fresh asparagus serves 1 portion.

Asparagus Three Ways

1. Fresh asparagus is superior served with clarified butter (see index), lemon juice, salt and freshly ground pepper.

2. Fresh asparagus, cut in 1-inch pieces, steamed with butter, salt and pepper. Serve with grated Parmesan cheese.

3. Mock Hollandaise for aspargus, fresh, frozen or canned. Add 3 egg yolks to 1 cup basic cream sauce, plus 2 tablespoons lemon juice, pinch cayenne.

Asparagus Angelique ★ ★ ★

2 pounds fresh asparagus
   or 2 boxes frozen
4 tablespoons butter
6 tablespoons bread crumbs
¼ teaspoon salt
⅛ teaspoon pepper
3 egg whites

¾ cup Pancake Batter
   (see index for recipe)
¼ teaspoon salt
2 tablespoons grated cheddar cheese
2 tablespoons grated
   Parmesan cheese

Parboil asparagus. Cut cooking time down to allow for time in oven. Preheat oven to 400° F. Heat a shallow baking dish with butter. Dish may be a 10″ x 1½″ round or a 10″ x 5″ oblong. When butter is melted add bread crumbs. Blend together with salt and pepper. Lay asparagus on bed of bread crumbs. Beat egg whites stiff but not dry. Stir cheeses and salt into the pancake batter. Fold in stiffly beaten egg whites. Spread mixture over asparagus and bake at 400° F. for 15 minutes. Serves 6 to 8.

With fresh spring asparagus, this is truly a heavenly vegetable. It is not half bad with the frozen variety. Substitute other vegetables for asparagus; the soufflé idea is really dramatic for a party.

For advance preparation, do everything up to (not including) the beating of egg whites. Twenty minutes before serving take 3 minutes in the kitchen to complete the recipe. It is well worth the effort!

Asparagus-Lemon Crumbs

See index for recipe.

THE BEAN GREEN

Buy green beans that are bright in color, firm in texture and thin in shape. Snap off both tip ends and wash. Green beans of good quality are most delicious when they are left whole and served with melted butter. They may be snapped into 1″ lengths or cut French style. Green beans are excellent served cold as well as hot, so that they provide a good leftover food for salads. One pound green beans serves 4..

Green Beans Three Ways

Top with finely minced bacon, rendered very crisp.

Serve cold with sliced Bermuda onion and vinaigrette (French dressing) sauce.

Toast sesame seeds in 2 tablespoons butter. Sprinkle seeds on whole beans.

BROCCOLI

Buy broccoli of a deep green color with tightly closed flowerets. Cut off the tough lower portion of the stalks and discard with the coarse leaves. Wash in cold water. Cut it in uniform lengths so that it will cook evenly. Broccoli may be steamed standing upright (like asparagus) in a deep saucepan or in a heavy waterless cooker with cover. It should be tender after 15 to 18 minutes of cooking. One bunch serves 4 to 6.

Broccoli Two Ways

Garlic crumb topping suits broccoli. Sauté 2 cloves of crushed garlic in 3 tablespoons butter. Add ½ cup dry bread crumbs. Stir until brown. Season with salt and pepper. Sprinkle on to cooked broccoli.

Blend together 2 tablespoons melted butter, 2 tablespoons lemon juice, 1 tablespoon chopped fresh tarragon, ½ teaspoon salt and ¼ teaspoon pepper. Pour over broccoli.

CABBAGE (GREEN AND RED)

Buy a cabbage with its outer green leaves. Inspect it for dark lines and holes which may mean inner deterioration. Use as many of the dark green leaves as possible. Wash cabbage in cold water and cut according to recipe. Choose a red cabbage that appears fresh and bright in color. Cabbage is highly nutritious and should be used more often in the daily menu. When quartered, cabbage cooks tender in 10 to 15 minutes. Shredded cabbage cooks much faster; allow 5 to 7 minutes. One pound cabbage serves 2.

Green Cabbage Two Ways

Steam 2 pounds shredded green cabbage about 7 minutes. Add butter, salt, pepper and ½ teaspoon caraway seeds.

Sauté 1 diced onion. Steam 2 pounds cabbage with onion. Thicken at the end of cooking with 2 tablespoons of flour blended with ½ cup cream. Season with salt, pepper and garnish with strip of pimento.

Red Cabbage

Stew 3 pounds of shredded cabbage with 1 sauteéd onion, 2 sliced apples and 2 teaspoons salt for 30 minutes. Add a paste of 2 tablespoons flour, 3 tablespoons sugar, 4 tablespoons vinegar, juice of a lemon and cook slowly for 1 hour.

THE CARROT

It is becoming almost impossible to buy carrots fresh with green tops. There are still some farms in the outlying areas of the suburbs where delicious young carrots are grown. Seek out these farmers; their vegetables are worth the hunt. If the carrots are young and clean, merely wash and brush them well. Sometimes they have to be peeled. Cut in uniform sizes and steam in a small amount of salted water until tender. Timing will depend on size. One pound of carrots serves 4.

Carrots Three Ways

Cook carrots in chicken broth with pinch of sugar.

Glaze cooked whole carrots with equal parts butter, sugar and a pinch of mace. This may be done in a skillet or a baking dish.

A mixture of 4 tablespoons melted butter, 1 tablespoon lemon juice and 1 tablespoon mixed parsley and mint may be poured over sliced or whole carrots.

CAULIFLOWER

Inspect the core of a cauliflower when buying it. Look for dark spots which indicate worms. Buy it unwrapped if possible. Discard only outer leaves that are bruised. Slice off a straight piece at the bottom so that cauliflower stands up securely. Pull off only outer leaves that are too heavy and ungainly. The green leaves are not only pretty, they make very good eating! Soak cauliflower for 30 minutes in cold water with 1 tablespoon lemon juice. One large head serves 4 to 6.

Boiled Whole Cauliflower

Boil enough water to cover the entire head. Add 1 tablespoon salt and 2 tablespoons lemon juice to the water. When the water boils, immerse cauliflower and cover. Simmer for 20 minutes. Timing depends on the size. Most heads take anywhere from 15 to 30 minutes. White vegetables remain whiter if the saucepan is covered during cooking. Whiteness also depends greatly on the quality and locale of growth. Cauliflower cut into flowerets cooks in a much shorter time; allow about 10 to 12 minutes. Serve with Hollandaise or Cheese Sauce (see index for recipes).

Cauliflower Casserole

Mix 1 cup sour cream, 1 tablespoon chives and 1 tablespoon parsley. Blend this lightly with 1 head cooked flowerets of cauliflower. Top with bread crumbs and bake for 10 minutes at 350° F.

CELERY

Celery is easy to buy and always available. Use for salad as well as a cooked vegetable. Celery should be brushed clean or pared with a sharp utensil to keep parings thin. Celery may be left whole, sliced or diced uniformly. One bunch celery serves 4 to 6.

Celery Two Ways

Sauté 1 diced onion, add cut celery and braise in small amount of chicken broth.

Add finely chopped mint or tarragon to buttered steamed celery.

THE CHESTNUT

Chestnuts arrive here every fall from Italy and sometimes from Spain and Portugal. They are most welcome for they provide us with many delicious food combinations both in vegetables as well as desserts. They are time-consuming to peel but rewarding to eat. Chestnuts may be bought dried, to be soaked and cooked according to directions. One pound chestnuts serves 4.

Fresh Roasted Chestnuts

Make a criss cross gash on the flat side of each chestnut. Place the nuts on a lightly oiled pan. Bake at 425° F. until outer shells pop open (about 7 to 10 minutes). Shell the nuts while they are hot. I sometimes use cotton gloves to prevent scorched fingers. These roasted nuts may be served in their shells for the family to enjoy.

Chestnuts Two Ways

1. Cook shelled roasted nuts in boiling water or chicken broth for about 20 minutes. Add pieces of chestnut to buttered green beans or peas.

2. Cook shelled roasted chestnuts in boiling water for 20 minutes. Purée chestnuts and use for soup or pie (see index).

CORN

Buy corn as fresh as possible. Remove the husks and trim the ends. Drop the corn into well salted boiling water. Bring to a simmer and cook for 5 minutes. Do not overcook. Serve with lots of butter and freshly ground pepper.

Barbecued Corn

See index for recipe.

EGGPLANT

Eggplant is a most versatile vegetable. It combines well with meats to make wonderful main courses. With other vegetables, it provides nutritious and tasty casseroles. Buy the eggplant firm and shiny. Do not peel unless recipe calls for it. It is not always necessary to salt down eggplant in order to extract the moisture. Each recipe is specific and each recipe is delicious! One medium eggplant serves 4.

Eggplant Two Ways

1. Coat sliced eggplant with one cupful of bread crumb flour mixture seasoned with ½ teaspoon salt, ¼ teaspoon pepper, ¼ teaspoon paprika, ½ teaspoon oregano and 6 tablespoons grated Parmesan cheese. Sauté in olive oil or butter until brown.

2. Bake eggplant, cut in cubes, with layers of tomatoes (canned) and onion, seasoned with salt, pepper, basil and cheese. Top with buttered bread crumbs.

Eggplant Florentine

1 large eggplant or 2 small	¼ cup bread crumbs
1 teaspoon salt	1 cup tomatoes
2 tablespoons butter	½ teaspoon salt
2 cloves garlic, crushed	½ teaspoon pepper
2 onions, diced	½ teaspoon basil
1 pound ground beef or veal, lamb, pork	½ pound mozzarella cheese, cut in slices

1. Split eggplant in half lengthwise. Scoop out inside, leaving intact ½″ shell. Cube eggplant, sprinkle with salt and set aside.

2. Melt 2 tablespoons butter in a heavy skillet. Add crushed garlic and diced onion and sauté till golden brown.

3. Add ground meat, separating pieces of meat with fork while browning.

4. Drain off juices from cubed eggplant. Turn eggplant in bread crumbs. Stir eggplant in with meat.

5. Brown eggplant and meat for 2 to 3 minutes. Remove from flame. Preheat oven to 350° F.

6. Blend in tomatoes, seasonings and basil. Fill eggplant skins

and set them in a buttered or oiled baking dish. Bake at 350° F. for 1 hour. Place cheese on eggplant 5 minutes before serving. Set under broiler for 30 seconds. Serves 4 to 6. Garnish with Creamed Spinach (see recipe later in this chapter). This recipe is illustrated in color.

Endive, Baked Belgian

See index for recipe.

THE MUSHROOM

The one vegetable that stands alone as most essential in all cookery is the mushroom. Selection of mushrooms is important. Buy them white and closed at the underside. Wash them lightly with cold water or use a soft cloth dipped in acidulated water to wipe each one clean. Fresh, high quality mushrooms need very little washing. Store in the refrigerator unwashed, wrapped lightly in paper. Keep them dry, away from moist foods, and for only a few days. If keeping them longer is desirable, blanch them in water seasoned with lemon juice. Keep them in a covered jar, refrigerated up to a week. Do not peel mushrooms; remember most of the flavor is in the outer skin. Tender mushrooms may be eaten raw as well as cooked. The test of doneness is in your personal preference.

Mushrooms Two Ways

1. Sauté 1 sliced onion in 1 tablespoon butter. Add 1 pound sliced mushrooms, 1 fresh tomato (skinned and seeded). Sauté all for 2 to 3 minutes. Season to taste with salt, pepper, ½ teaspoon basil and 1 teaspoon parsley. Blend in 1 tablespoon butter at the end.

2. Heat skillet, add 2 tablespoons butter. Sauté 1 pound mushroom caps till brown, but not soft. Add ¼ cup cognac and flame. Season with salt and pepper to taste.

Mushrooms Copenhagen

See index for recipe.

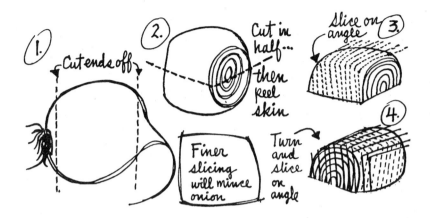

THE ONION

The common onion is perhaps the most used of all vegetables. A small amount of sautéed onion enhances a multitude of dishes. Be sure to cut ¼″ off either end of onion before peeling. This releases the skin for easy peeling. Dice onion, *flat* side down on wooden board.

Small white onions are traditional with turkey. They also combine well with peas and green beans.

The Onion Two Ways

1. Combine cooked onions, French-style beans and mushrooms with a cream sauce. Sprinkle with Parmesan cheese.

2. Combine 1 pound of cooked onions with 1 cup of Cheese Sauce (see index). Sprinkle with 1 tablespoon chopped parsley and ¼ cup buttered bread crumbs. Bake at 350° F. One pound of onions serves 4.

PEAS

When fresh peas are available, buy them. Shell the peas just before cooking. Wash and steam in a small amount of salted water. Depending on age and size they should cook anywhere from 10 to 15 minutes tightly covered. One pound serves 2.

Peas Four Ways

1. Add sautéed onion to freshly cooked peas.
2. Add 1 tablespoon chopped fresh mint or 1 teaspoon dried mint.
3. Smother peas with a layer of lettuce below and lettuce to cover. Steam, with little water, tightly covered. (The books say to discard the lettuce, but I enjoy its flavor.)
4. Add finely minced pimento and ham.

THE POTATO

The potato, a basic staple and generally considered an unpoetic food, is perhaps the most satisfying vegetable of all. Do not underestimate the potato. It is not only economical but it is highly nutritious. There are three standards for purchasing potatoes. Idaho potatoes are generally used for baking; Maine and Long Island (old) potatoes are used for mashing and sautéing; new potatoes (from California and the East too) are perfect for serving whole, buttered and parslied. New potatoes are excellent for salad too.

Translated into the French, the potato has a lovelier sound, pomme de terre, *and an even lovelier flavor. Monsieur Thuilier of Baumanière, one of the great inns of France, says that the following potato dish is the finest accompaniment for his special leg of lamb. I agree that it is all that. Take it alone and this casserole provides a filling and nutritious vegetable main dish. Serve a good salad with it and the meal is made.*

Pommes de Terre Gratin

4 tablespoons butter
2 large onions, very thinly sliced
6 potatoes, sliced thin (⅛")
6 ounces Swiss or Gruyère cheese, grated or sliced

2 to 3 teaspoons salt
½ teaspoon pepper
1½ cups sweet cream

Line a shallow baking dish (preferably one that has a cover) with bits of butter. Preheat oven to 350° F. Cover the bottom of dish with some of the sliced onion then a layer of potatoes and Swiss cheese. Sprinkle salt and pepper as you make layers. Continue with another layer until onion, potato, butter and cheese are entirely used. Pour sweet cream over all. Cover and bake for one hour at 350° F. Uncover and bake for 30 minutes until brown. Serves 8.

Teacher says:

Pommes de Terre Gratin is served in the French provincial inn as well as the sophisticated Parisian restaurant. It is cloaked in a variety of names and seasonings. Some say it should contain garlic and no cheese and others say no onion. Trust your better taste and choose your own combination. To protect your oven, set a cooky sheet under casserole. It sometimes leaks over. Your men can ask for no better assist on a barbecue day than an offer from you to prepare this marvelous potato dish for their charcoal grilled meats.

Potato and Onion Packets

See index for recipe.

Duchess Potatoes

See index for recipe.

SPINACH

Spinach can still be bought loose but the trend is definitely towards washed package spinach. Inspect the bag! Be sure spinach looks fresh (no dark spots and no yellowing). Cook spinach with only the water that clings to its leaves. Cover it tightly and cook for approximately 5 minutes. Add butter, salt and pepper for the simplest yet most delicious cooked green! One pound fresh spinach serves 4.

Creamed Spinach, an Attractive Garnish

2 tablespoons butter
1 onion chopped
2 pounds fresh spinach or 2
   packages frozen chopped spinach
2 tablespoons butter
2 tablespoons flour

1 cup milk or cream
½ teaspoon nutmeg
⅛ teaspoon allspice
½ teaspoon salt
¼ teaspoon pepper

Melt butter in saucepan large enough to hold spinach. Sauté onion in butter until brown. Add washed drained spinach to onion and cook covered for 3 to 5 minutes. Spinach should just be tender and still very green. Drain and chop it. Return spinach to saucepan. While spinach is cooking, knead the butter and flour together with your fingers (beurre manié). When spinach is cooked, lower flame and add beurre manié bit by bit until it is all smoothly incorporated. Add milk or cream and seasonings. Use to garnish Eggplant Florentine and other vegetables. Serves 6.

Spinach Three Ways

1. Cook 2 cups spinach with a little onion and flavor with ¼ teaspoon marjoram.

2. Try ¼ teaspoon nutmeg to 2 cups of cooked spinach.

3. *Quick Cream of Spinach Soup:* Knead 2 tablespoons flour and 1 tablespoon butter with your fingers. Add this bit by bit to 1 cup chopped cooked spinach, over a low flame. Add cream or milk, a little at a time until soup reaches desired consistency. Adjust seasonings.

SQUASH

The squash family is extensive. Some form of squash is available to us all year round. The soft moist squashes such as zucchini and yellow summer squash must be scrubbed well (peeled only if recipe calls for it) and cooked rapidly (7 to 10 minutes). Butternut and acorn squash may be treated just as potato. They can be pared, cubed and boiled or baked in their skins. Both these yellow squash are excellent substitutes for the potato.

Stuffed Baked Zucchini

See index for recipe.

Zucchini Two Ways

1. Add butter and 1 tablespoon mixed herbs (basil, chervil, parsley) to cooked zucchini. One pound serves 3.

2. Combine zucchini, cut lengthwise, with frying peppers, cut the same way. Sauté both with sliced onion and a touch of garlic. Go Italian all the way and use olive oil. Add a pinch of oregano.

Squash Two Ways

1. Butternut squash, peeled, cubed and cooked till soft, takes especially well to 1 tablespoon of butter and a large spoonful of maple syrup.

2. Acorn squash is most delicious when halved, seeded and baked for 45 minutes in small amount of water. Fill cavity with 1 tablespoon butter and 1 tablespoon brown sugar.

Olive oil, tomatoes and garlic add excitement to many garden vegetables. "Garden" is used qualifiedly hoping that some of you do have summer gardens. Your less-beautiful garden yield makes an excellent stew, helped much by these three basic seasonings of southern France (the Provence).

Any combination of fresh vegetables, at least a variety of five, makes for a fine baked casserole dish. The stew below is a slight adjustment since the eggplant is layered separately and smothers the other vegetables. Words can't explain the sweet aroma; find out for yourself.

Vegetable Stew Provençale

1 eggplant unpeeled, ⅛" round slices	2 carrots diced
½ cup flour	2 zucchini, diced
¼ teaspoon salt	¼ pound green beans cut in pieces
¼ teaspoon pepper	1 pepper, diced
¼ teaspoon paprika	(sweet or frying pepper)
3 tablespoons olive oil	3 ripe tomatoes, peeled,
3 tablespoons butter	seeded and diced
2 onions, diced	3 cloves garlic, crushed or minced
2 potatoes, diced	1½ teaspoons salt
1 pound peas shelled	½ teaspoon pepper
	3 tablespoons olive oil

Prepare a 1½-quart casserole or shallow baking pan. Dredge eggplant in a mixture of flour, salt, pepper and paprika. Preheat oven to 350° F. Heat 1 tablespoon oil and 1 tablespoon butter in a skillet. Brown eggplant on both sides until all slices are browned. Use more oil and butter as needed. Layer half of the slices along the bottom of the baking dish. Reserve the other half. Blend all other vegetables, seasonings and oil. Place vegetables on eggplant. Cover with the layer of reserved eggplant. Bake covered at 350° F. for 45 minutes, uncovered for 15 minutes. Serves 6 to 8.

Broiled Yam and Apple Rings

See index for recipe.

THE GRAIN

Rice

If statistics were collected from the women and men who are the cooks of today, I venture to say that rice would be recorded as one of the best liked and most used of all the starches. It deserves to be on top of the list for its texture and blandness combine so well with a vast variety of foods.

Many types of rice are sold today but I will suggest only the ones that are most used in rice recipes. The long-grained rice such as the Carolina is used mainly for Chinese-style rice but may be used for pilaff and most rice dishes. The converted rice is the one I find the simplest to use for steamed rice, pilaff and risotto. You might like to try the Italian rice for risotto; it is a short grained rice. Although I am not including any rice desserts here, I must tell you that neither Carolina nor converted rice is good for creamy puddings. A short-grained, glutinous rice must be used for all rice desserts. Converted rice requires no washing; Carolina rice very little. You will need a heavy-weight 2-quart tightly covered saucepan for grain cookery.

Steamed Rice

1 tablespoon butter	2 cups salted boiling water
1 cup converted rice	

Use a heavy saucepan with a tight fitted cover. Melt butter in saucepan. Toss rice in butter so that the grains are coated. Add boiling water to the rice. Cover and cook over low heat for 20 minutes. At the end of cooking time all the water should be absorbed. Do not stir rice with a spoon or fork. Invert pan on to a hot plate. Wait one minute, then toss rice with additional butter if desired and serve. Serves 4.

Rice, Chinese Method

Wash Carolina rice in cold water by rubbing grains between palms of hands. Place in a heavy saucepan; add cold water to stand about 1 inch above rice. Start on a high flame, uncovered. When water evaporates and "fish eyes"—air bubbles that show on top of rice when water is absorbed—appear, cover with a close fitting cover and lower flame. Never stir rice. Cooking time is 25 minutes. One cup raw rice yields 4 servings.

Rice Pilaff

2 cups stock, consommé or broth　　1 cup rice
3 tablespoons butter

Heat stock in a 1-quart casserole in an oven set at 350° F. Melt butter in a skillet. Brown rice in butter, stirring constantly. This should take only 3 or 4 minutes; rice should be lightly browned. Turn rice into heated stock, cover closely and bake in oven for 25 to 30 minutes. Serves 4.

Teacher says:

This can be cooked just as well on the stove. Cook the rice in a closely covered heavy saucepan.

Onion may be sautéed with the rice when it is browned.

Mushrooms and/or green peppers may be added too.

Use the basic recipe. Variations may be made after the rice is cooked as in the following ring.

Rice Pilaff Ring

4 cups stock or consommé　　　　1 green pepper, diced
6 tablespoons butter　　　　　　½ cup diced ham
2 cups rice　　　　　　　　　　½ teaspoon salt
3 onions, diced and sautéed　　　¼ teaspoon pepper

Heat stock in a 2-quart heavy saucepan. Melt butter in a skillet. Add rice and brown rice lightly stirring constantly. When rice is evenly browned, turn rice into stock. Cover and cook over low heat for 20 to 25 minutes. When rice has absorbed all the liquid, add sautéed onions, pepper, ham and seasoning. Pack rice mixture into a 1½-quart ring mold and unmold immediately for serving. If you prefer to prepare this in advance, reheat the ring by setting it into a pan of hot water. Heat it in a 350° F. oven or on the stove. Serves 8 to 10.

Teacher says:

You may have noticed that the ring mold was not greased. Greasing is unnecessary since there is enough butter in the rice. If the ring should fall apart when you unmold it, nothing is lost. With a spatula smooth the outer edge to a sloping edge instead of a vertical one. Some say it looks even better this way.

Fill the center of the ring with any of the many creamed vegetables, chicken or sea-food dishes in this book.

Instead of the green pepper and ham, or in addition to them, use bits of leftovers. Make it a main course rice ring filled with a creamed vegetable.

Casserole dishes can be created with a basic rice pilaff. Shrimp and crabmeat turn the rice into a tasty sea food combination. Two cups leftover turkey, ½ cup diced celery, a cup of cream sauce added to a casserole of rice and a post-Thanksgiving casserole is ready!

Risotto alla Milanese

3¾ cups chicken broth
½ cup dry Marsala wine
4 tablespoons butter
1 large onion, diced
2 cups rice

¼ teaspoon saffron (dissolved in 2 tablespoons hot water)
½ cup freshly grated Parmesan cheese

In a 2-quart heavy saucepan, heat broth and wine. Melt butter in skillet and sauté onion. When onion is golden, add rice; brown lightly, stirring well. Turn rice into broth and cover. Cook for 20 minutes or until liquid is absorbed. (This may also be baked in a covered oven dish 350° F. for 25 minutes.) When rice is finished add saffron and cheese. If you are not acquainted with saffron, use just a pinch to educate yourself to its aroma and flavor; it may seem medicinal to you at first. Saffron is used in many Spanish and Mexican dishes. Frequently, it is used to color the traditional chalah (egg bread).

Wild Rice

See index for recipe.

WHEAT

Grains other than rice are a staple food all over the world but not until recently have we in the United States recognized them for their true worth. Not too long ago our western grainaries started to market bulghour, a cracked wheat which has been used in the middle east for many, many years. Bulghour may be served in the same way as rice. It is such a pleasant change from and addition to our list of starches; full of natural vitamins too! I enjoy it best cooked like pilaff. Treat it like rice, but remember that it needs much seasoning, for it is very bland.

Bulghour

| 4 tablespoons butter | 1 cup bulghour |
| 1 onion diced fine | 2 cups beef broth |

Melt butter in a skillet. Sauté onion until golden. Add bulghour. Brown it very lightly, stirring constantly. In the meantime heat broth in a heavy saucepan. Add bulghour. Cover tightly, lower flame and cook for 20 minutes. Adjust seasonings after tasting. Additional butter and sautéed mushrooms may be added if desired. Serves 4.

VEGETABLE QUESTIONS ANSWERED

Q *Can seasonal vegetables such as mushrooms and asparagus be frozen?*
A I have found that mushrooms change in texture if frozen raw. They are acceptable if blanched first. Apply the same method for asparagus. Immerse mushrooms or asparagus in salted acidulated boiling water for 2 or 3 minutes. Drain them, cool rapidly and package for the freezer.

Q *Do you think the pre-packaged vegetables are as good as the loose fresh vegetables?*
A Sometimes the quality of the pre-packaged vegetable is very good, but the packaging conceals the freshness of the vegetable itself. In this case you must depend on your produce dealer. I always do my best to find radishes and carrots with their green leaves. Unfortunately this is becoming more and more difficult.

Q *Which vegetables can be made in advance without loss of flavor?*
A The vegetables that keep well when made in advance and reheated before serving are: white onion, carrot, sweet and red cabbage, butternut squash, Vegetable Stew Provençale, Eggplant Florentine, Pommes de Terre Gratin and Artichoke Hearts Surprise.

Q *Are vegetables necessary to one's diet? I am concerned because I cannot get my children to enjoy them.*
A Yes, vegetables contain necessary vitamins and minerals. Remember that most children enjoy uncooked vegetables. Try them this way! See the next chapter for suggestions. Offer small amounts of cooked vegetables at the table daily, using as many varieties as possible. Children do eventually grow into adulthood and will become more interested in variety as they grow older. This education in eating must start when they are young. Do not be discouraged; your son may be 14 before he will venture to taste eggplant!

Q *What are the names of the vegetables most used in Chinese cooking and where can they be bought?*
A The most popular vegetables are bean sprouts, water chestnuts, bamboo shoots, snow peas (Chinese pea pods) and bok choy. Canned bean sprouts, water chestnuts and bamboo shoots may be purchased in any supermarket. Snow peas are now frozen so that they too are sold in many supermarkets. Bok choy must be purchased fresh at a Chinese grocery. For a real taste sensation buy water chestnuts fresh. Their flavor is completely different from the canned variety.

Holiday Hors D'oeuvres Tray, page 22

Filet Wellington, page 121

Eggplant Florentine, page 149, on Creamed Spinach, page 153,
with Danish Pastry, page 213

Gâteau Saint Honoré, page 189

The Salad and Its Dressing

Salads hold an important place in menu planning. The appetizer salad, offshoot of the European hors d'oeuvres tray, is tremendously successful with most adults. In California, the first-course salad plays a useful role in satisfying guests who are hungrily awaiting the barbecued steak. For children, salad is a welcome change from tomato juice or grapefruit. They will more often eat and enjoy salad when hungry too. Best of all, a first-course salad whets the appetite without completely satisfying it.

During the high temperature days of summer, some of the salads given in this chapter do beautifully as main-course dinners. All year 'round, they are excellent as luncheons or suppers. With hot soup and crunchy bread, they make a satisfying departure from the usual blue plate dinner.

Let us not forget that salads are always in order with the main course or served just after. They are important on the buffet table. Wherever and whenever you serve salads, do not neglect locally grown greens, including young spinach.

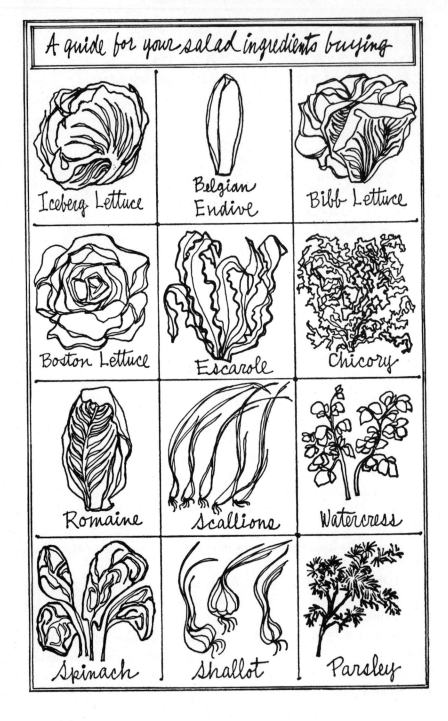

A guide for your salad ingredients buying

Iceberg Lettuce | Belgian Endive | Bibb Lettuce

Boston Lettuce | Escarole | Chicory

Romaine | Scallions | Watercress

Spinach | Shallot | Parsley

THE SALAD

Crisp Greens:

Tossed green salad is superb when greens are crisp and dressing is properly seasoned. Its success will depend greatly on the dryness of your leaves since oil will not adhere to wet leaves. Buy several varieties for a four- or five-day supply. Buy the greens that look freshest. Your choice may be Simpson or Iceberg lettuce, Boston lettuce, Bibb when you can get it, Romaine, escarole, chicory and watercress. Wash thoroughly, separating leaves with your hands. Cutting with a knife browns the edges. Permit greens to drain off their water for at least an hour. Dry greens as well as you can. Wrap them lightly in paper toweling and store in a covered plastic vegetable bin. Once dried and refrigerated, they will crisp in a few hours, and keep crisp up to a week. This is one chore that can be done well in advance when expecting guests.

The dressing: The simple tossed salad is best with a simple French dressing. The flavor of your dressing is dependent on your choice of olive oil and wine vinegar. There are excellent olive oils imported from Spain, France and Italy; each with its very own flavor. Change oils till you find your preference. The same applies to the wine vinegars. Some of the better spice companies bottle wine vinegars. Look for wine vinegar unadulterated with herb and garlic. You should make these additions yourself. My vinegar always gets added fillip when I add wines used at the table!

Artichoke and Tomato Salad

1 package frozen artichokes or 1 medium can artichokes	3 tomatoes cut in wedges
2 tablespoons lemon juice	1 can anchovy filets
¼ teaspoon salt	1 cup French dressing (see index)
⅛ teaspoon pepper	1 tablespoon chopped parsley
1 head Boston lettuce	1 teaspoon chervil
1 heart Romaine lettuce	2 tablespoons capers

If you are using frozen artichokes cook them according to the directions. Sprinkle with lemon juice, salt and pepper. Allow to cool. Make a bed of lettuce in a salad bowl. Place artichokes and tomato wedges on lettuce. Top tomato wedges with anchovy filets. Blend French dressing with parsley, chervil and capers. Mix well. Top salad with dressing and serve. Serves 6.

Artichoke and Shrimp Bowl

Guacamole

Holiday Hors d'Oeuvres (A Salad)

See index for recipes.

~~~~~~~~~

Cabbage is almost always available. It is easy to prepare, and the tedium of washing lettuce is eliminated. The cabbage may be shredded an hour or two ahead of time and lightly salted. When ready to toss with dressing, drain off any water that accumulates.

Green Cabbage Salad

1 head cabbage 3-4 pounds, shredded
1 teaspoon salt
½ Spanish onion, thinly sliced
1 dozen pimento olives, sliced

½ cup oil
¼ cup wine vinegar
1 teaspoon sugar
salt and pepper to taste

Salt cabbage and allow to stand for at least a half hour. Drain off water that may have accumulated. Add all ingredients, adjust salt and pepper. Toss and serve. Serves 8.

~~~~~~~~~

Red and Green Cabbage

1 small head red cabbage
(1½ to 2 pounds)
1 small head green cabbage
(1½ to 2 pounds)
1½ teaspoons salt
2 green peppers, diced
4 stalks celery, diced

1 onion grated
4 scallions, minced
½ cup oil
2 tablespoons wine vinegar
2 tablespoons lemon juice
1 tablespoon sugar
¼ teaspoon pepper

Slice cabbage and salt it. After 30 minutes drain off water. Add all other ingredients. Correct seasoning. Serve immediately. Very colorful for a buffet table, it is easy to make and is generally compatible with poultry and fish dishes. Serves 12.

If the man in your house enjoys a bit of showmanship, let him toss this impressive salad for your family and guests. He may enjoy the actual preparation of the dressing at the dinner table. Supply him with a tray of vinegar, oil and seasonings. You will be in for a real surprise. Most men are uninhibited with seasonings and come up with the most original combinations. Be the good woman behind the scenes; crisp the greens a day ahead and sauté fresh croutons in garlic and olive oil. Supply only freshly grated Parmesan cheese. He couldn't possibly miss now!

Caesar Salad

TO MAKE CROUTONS:

4 slices white bread, crusts removed and cut in cubes

¼ cup olive oil
2 cloves garlic crushed

Sauté cubes of bread in olive oil and garlic until lightly toasted. Set aside to cool.

ON THE TRAY PREPARE:

½ cup olive oil
2 tablespoons wine vinegar
1 egg, coddled (bring water to a boil and remove egg)
1 tablespoon lemon juice
½ teaspoon dry mustard
1 clove garlic crushed

½ teaspoon salt
¼ teaspoon freshly ground pepper
1 small can anchovy filets, diced
½ cup freshly grated Parmesan cheese
fried croutons

IN THE SALAD BOWL:

Tear leaves of 2 small heads of washed and dried romaine lettuce into mouth-sized pieces.

Toss greens with oil and vinegar. Break egg into a small bowl. Stir in lemon juice, mustard, garlic, salt, pepper and anchovy filets. Mix well and toss into salad. Toss salad well. Add cheese and croutons last. Toss again and serve immediately. Serves 6 to 8.

An Alternate Dressing

For the man who prefers the dressing a "fait accompli."

Yolks of 2 eggs
½ cup olive oil
¼ cup wine vinegar
1 clove garlic, crushed
1 small can anchovies, diced
1 teaspoon prepared mustard

½ teaspoon salt
¼ teaspoon freshly ground pepper
½ cup Parmesan cheese,
    freshly grated
4 slices bread, cut in cubes
    and fried in garlic oil

Blend together all ingredients except cheese and croutons. Toss salad with dressing. Stir in cheese and croutons. Toss thoroughly and serve. Yields enough dressing for 2 small heads of romaine lettuce.

The large-bowl salads make beautiful buffet foods. There are occasions though when more stylized arrangements are required. Chicken salad, though often used, takes on an elegant air with the next arrangement.

Festive Chicken Salad

5- to 6-pound chicken, poached,
    boned and diced
1 cup finely diced celery
¼ cup white wine
2 tablespoons lemon juice
¾ cup mayonnaise
1 teaspoon salt

¼ teaspoon white pepper
1 cup seedless grapes or grapes
    cut in halves, and seeded
½ cup toasted slivered almonds
1 pineapple
parsley, grapes and crabapples
    for decoration

Toss chicken with celery, wine, lemon juice, mayonnaise, salt and pepper. Add seedless grapes and blend lightly. Pack into 1½-quart ring mold. Refrigerate. Cut top off pineapple and keep leaves intact. Skin pineapple and score it with sharp knife to remove all the prickly eyes. Slice pineapple across in round slices, being sure to keep shape of pineapple. Reform pineapple to stand straight. Unmold chicken salad on a large round platter. Place pineapple in the center of the ring, propping it up with crushed Saran wrap if necessary. Attach top leaves with toothpicks to reshape pineapple. With spatula, flatten

Cut off and save

Cut off all skin of pineapple

Score on angle... then lift out to remove 'eyes'

Slice through

Replace top

Flatten sides of salad to meet sides of pineapple.

Chicken Salad

salad to meet the sides of the pineapple. Sprinkle almonds over chicken salad; surround chicken salad with clusters of grapes and crabapples garnished with parsley. Serves 8 to 10.

Cucumber Salad

2 cucumbers unpeeled,
   very thinly sliced
2 onions, thinly sliced in rings
½ cup mayonnaise
½ cup sour cream

2 tablespoons white vinegar
½ teaspoon salt
¼ teaspoon pepper
pinch sugar

Blend cucumbers and onions with all other ingredients. Allow mixture to stand a few hours to blend. Serves 8.

Avocado with Lobster Dressing

Salade Mimosa

Green Beans, Onions and Capers Vinaigrette

Watercress, Lettuce and Radish Salad
   See index for recipes.

Eggplant and Mushroom Salad

2 tablespoons olive oil
2 cloves garlic
1 onion, diced
½ pound mushrooms sliced

½ eggplant, unpeeled, thinly
   sliced and cut in quarters
1 teaspoon salt
½ teaspoon pepper
½ teaspoon basil

Heat olive oil in skillet, then add garlic and diced onion. When onion is browned add mushrooms. Sauté till brown. Set mushrooms and onion in a bowl on the side. Discard garlic. Brown eggplant in the same skillet. Eggplant will soften and turn brown. Turn eggplant into bowl with onions and mushrooms. Season with salt, pepper and basil. Refrigerate until very cold. Serve a mound of this mixture on slices of tomato. Dribble a little olive oil over all and sprinkle with fresh parsley. This makes a perfect first course salad. Serves 4 to 6.

Green Bowl Ravigote

1 head Simpson lettuce
1 small head Boston or
   Romaine lettuce
1 red onion thinly sliced

1 pound fresh spinach
   (discard heavy stems)
2 to 4 lobster tails, cooked and sliced
2 tablespoons capers

Toss both lettuce greens with rings of onion. Place these at bottom of the salad bowl. Place spinach greens around outer edge of lettuce. Decorate on top with lobster slices and capers. Serve with Ravigote Sauce and crusty rolls. Serve 4 to 6.

RAVIGOTE SAUCE

¼ cup wine vinegar
⅔ cup olive oil
1 finely diced shallot
1 tablespoon prepared mustard
1 chopped hard-cooked egg

1 teaspoon parsley
1 teaspoon mixed herbs
   (chervil, chives, tarragon)
½ teaspoon salt
¼ teaspoon pepper

Stir all ingredients together well. Use desired amount for salad above. Yield: 1¼ cups.

Chef's Salad

The chef's salad is one of the most popular luncheon dishes and a mainstay for restaurant menus. It is a gift for the bright homemaker who enjoys making use of leftovers. Although a showcase chef's salad can be composed of especially bought ham, cheese, etc., it can be just as good with leftover chicken, tongue, roast beef and bits of cheese and vegetables.

The chefs' salad as we know it is an arrangement of tomatoes, green pepper, cucumbers, cheese, ham, turkey, hard-cooked eggs, etc., on a bed of lettuce. The salad can be made in one large bowl or individual bowls, with a choice of dressings usually passed around.

~~~~~~

I am not sure if the chef's salad came after the Salade Niçoise or at the same time. Nevertheless, following is a French version and a novel way of serving from the large bowl.

Salad Niçoise ★ ★ ★

6 tablespoons olive oil
2 tablespoons wine vinegar
½ teaspoon salt
1 clove garlic, crushed
¼ teaspoon freshly grated pepper
1 head lettuce, any variety,
  torn into bite-size pieces
1 onion, chopped

1 tablespoon each chopped tarragon,
  chives, parsley, (¼ teaspoon each
  of dried variety)
1 green pepper cut in rings
1 can tuna fish (7 ounces)
1 can flat anchovies
12 black olives
4 tomatoes, quartered
4 hard-cooked eggs, cut in quarters
1 cup cooked whole string beans

Place first five ingredients in salad bowl and stir vigorously. Make a bed of lettuce in bowl. Toss greens well in dressing and sprinkle with onion and herbs. Arrange other ingredients on top. Serve tuna, eggs, tomatoes, string beans and anchovies first. Serve the tossed greens next to the tuna, eggs, etc. You may make substitutions or additions such as cooked potatoes, celery and raw vegetables of any kind. Serves 4 to 6.

~~~~~~~~~

*The following platter combines salads but each salad may be used
alone. The pretty Deviled Egg Orleans is a tasty hors d'oeuvres and
something of a conversation piece. Executed properly with its gay
pimento tulip, this platter will be a big attraction on the buffet table.*

Sea-food Platter

POTATO SALAD

2 pounds potatoes
¾ teaspoon salt
¼ cup vinegar
¼ teaspoon salt
⅛ teaspoon pepper

⅛ teaspoon dry mustard
⅛ teaspoon sugar
1 grated onion
½ cup mayonnaise

Boil potatoes in salted water to cover. Peel carefully while hot,
slice, and salt lightly between layers. Heat vinegar with salt, pepper,
mustard and sugar; then sprinkle this hot vinegar combination and
grated onion over potatoes. Toss well. Blend in mayonnaise and adjust seasoning to taste.

LOBSTER SALAD

4 large lobster tails, boiled
2 stalks celery, chopped
2 tablespoons lemon juice

½ teaspoon salt
½ teaspoon pepper
2 tablespoons capers

With scissors, remove lobster meat by cutting the membrane on
either side of the hard shell. Dice lobster in large chunks. Mix with
celery, lemon juice, salt, pepper and capers. Taste and adjust seasoning.

DEVILED EGG ORLEANS

6 eggs
2 tablespoons mayonnaise
2 tablespoons butter
¼ teaspoon salt

⅛ teaspoon pepper
⅛ teaspoon dry mustard
⅛ teaspoon curry powder

Start eggs cooking in salted cold water. When water starts boiling, cover pan tightly and remove from flame. After 20 minutes,
douse eggs in cold water. Let stand in cold water. Roll cooled egg on
counter to crush shell all over. Eggs should shell easily this way. Cut

each egg in half. Remove yolks to a bowl. Add mayonnaise, butter and seasonings to egg yolk. Mash well. Consistency should be soft and smooth but thick enough to hold a shape when piped out of a decorating bag. Pipe egg yolk mixture into each white of egg.

GARNISHES

12 shrimps cooked and cleaned
  so that tail remains when shell
  is removed
4 leek leaves, blanched

1 pimento
½ green pepper, cut the long way
2 lobster shells

Place a shrimp on each egg, curved side down. This will resemble a chicken sitting on an egg; it makes a beautiful garnish. Place lobster and potato salads side by side in the center of the tray. A 16″ round tray would be desirable. Set deviled eggs around top half. Set two lobster tails on either side below eggs. Now drape leek leaves up across both salads to resemble a plant. Cut pimento with pointed edges, tulip like. Place on top of tallest leaf. Set green pepper at the bottom between lobster shells. The green pepper acts as holder for leaves and flower. Serves 6.

Teacher says:

Use new potatoes for salad when they are available. New potatoes dice evenly. Old potatoes have a tendency to mash.

No dressing is added to the lobster salad because both the potato salad and deviled eggs are rich in dressing. Serve salad dressing on the side for those who desire it.

To blanch leek leaves, pop them into boiling water for a few seconds, then into cold water. This lightens their hue and makes them pliable for leaf formation.

The individual parts of this salad may be prepared a day in advance. Assemble it on your serving platter early in the day. Be sure to cover it closely with Saran wrap.

See Lesson 19 (Dinner Menus) for more salad recipes.

~~~~~~~~

Tomato and Cucumber Salad

1 tomato, whole
1 tablespoon capers
2 tablespoons chopped parsley
2 tablespoons chopped chives

2 tablespoons chopped watercress
½ head lettuce, shredded
3 ripe tomatoes, sliced
1 or 2 cucumbers, sliced

Cut a slice across stem end of a tomato which will serve as holder of the herb topping. Scoop out center and fill with mixture of capers, parsley, chives, and watercress. Choose a flat, round or oval serving platter. Cover the surface with shredded lettuce, place filled tomato in center and surround with alternating slices of tomato and cucumber. Top each serving of tomato and cucumber with a spoonful of mixed herbs. Serve with French dressing. Serves 6 to 8.

THE DRESSING

~~~~~~~~

Basic French Dressing

1 cup oil
¼ cup wine vinegar
   (lemon juice or a combination
   may be substituted)

1 teaspoon salt
½ teaspoon freshly ground pepper

Beat all ingredients together until mixture is creamy. You may use an electric blender. Add dry mustard, paprika, garlic or herbs to taste. Yield: 1¼ cups.

~~~~~~~~

Chiffonade Dressing

1 cup French dressing (see index)
3 hard-cooked eggs
   or 3 to 6 hard-cooked yolks,
   chopped fine
1 onion, chopped fine

1 tablespoon chopped parsley
2 tablespoons pickled beets, chopped
2 tablespoons green olives, chopped
½ teaspoon salt
⅛ teaspoon pepper

Combine all ingredients by hand. Do not use blender. This is an excellent dressing for hearts of lettuce. Yield: 2 cups.

Since we all strive to please our man, it is appropriate to note that the Green Goddess is always the big salad hit of my barbecue class for men. Word gets around town that this is the favorite.

Green Goddess Dressing ★ ★ ★

1 cup mayonnaise
¼ cup French dressing
4 anchovy filets, chopped

2 tablespoons minced scallion (white)
1 tablespoon each fresh tarragon and chives, chopped

Beat all ingredients together until mixture is creamy. You may use an electric blender. Serve over crisp greens in variety. Yield: 1¼ cups.

Sauce Verte — Green Dressing

1 tablespoon chopped parsley
1 tablespoon chopped watercress
1 tablespoon chopped capers
1 clove garlic, crushed

¼ teaspoon salt
⅛ teaspoon pepper
6 tablespoons oil
3 tablespoons lemon juice

Mash the first six ingredients with a fork. Gradually add oil. Stir briskly, then add lemon juice. Excellent dressing for hot or cold fish, pastas and vegetables.

Sour Cream Dressing

1 cup sour cream
2 tablespoons mayonnaise
2 hard-cooked eggs, chopped fine
2 tablespoons lemon juice

1 tablespoon chopped chives
½ teaspoon salt
½ teaspoon pepper

Combine all ingredients by hand. Do not use blender. Use for seafood, chicken and vegetables. Yield: 1½ cups.

~~~~~~~~~

Tomato Dressing

1 cup oil	1 clove garlic, crushed
⅓ cup wine vinegar	1 tablespoon ketchup
1 teaspoon salt	2 tablespoons chili sauce
½ teaspoon pepper	1 tablespoon chopped parsley

Beat all ingredients together, except parsley. You may use an electric blender. Stir in parsley by hand. This is especially good with cold cooked vegetables. Yield: 1¼ cups.

SALAD QUESTIONS ANSWERED

Q *Why must salad greens always be torn by hand, not cut?*
A If the greens are cut with a knife, the edges brown especially if they are stored.

Q *Can salad tossed with dressing be used as a leftover?*
A One of the secrets of a good green salad is to toss greens lightly *just before* serving. Greens that are coated with dressing become soggy and are not edible the next day. Very poor for leftovers.

Q *Should dark heavy greens on the outside of lettuce leaves be used?*
A Absolutely! Tear away brown spots. Sometimes these are beautiful for garnishes. These green leaves are wonderful tossed in with lighter leaves.

Q *May other oils be used besides olive oil?*
A Yes, corn and peanut oils may be used or combinations of them with olive oil. Olive oil has a wonderful flavor for greens and salads. Use it in moderation at first if it tastes foreign to you. Before you realize it you will never be able to use anything but olive oil!

Q *May white vinegar or lemon juice be substituted for wine vinegar?*
A Yes, but be sure your white vinegar is mild.

Q *Is it necessary to blanch skin and seed tomatoes?*
A I know that in classic cuisine this is often recommended. If tomatoes are beautifully ripe give them to me as they come off the vine complete in their covering. There are however some special dishes where seeded and skinned tomatoes are necessary in order to remove the juices. The skin and seeds are not good-looking in many cooked dishes.

Q *Should oil be stored in the refrigerator?*
A No it becomes cloudy in the refrigerator. Store it in a relatively cool pantry closet. Always keep it tightly covered.

LESSON 12

Puff Pastry and Pâte à Chou

If you have never made pastry, please start now. This puff paste recipe is a gem because it is actually easier to handle than pie pastry. Most amateur bakers read the lengthy puff pastry recipes included in all comprehensive cook books and quickly turn the page. This is one that you can stay with and successfully perform. The versatility of this pastry is amazing. Use it for hot hors d'oeuvres or an apple turnover, a cheese stick or an apricot strip.

Important pointers for preparing dough:

1. Use a pastry cloth and a cloth cover for your rolling pin.

2. Prepare pastry in a cool room using cold ingredients.

3. Butter should be cold but *pliable*.

4. If vinegar is strong, decrease the amount to 2 tablespoons. Lemon juice may be substituted for vinegar.

5. Work as quickly as possible; the entire process of making the dough takes 4 minutes!

6. Lastly, try not to be discouraged if the first batch is imperfect. Pastry making deserves *practice*.

Important pointers for storing dough:

1. Dough can be kept refrigerated up to 3 weeks. Do not freeze dough.

2. For delicate dessert pastries, try to use dough within a week.

3. Dough can be cut for use in any amount desired. With short notice your guests may be treated to hot hors d'oeuvres or to an oven warm dessert pastry.

4. Freeze completed hors d'oeuvres unbaked, assembled in dozens and ready for the oven.

5. Hors d'oeuvres freeze well up to 3 months. Place frozen product immediately into hot oven allowing at least 10 minutes longer for baking time.

6. Apple pastries are better when baked first and then frozen. When they are frozen pop them into a 425° F. oven to defrost and reheat. Dessert pastries are by far best when freshly baked and the sweet scent pervades the home.

7. Dough for dessert rolls and strips may be rolled out and frozen. The roll will have to be slightly defrosted to make it pliable; the strip can be filled and baked immediately. The faster pastry is baked from the freezer, the better its quality.

QUICK PUFF PASTRY

Quick Puff Paste ★ ★ ★

1 pound sweet butter   ¾ cup water
4 cups all-purpose flour, unsifted   ¼ cup white vinegar
½ teaspoon salt   1 egg

1. Prepare pastry cloth (or board) and rolling pin.

2. Place butter in a large bowl. Add flour and salt. Using one hand for working, blend butter and flour together for 30 seconds, breaking butter into large lumps.

3. Make a well, add water, vinegar and egg. Stir wet ingredients and gradually blend in butter and flour. Combine all very lightly with hand for 1 minute. The mixture may be uneven, lumpy and somewhat unmixed.

4. Turn mixture onto cloth (or board).

5. Roll mixture back and forth with rolling pin to as near an oblong shape as possible. This first rolling will appear somewhat messy, yet dough will begin to take shape. Scoop up any loose bits of butter or flour and place on center of dough.

6. Fold by placing top third over center third. Then fold bottom third over center. You now have 3 layers of dough. As in closing a book, fold dough in half from right to left. Now you have six layers.

7. At this point turn dough around once to the left. Now roll dough again into a long thick (½″) strip.

8. Repeat folding and turning as above 4 times or until dough is solid and somewhat elastic.

9. If during the rolling out process, the dough becomes sticky, refrigerate it for 30 minutes and then continue the same rolling and folding.

10. Cover dough well and refrigerate overnight before using. This dough may be kept up to 3 weeks in your refrigerator.

GENERAL BAKING DIRECTIONS

1. Always preheat oven to 425° F.

2. Shaped pastries bake best when they are refrigerated before baking time.

3. Place pastries on ungreased jelly roll pans. The use of silicone-treated paper is highly recommended.

4. Before baking, brush all pastries with a mixture of 1 beaten egg yolk and 2 tablespoons water.

5. Bake all pastries at 425° F. for 10 minutes. Then lower temperature to 375° F. for remainder of time.

6. Bite-size hors d'oeuvres take about 20 minutes for complete baking time. Medium size turnovers may take 30 minutes. Large forms may bake for as long as 40 to 50 minutes.

7. Do not open door of oven for at least the first 10 minutes.

Puff Paste Hors D'oeuvres

For bite-size hors d'oeuvres, cut a 1″ strip of dough. Flatten with rolling pin; then roll into a long strip, ⅛″ thick. Place desired filling down the center and bring one side of dough over filling to meet the other. Pinch together. Cut this long strip into 1″ pieces. This entire recipe makes 125 hors d'oeuvres.

LIVER FILLING

Sauté 2 finely diced onions in 1 tablespoon butter or fat until brown; add ½ pound chicken livers. When livers are browned and cooked, put through a sieve or grinder. Add 3 hard-cooked egg yolks. Season with salt, pepper and freshly rendered chicken fat if you are lucky to have it. If chicken fat is not available use butter, oil or mayonnaise. Use a very small amount of fat because pastry is rich. This makes about 3 dozen small hors d'oeuvres.

POTATO FILLING

Boil 4 large potatoes until tender. In the meantime sauté 2 finely diced onions. Mash potatoes, add onions, 1 tablespoon butter, salt and pepper to taste. Cool mixture before filling pastry. Fills 3 to 4 dozen small pastries.

SHRIMP FILLING

Marinate shrimp in your favorite French dressing for 3 hours. Drain and wrap pastry around each shrimp.

SEA-FOOD OR FISH FILLING

Use 2 cups minced cooked shrimp, lobster, crabmeat or cooked fish (such as halibut, haddock, flounder) and combine with ¼ cup each of minced celery and green pepper, 1 tablespoon chopped parsley, 1 tablespoon chopped chives, 2 tablespoons mayonnaise, 1 tablespoon lemon juice, 1 teaspoon Worcestershire sauce. Salt and pepper to taste. This filling makes about 3 dozen.

〰〰〰〰

Cheddar Cheese Sticks

1 cup sharp cheddar cheese, grated
½ teaspoon dry mustard

¼ teaspoon paprika
¼ teaspoon chili powder

Blend all ingredients together. Roll out pastry approximately 6 x 10 to ⅛″ thickness. Sprinkle all over with cheese mixture. Fold pastry as in making original dough. Roll again and repeat. Cheese should blend in by third rolling. Cut into ½″ strips then cut into 2″ lengths and twist them. Leave them plain or turn them into a snail. Cheddar cheese pastries are the only ones that should bake at even temperature 375° F. throughout. Keep your eye on them. Remove from pan *immediately*.

〰〰〰〰

Meat Pastries

2 onions finely chopped
1 tablespoon butter
½ pound mushrooms finely chopped
1 pound ground chuck
½ teaspoon salt

¼ teaspoon pepper
1 teaspoon tomato paste
½ teaspoon savory
1 tablespoon flour

Sauté onions in butter until brown. Add mushrooms. Cook rapidly to reduce moisture. Add meat and brown it by stirring it with a fork to break it up. Add seasoning, tomato paste and savory. Taste and adjust seasonings. Remove from flame and add flour to bind mixture. Cool before using it as a filling for pastry.

This filling is fine for medium-sized turnovers. Roll out dough ⅛″ thick then cut squares of 2½″ by 2½″. Make turnovers; place 1 tablespoon of mixture near center and bring one corner over to meet its opposite corner. Pinch together. Yield: 20 medium turnovers.

DESSERT PASTRIES

For a midnight snack, prepare turnovers early in the day and refrigerate. Bake one-half hour before serving. Your guests will enjoy not only the pastry but also the aroma as it wafts through the house.

Apple Turnovers

3 apples, unpeeled, grated coarsely
⅔ cup sugar

¼ teaspoon cinnamon
1 tablespoon lemon juice

Combine ingredients using only ⅓ cup sugar. Roll out strip of dough about 15″ by 5″. Sprinkle with remaining sugar. Cut into squares 2½″ by 2½″.

Place 1 tablespoon of apple mixture in center of each square and fold one corner over to meet the opposite. Pinch together. Don't be concerned if dough does not stick together.

Bake on ungreased jelly roll tins for 10 minutes at 425° F., then for 15 minutes at 350° F. These may be dusted with powdered sugar after they are cool. Yield: 12 turnovers.

The pastry strip is one of my best desserts when baked as close to serving time as possible. Nothing beats pastry which is freshly baked.

Pastry Strip (see drawing page 175)

Cut a piece of dough approximately ¼ of Quick Puff Paste recipe and flatten it with rolling pin, on top side, not on cut side. Roll out to ⅛″ thickness about 15″ long and 7″ wide. Using a pastry wheel (fancy edger), cut two 1″ strips down the length of the pastry. Now you have one pastry strip 5″ wide and two pastry strips 1″ wide. Brush a little beaten egg white along the edge of both sides of 5″ strip. Place each 1″ strip on the two edges of the 5″ strip. Refrigerate or freeze until ready to use. Bake pastry unfilled on cookie sheet at 425° F. for ten minutes; at 375° F. for 35 minutes. When cool, fill center with custard (see index for recipe). Cover with fresh blueberries or sliced strawberries.

Apple Roll

1 can sliced apples   1 tablespoon lemon juice
   or 6 pared and sliced raw apples   ¼ teaspoon cinnamon
¾ cup sugar

Roll dough ⅛" thick to an oblong about 6" by 16". Place dough on ungreased jelly roll pan. Sprinkle 3 tablespoons of sugar over entire dough. Mix together apples, remaining sugar, lemon juice and cinnamon. Spread apple mixture over the long side of dough. Bring furthest edge of dough over to enclose apples. Cut dough on top at 2" spaces. Sprinkle top with sugar and bake at 425° F. oven for 10 minutes. Lower oven to 375° F. and continue baking for 35 minutes. If juices ooze out of pastry, use a brush to baste the pastry with the apple juices.

Apple is delicious in combination with many other ingredients. Sometimes vary your apple pastries with the addition of apricot jam.

Use a mixture of apples and raisins or apples and nuts. Raisins add natural sweetness to pastries, so use them when you prefer to be sparing with the sugar.

Berry Roll

Roll dough as for Apple Roll. Toss lightly 1 pint blueberries, ½ cup sugar, 1 tablespoon cornstarch, and 1 tablespoon lemon juice. Use as filling, proceeding as for Apple Roll.

Cheese Turnovers or Roll

8 ounces cream cheese   1 tablespoon grated orange rind
½ cup sugar   1 egg yolk
1 teaspoon vanilla   2 tablespoons flour

Cream all ingredients together and proceed to make pastries as for apple.

~~~~~~~~

Sweet Bits

½ cup raspberry jam   ½ cup chopped walnuts
½ cup raisins

Roll out dough ⅛″ thick into a rectangle 2″ by 12″. Spread mixture along front half of 12″ side. Bring one side of pastry over to meet the other. Pinch together. Cut slits on top of pastry to later make 1″ size pieces. Bake on ungreased pan at 400° F. for 25 minutes. Brush top of pastry with juices that run out while baking.

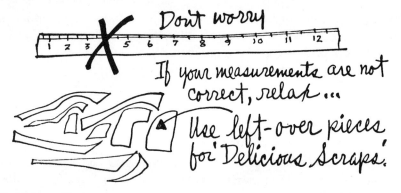

Don't worry

If your measurements are not correct, relax ...

Use left-over pieces for 'Delicious Scraps'.

Delicious Scraps

Do not worry if your measurements are not exact in rolling dough!

Use all ends that you have trimmed off pastry. Do not discard them. Put them all together and refrigerate for a few hours.

This dough may be used as a topping for beef stew or chicken pie. You may also use scraps for cheddar cheese sticks.

One of the simplest pick-up cookies can be made with these left-over bits of dough. Roll out dough to ⅛″ thickness. Sprinkle heavily with sugar. Prick it all over many times. Cut into ½″ strips. Bake strips in 3″ pieces or swirl strips to resemble a snail.

Bake at 425° F. for 10 minutes. If you like these with a glazed look, turn them over and bake for 5 minutes longer.

PÂTE À CHOU (CREAM PUFF PASTRY)

I always marvel at the wonderful basic pastries that come to us from the classic French cuisine, each with its special uses, each with its own texture and each requiring a different technique. Pâte à chou, the cream puff paste that expands with heat, is perhaps the most fun of

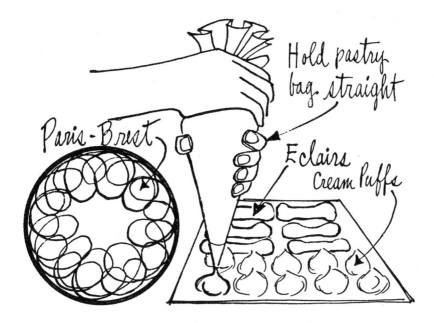

all because it can be made so effortlessly. The fact that it requires only a little effort is hardly reflected in the results which vary from the delectable cream puff to the stupendous croquembouche.

Facts about Pâte à Chou

1. This paste may be cooked, covered well and refrigerated for 3 days.

2. The paste bakes best when it is cold.

3. This paste may be dropped on a greased baking sheet with 2 spoons to form a shape. Keep shape high not flat. For more uniformity, pipe out puffs. Use plain tube, any one from #5 to #9. I find that the #5 can be used for various sizes depending on the amount of pressure put on the bag.

4. Hold the decorating bag at right angles to the baking sheet. Press paste directly down on to sheet. Make small mounds about 1 inch in diameter with at least 1 inch in height. These will almost double when baked so judge your size accordingly.

5. Cream puffs and *éclairs* may be prepared in advance, dropped on to cooky sheets and refrigerated raw. They may be baked any time the same day.

6. Cream puffs and *éclairs* may be completely baked and frozen. Pop them into the oven directly from the freezer. Bake at 400° F. for 10 minutes. Watch the tiny ones as they may need less time. These frozen puffs make quick hors d'oeuvres and desserts for unexpected guests and unexpected appetites.

7. Like the puff paste, this pastry can be used as an hors d'oeuvres or luncheon dish as well as a dessert. There is still another aspect to the Pâte à Chou. It may be fried and then it becomes the Beignet. What a bonus!

Pâte à Chou — Cream Puff Paste

¼ pound butter
1 cup cold water
1 cup all-purpose flour

⅛ teaspoon salt
4 eggs

1. Place stick of butter and water in a heavy saucepan over low flame.

2. Water will heat as butter melts. When water starts simmering butter should be completely melted. If butter is not melted when water is close to boiling, either lower flame or remove from stove for a few seconds.

3. As soon as butter is melted and water is boiling, lower the flame and add flour and salt. Using a wooden spoon, stir vigorously until mixture forms a ball of paste and leaves the sides of the pan. This usually takes 3 or 4 minutes.

4. Remove saucepan from stove. Blend in one egg at a time. Beat each egg vigorously into paste. This part of the recipe may be done in the electric mixer. The mixture when finished is very smooth, glossy but pasty.

Cream Puffs

Prepare 1 recipe Pâte à Chou. With 2 spoons, or, better still, using a large decorating bag with #5 plain tube, drop paste onto a lightly greased cookie sheet. Bake at 400° F. for 25 minutes. To test for doneness, place one puff on a rack. If it holds its shape after one minute it is done. If it collapses and becomes soft, give all the puffs another five minutes. When puffs are cool, cut in half and fill with custard or whipped cream. One way to fill: make a small hole at the bottom or side of puff and squeeze in custard from a decorating bag with #0 plain tube. Serve heavily dusted with confectioners' sugar. Yield: 6 dozen small; 4 dozen medium; 1 dozen large puffs.

Chocolate Floats

Select a round flat serving tray with a rim. Pour hot chocolate coating (page 246) over entire surface of tray. Place small whipped cream filled puffs in chocolate and serve.

Éclairs

Prepare 1 recipe Pâte à Chou.

1. Using a decorating bag with a #5 plain tube, pipe out a line of paste about 2½" long, ¾" wide. Hold bag vertically, start to release paste as though dropping a cream puff. Continue in a straight line for an inch and then repeat another puff. What you will get are 2 small puffs connected by a line of paste. This makes a perfect small éclair.

2. Bake at 425° F. for 20 minutes. Then lower temperature to 375° F. for 20 minutes more.

3. Cool. Prick a tiny hole in either end of *éclair* and fill from both sides by using a decorating bag fitted with a #0 tube. The fillings may be custard, Bavarian cream or whipped cream (see index). Yield: 3 dozen small, 18 large.

Bill Greenberg, Jr., the most Ivy League looking baker I know, calls this the Royal Crown, which is most descriptive, because that is exactly what this pastry looks like. I have always known it as Paris-Brest, a less descriptive but more nostalgic title. Make it and enjoy a really exquisite pastry.

Paris-Brest ★ ★ ★

1½ recipes Pâte à Chou	2 cups heavy sweet cream, beaten
1 recipe Chocolate Pastry Cream	stiff with 2 tablespoons sugar
(recipe follows)	and 1 teaspoon vanilla

1. Prepare a 9-inch lightly greased round layer pan.

2. Fit a decorating bag with a #5 plain tube, pipe out paste in overlapping swirls going completely around edge of pan, close to side. This swirl should be about 1½ inches in diameter. Now pipe a second layer on top of this, next to side of pan. Make the second layer of swirls, half the size. You now have a double decker ring.

3. If you can allow the time, place in the refrigerator for almost an hour. In the meantime, prepare the Chocolate Pastry Cream.

4. Preheat oven to 450° F. Bake the pastry when it is very cold for 30 minutes at 450° F. then 30 minutes at 400° F. and then 20 minutes at 375° F.

5. Cool thoroughly. Split in half, remove the top section and take out moist inner portions. Spread the Chocolate Pastry Cream in the bottom cavity of the pastry. With a spoon, mound whipped cream on top of chocolate cream. Place crown (top portion of pastry) on whipped cream. Dust all over with confectioners' sugar. Serves 10 to 12.

Crème Pâtissière Chocolate (Chocolate Pastry Cream)

1½ cups milk
1 vanilla bean
½ cup sugar

4 egg yolks
4 tablespoons flour
2 tablespoons cocoa (unsweetened)

Scald milk with vanilla bean. While milk is warming, cream sugar and yolks together. Blend in flour and cocoa. When milk is hot, pour it a little at a time into second mixture. stirring constantly. When well blended, turn mixture back into saucepan and cook over low heat until thickened. This takes about 5 minutes. Be sure to stir constantly. If you notice any lumps, use whisk wire. Remove to a bowl and cool thoroughly. Beat cream with whisk occasionally to prevent a skin from forming.

Vanilla Pastry Cream

Follow preceding recipe. Omit the cocoa and add 1 teaspoon vanilla when the mixture is cool.

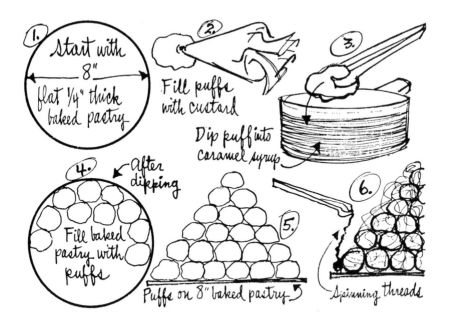

1. Start with 8" flat ¼" thick baked pastry

2. Fill puffs with custard. Dip puff into caramel syrup.

3.

4. After dipping. Fill baked pastry with puffs.

5. Puffs on 8" baked pastry

6. Spinning threads

The croquembouche literally translated means "crunches or crumbles in the mouth." The composition of the pastry may be varied as long as the ingredients are crunchy and are coated with a caramel glaze cooked to the hard candy stage. The croquembouche most popular with us is the pyramid of cream puffs on a pastry base. The filling is usually soft custard or whipped cream. What a taste sensation! Of the many French and Italian restaurants we visited, no two bakers seemed to make them exactly alike. I am sure no two American enthusiasts will do so either. More credit to you if you can create your own masterpieces.

Croquembouche

1. Prepare one recipe Custard or Crème Pâtissière (see index).

2. Prepare 1 piece of pie pastry or puff pastry rolled ¼ inch thick, cut into an 8-inch circle. Prick dough and place on a cookie sheet. Bake at 425° F. for 12 minutes or until golden. Remove from oven and cool.

3. Prepare 1 recipe Pâte à Chou. Pipe the paste on to lightly greased cookie sheet in the shape of cream puffs (50 to 60). Bake at 400° F. for 25 minutes. Cool thoroughly. Make a tiny hole on the side of each puff using #0 plain tube. Pipe custard into each puff using a decorating bag with this same point.

4. Prepare the following Caramel coating when cream puffs are filled: Blend together 1½ cups sugar, ½ cup water, ½ teaspoon cream of tartar in a saucepan. Bring to boil, only stirring until sugar is completely melted. Allow to boil until syrup just starts turning color (about 5 to 7 minutes).

5. In the meantime set up next to stove: Baked pastry round on turntable or tray, rack of filled cream puffs, tongs, and asbestos gloves if you can work with them. Before caramel starts turning color, turn off the flame but leave saucepan on the burner. Pick up one puff at a time with tongs. Dip each one into the hot syrup and place on to pastry. Cover the entire pastry with puffs. Syrup will act as a glue. Start second layer ½ inch in from the edge. Keep turning the pastry so that you can build the pyramid as evenly as possible.

6. If you are patient enough to wait about 2 or 3 minutes, the glaze will be cooled off enough for you to spin threads around the pastry. With the tongs, test the syrup. When it starts to become heavy, with the tongs, place a drop of caramel at the bottom side of the pyramid. Gently pull the caramel syrup with the end of the tongs, and you will start spinning threads. Start at the bottom of the pyramid and work your way around. Repeat this procedure. When finished, the croquembouche will be encased in the wispy caramel. This is a last touch; you can perform it *only* with patience and love. Serves 12.

Teacher says:

Since this caramel syrup hardens after a while and is no longer usable, start dipping the puffs before the syrup is caramel color. If you begin to place them when syrup just turns color you can take time to place the puffs with no danger of the syrup hardening before you place your top cream puff.

Work with asbestos gloves if you can. Never touch syrup with bare fingers. This is not for tasting!

A very attractive arrangement of puffs in a pyramid may be set up with chocolate coating. Of course it won't be a true "croque," not as crunchy as caramel brittle, but very good nevertheless.

Serving the croquembouche is a problem to some. If you explain the name to your guests, they will understand that it should crunch and crumble. It is best to cut portions for each one. The traditional method of breaking off each puff does make them too "crumbly."

Gâteau Saint Honoré

1 9″ round of Basic Pie Pastry   1 recipe Pâte à Chou
  (see index)   (first recipe in this chapter)

1. Place round of pastry in a 9″ layer pan with a removable bottom or on a cookie sheet.

2. Using a pastry bag fitted with a #5 (#6 or #7) plain tube, press out a ring of paste about 1″ wide around the edge of the pastry. Bake at 450° F. for 15 minutes. Reduce to 375° F. and bake for 30 minutes more. Remove and cool.

3. Use remainder of cream puff paste to make small cream puffs. Bake them at 375° F. for 30 minutes. Remove and cool.

1 cup cream, beaten stiff   1½ cups sugar
1 recipe Custard (see index)   ½ cup water
meringue made of 3 egg whites   ½ teaspoon cream of tartar
  and ⅓ cup sugar (see index)

Fill the small puffs with the whipped cream. Blend the custard with the meringue. Fill the cavity of the pastry with the combination and refrigerate.

Prepare the caramel glaze by blending together sugar, water and cream of tartar in a saucepan. Boil and stir until sugar melts completely. Stop stirring and allow syrup to boil until color starts to turn amber. Remove from flame. Dip puffs into syrup (as for the croquembouche).

Place each puff next to the other onto the ring of cream puff. Decorate all with crushed crystallized violets, rose petals and mint. Serves 10 to 12. This recipe is illustrated in color.

The cream puff paste becomes something unlike itself when it is fried. It turns into the Beignet, known to us as the fritter. As a dessert it is a delicate rich delight. The same recipe may be used or, if you wish, use 2 tablespoons less butter.

Dessert Beignet

1. Oil a cookie sheet and drop Cream Puff Paste in small mounds onto it. Use your decorating bag with # 5 plain tube or use 2 spoons. Refrigerate if possible.

2. Heat 1 quart peanut oil (corn oil if you wish) to the frying point of 375° F. Drop beignet from cookie sheet into hot oil. They will fry in 3 to 4 minutes to a golden crisp brown. Fry no more than 10 to 12 at one time. You will notice that they expand and almost crack. Remove with a slotted spoon. Drain on absorbent paper. Arrange on a lovely silver tray or bowl. Dust them generously with powdered sugar. Serve immediately with the following sauce.

APRICOT MADEIRA SAUCE

6 ounces apricot jam   4 ounces Madeira wine

Melt down jam on a low flame. Add wine, heat and serve with beignets.

PUFF PASTRY QUESTIONS ANSWERED

Q *May another shortening be substituted for butter?*
A Substitute margarine if you absolutely must, but nothing replaces the fine flavor of butter.
Q *What can be done to prevent puff pastry edges from separating during baking?*
A Nothing! This is the nature of puff pastry and is a sign that your pastry is baking the way it should. Puff pastry should puff up and so it shrinks from the sides.
Q *Can puff pastry be used for a pie shell?*
A No, not in the same sense that we think of pie shells. It does not keep its shape when fitted to a pie tin. It may be rolled and baked round to cover a deep dish fruit pie or meat pie.

Q   *May canned fruit be used in place of fresh?*

A   Fresh fruit is best but if you use canned fruit, drain off the moisture. Canned sliced apples (without sugar) are very good for the Apple Roll.

Q   *How far in advance can the large pastries (Gateau St. Honoré, Croquembouche, etc.) be made?*

A   All pastries filled with creams should be made as near to serving time as possible. The basic dough can always be made the day before. The pastry is superior when it is baked and filled the day it is to be served.

Q   *Can puddings be used to fill these pastries?*

A   Yes, use whatever fillings you enjoy most.

LESSON 13

The Pie

Pie pastry attracts the new baker and at the same time intimidates her. My first attempt at baking the year I was married was no great success. I attempted pie pastry and found the rolling pin deficient. Why didn't the dough stay in one lovely piece? Now many years later, I know it is mostly a matter of experience and feeling master of the situation. This is my basic recipe for pie pastry. Aside from seriously taking the hints that I will add to the recipes later, start a campaign of practice.

Important facts about pie pastry

1. Be sure that ingredients are cold and room is cool.

2. Pastry will turn out flakier when handled quickly. It also improves when it is allowed to rest in the refrigerator.

3. The secret of fine pastry is knowing how far to work it in order to make it roll out easily. Be sure to work the flour well into the fat so that the particles are small and all the dry flour disappears. At first you may have to use more water but try to cut it down as you become experienced.

4. Do not worry about touching the dough. It is better to feel it

to understand the desired texture. It should be soft, semi-dry, not sticky and doughy, but moist enough to hold its shape. Pastry making is a personal experience. Knowing your dough is a challenge to you. The better your understanding of it, the worthier the baked product.

5. Pastries are versatile. They are used as often for appetizers and luncheon dishes as they are for dessert. In this lesson, I will include some of those pies most favored by my students.

6. Pie crusts freeze perfectly, no ifs, ands or buts. Freeze them unbaked in their pans. Aluminum foil pans may be used. If you own a freezer, you can always have on hand the base for one of the best loved of all desserts, the pie.

Basic Pie Pastry

¼ pound butter
½ cup vegetable shortening
2½ cups all-purpose flour

½ teaspoon salt
1 teaspoon sugar
5 to 6 tablespoons ice water

1. Place butter and shortening in a large bowl.

2. Sift flour, salt and sugar on to butter and shortening.

3. Cut flour into fat with a pastry blender or two knives. The mixture starts looking like tiny balls. When the white flour look is gone and each tiny particle of fat is combined with a bit of flour, start adding water.

4. Add up to 4 tablespoons of water, working it in with your pastry blender. If the dough begins to form a ball, do not add any more water. Feel it with your hand. The pastry should not be dry and mealy now. If it still falls apart add some more water (one-half cup of water is the positive limit).

5. Roll out a sheet of waxed paper. Dump dough on paper. Fold waxed paper around dough and press into a ball. Do not handle dough directly with your hands. The less handling, the better the pastry. Divide dough into pieces to suit the size pies or pastries you intend to make. For example divide dough in half for a covered 10″ pie; divide dough into four parts for four 8″ pie shells.

6. Wrap balls of dough in waxed paper and refrigerate for 1 hour.

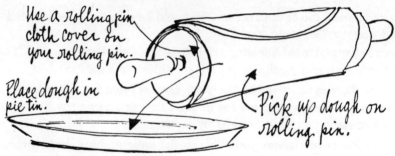

Use a rolling pin cloth cover on your rolling pin.

Place dough in pie tin.

Pick up dough on rolling pin.

TO ROLL PIE PASTRY

1. Set out a well floured pastry cloth or board.

2. Use a cloth covered rolling pin.

3. If dough is very firm from refrigeration allow it to soften slightly for a few minutes. Start at the center and flatten the dough with the rolling pin; roll to the outer edge moving the dough around as you roll. Try to roll so as to keep the shape of the circle.

4. Roll from the center to the outer edge, always being sure that the pastry is free from the cloth. In order to avoid breakage roll in one direction. If you roll lightly and keep turning the dough you will prevent stickiness.

5. *For a 2-crust pie,* cut the bottom pastry at least 1½″ larger than the pan and the top pastry ½″ larger than the pan. *For a shell* (single crust) cut the pastry 1½″ larger than the pie plate.

6. Roll dough over rolling pin. Place pie plate near rolling pin. Pick up dough with pin and place it on the pie plate. Fit dough into pan very loosely. If there is an uneven edge hanging over sides, cut it with a scissors to even it off. Occasionally dough will break; patch it. Breaking generally forecasts a fine short pastry to come.

For a two-crust pie, bottom crust may be trimmed just over the edge, top crust may be larger so as to fold over and enclose bottom edge. Flute around the edge or press edge down with the tines of a fork. Yield: 1 covered 10″ pie, 3 9″ pie shells, 4 8″ pie shells or 20 tartlette shells (2½″).

TO BAKE PASTRY

1. Brush edge of pastries with beaten egg yolk and 1 tablespoon of water.

2. Bake a 2-crust pie 20 minutes at 425° F., then continue for 35 minutes at 375° F. For single unfilled shell: Prick bottom and sides all over with a fork. Bake at 425° F. for 10 to 12 minutes.

Chocolate Mousse Pie ★ ★ ★

1 8" or 9" baked pie shell
4 egg yolks in large bowl
  (bowl from electric mixer)
¼ cup sugar
4 egg whites in smaller bowl
pinch of salt

4 ounces semi-sweet chocolate
  (melted and slightly cooled)
1 teaspoon vanilla
1 cup cream, whipped stiff
  for decoration

1. Beat egg yolks; add sugar gradually and beat till mixture is light colored and thick (about 3 minutes).

2. Beat egg whites with pinch of salt until stiff.

3. Add melted chocolate to egg yolks and beat just enough to blend in thoroughly.

4. Remove from beater. Fold in beaten egg whites and vanilla by hand. Pour into baked pie shell and refrigerate.

5. Allow to set for 2 hours. Cover with whipped cream. Use decorating bag for a fancier look. Serves 8.

Lemon Mousse Pie

1 9" or 10" baked pie shell
1 cup heavy cream
1 envelope unflavored gelatin
¼ cup water
4 egg yolks in large bowl
  (bowl from electric mixer)

⅔ cup sugar
4 egg whites
2 tablespoons grated lemon rind
¼ cup fresh lemon juice
1 cup whipped cream for decoration
4 paper thin slices of lemon

1. Beat cream to stiff consistency and refrigerate.

2. Soften gelatin with ¼ cup cold water in a cup. Place cup in a saucepan of boiling water until gelatin becomes a clear liquid. Remove from flame.

3. While gelatin is dissolving beat egg yolks. Add sugar gradually and beat until mixture is thick and lemon-colored, about 5 minutes.

4. Beat egg whites until stiff and set aside.

5. Add lemon juice, rind and dissolved gelatin to beaten egg yolk mixture using the electric mixer.

6. Remove from mixer and fold in egg whites, then whipped cream. Do this by hand.

7. Pour mixture into baked pie shell and refrigerate for at least 2 hours. Decorate with whipped cream before serving. Place thin lemon slices on the center. Serves 8.

Teacher says:

Both mousse pies will be soft-textured but they will jell firmly after 12 hours.

Serve the chocolate mousse in individual soufflé dishes or demi-tasse cups.

Pour the lemon mousse into a 1-quart mold. Unmold and surround with clusters of grapes or fresh strawberries when set.

The lemon mousse pie is a real taste sensation when garnished with sliced fresh strawberries.

Both the lemon and chocolate may be used as the filling for what the English call a trifle. Layer rum-soaked sponge cake with either chocolate or lemon mousse. Present it in a beautiful crystal bowl. Pipe rosettes of whipped cream on top. *Voila;* a picture-book dessert and a true company delight.

Custard Fruit Pie

1 8″-baked pie shell	2 eggs
2 cups milk (in a 4-cup pyrex measuring container)	2 tablespoons cornstarch
	1 envelope unflavored gelatin
½ cup sugar	¼ cup cold water
pinch salt	1 teaspoon vanilla

1. Pour 1½ cups milk into a heavy saucepan, keeping ½ cup in pyrex container. Blend sugar and salt with milk in saucepan. Set on low heat.

2. Beat the remaining ½ cup milk with 2 eggs and cornstarch.

3. When milk and sugar mixture are hot stir in milk, eggs and cornstarch slowly. Keep over low flame.

4. Stir constantly until mixture simmers; simmer for a few minutes. If any lumps appear use your wire whisk. Set custard in a bowl to cool.

5. In a cup, soften gelatin with cold water. Place cup in a saucepan with an inch of water. Heat water and wait for gelatin to dissolve. When gelatin is a clear liquid, add it to the custard with the vanilla. Unless the custard is beaten every once in a while until cool a skin will form on the top.

6. When custard is cool, fill the pie shell. Refrigerate until set.

Top the custard with any desirable fruit or combination of fruits. Use the red glaze for red and dark berries; use the light glaze for bananas, peaches and grapes. Serves 8.

RED GLAZE

1 cup red berry juice	1 tablespoon cornstarch
(raspberry is delicious)	mixed with 2 tablespoons water
2 tablespoons currant jelly	few drops red coloring

Bring berry juice and currant jelly to a boil. Lower heat. Add cornstarch mixture and coloring. Stir briskly until mixture thickens. Mixture should coat the spoon. Cool the glaze before coating the fruits.

LIGHT GLAZE

½ cup apricot jelly	1 tablespoon cornstarch
¾ cup peach or apricot juice	mixed with 2 tablespoons water
	few drops yellow coloring

Melt jelly in peach or apricot juice. When mixture simmers, lower flame. Add cornstarch and water and then stir briskly. Blend in coloring. Set aside to cool after mixture is thickened and has cooked about 3 minutes.

For the simplest glaze, red or light jellies can be melted down with a small amount of water. Cognac or other brandies may be used in place of water.

Chocolate Tartlette

See index for recipe.

━━━∿∿∿━━━

There are many obviously simple recipes that most people never attempt. Easier to bake than most people suppose, the coconut custard pie is one of those favorites. As a fine teaching point, compare it to the preceding Custard Fruit Pie. The custard in the fruit pie is boiled. The custard in the coconut pie is baked. Coconut Custard Pie is the dessert counterpart of "quiche Lorraine," which is a baked appetizer pie (like the Onion and Cheese Pie—see index). Both are baked in an unbaked pie shell.

Coconut Custard Pie

1 unbaked 8" or 9" pie shell   ½ teaspoon salt
   in refrigerator   1 teaspoon vanilla
2½ cups milk   4 tablespoons coconut,
4 eggs   shredded or canned
½ cup sugar

Preheat oven to 400° F. Heat milk to scalding. Beat eggs, sugar, ½ teaspoon salt, vanilla together. When milk is hot, add it gradually to egg mixture. Place cold pie shell on lowest rack in the oven. Then pour milk mixture into pie shell. Bake for 30 minutes. Five minutes before pie is finished, sprinkle 4 tablespoons coconut over the top. Set back into oven to complete baking. Serves 8.

Many years ago I promised a friend that I would not circulate her recipe. The secret is out! For 12 years I kept it under my hat or hidden in my file box. Whatever the legal limit for keeping secrets, the time for this one has passed.

Fresh Coconut Cream Pie

1 10" baked pie shell   ¾ pound marshmallows
1 cup fresh or canned coconut   3 cups heavy cream, whipped stiff
1 cup milk   2 cups freshly grated coconut

1. Soak 1 cup coconut in milk for an hour. Strain mixture through a double thickness of cheesecloth. Press out all the milk.

2. Cook this coconut milk with marshmallows over low heat until marshmallows melt. Cool in a bowl. Set in refrigerator until mixture starts to jell (about 1 hour).

3. Beat the jellied mixture till frothy with the electric mixer. Combine this with the whipped cream.

4. Blend in 1 cup of freshly grated coconut with the cream mixture. Pile the mixture into the pie shell. Cover the entire top of the pie with the remaining cup of coconut. Refrigerate for at least 6 hours. Serves 8 to 10.

Fresh berries perform a miracle for the cheese pie. The tart and juicy berry is a perfect complement for this creamy filling.

Strawberry Cheese Pie

1 10″ partially baked pie shell (5 minutes at 425°F)	4 eggs 1 teaspoon vanilla

1½ pounds cream cheese,
   room temperature
	1 quart strawberries,
	   fresh and cut in half

1 cup sugar	1 cup red glaze (see index)

Soften cheese and beat in electric mixer with sugar (3 minutes). Beat in one egg at a time (total time about 8 to 10 minutes). Add vanilla. Pour into crust and bake for 50 minutes at 350° When pie is cool, lay halves of fresh strawberries on top to completely cover surface. Coat berries with red glaze. Blueberries or raspberries may be substituted. Serves 8 to 10.

Note: A zweibach or graham cracker crust may be used instead of pie pastry. If time allows, be patient and allow pie to cool in the oven without opening oven door; this prevents an immediate fall. Cheese cakes are known to drop. Cheese cakes sometimes crack on top and may flatten, but the berries cover all sins and the flavor remains superb.

Many times I meet the husband or friend of a student who exclaims about the excellent fruit pastries the student prepared. "Were they really home-made?" is a frequent question. Yes, blue ribbons to all these students who baked them so well! You can earn your culinary blue ribbon too with this recipe.

French Pastry Tartlettes

Prepare one basic pie pastry recipe (first one in this lesson). Use 3-inch fluted tartlette tins. Cut out rounds of pastry ½ inch larger than tin. Fit pastry into tin very loosely. Press pastry against curved sides. With a small sharp knife trim pastry to the edge of the tin. Prick all over with a fork. Brush the edges with beaten egg yolk and water. Bake at 425° for 10 minutes. Yield: 20 tartlettes.

Caution: Look at pastries after 4 or 5 minutes in the oven. Sometimes they puff up. If not too much baking time has elapsed to make them crusty, it is possible to prick them where they bubbled. This will release air and flatten them.

TO FILL TARTLETTES:

Prepare 1 recipe custard as for Custard Fruit Pie. Whip 1 cup heavy cream very stiff, fold into custard and flavor with 1 teaspoon vanilla or 1 tablespoon cognac. You now have a Bavarian cream. Place a heaping spoon of Bavarian cream in each pastry. Cover with fresh strawberries, blueberries, seedless grapes, sliced bananas, or peaches. Use appropriate red or light glaze for the different fruits.

Comes the fall and our culinary thoughts turn to chestnuts. This nut, unique in texture and taste, is as popular along the sidewalks of New York as on the table of royalty. It is as splendid in its simple roasted state as in glorious continental creations. The Rum Chestnut Pie concluded a recent Hillman Thanksgiving dinner, a perfect ending to my favorite day.

Rum Chestnut Pie

1 8-ounce can chestnut purée (unsweetened)
2 egg yolks
1 cup evaporated milk
¼ cup sugar
¼ teaspoon salt

1 envelope gelatin softened in ½ cup water
¼ cup rum
1 cup heavy cream, whipped
3 marrons (chestnuts in syrup)
1 baked 9" pie shell
1 baked 9" thin sponge layer

1. Blend chestnut, egg yolks, milk, sugar and salt in a heavy saucepan till smooth. Bring mixture slowly to a boil, stirring constantly until a heavy custard is formed. Set aside.

2. Place cup of softened gelatin in a pan of hot water. Heat until gelatin becomes clear.

3. Pour gelatin into chestnut mixture. Stir thoroughly. If any lumps appear use a wire whisk. Refrigerate chestnut custard until it is almost set.

4. When chestnut is practically set, beat egg whites. Add ¼ cup of sugar gradually. Fold stiffly beaten egg whites into chestnut mixture. Flavor with 1 tablespoon rum.

5. Pour mixture into pie shell. Cover with sponge layer. Sprinkle remainder of rum over sponge.

6. Decorate top of sponge with whipped cream and marrons. Serves 8.

~~~~~~~~

Italian Cheese Pie

1 recipe Basic Pie Pastry	4 eggs
1½ pounds ricotta cheese (sieved)	1 teaspoon vanilla
4 ounces toasted almonds chopped	2 tablespoons marsala wine or rum
1 tablespoons grated orange rind	1 egg yolk beaten
⅛ cup sugar	with 1 tablespoon water

1. Cut off a little less than half the dough and roll it out to fit a 9″ or 10″ round pie pan. Roll out remaining dough into an oblong ⅛″ thick. Using a fancy pastry wheel or knife, cut at least eight 10″ strips, each ½″ wide. Set pastry in refrigerator.

2. Combine cheese, nuts and rind. Add sugar and beat for 2 minutes. Add eggs one at a time, beating each egg for a minute or two. Blend in vanilla and wine, then pour mixture into lined pie plate.

3. Brush pastry strips with beaten egg yolk. Place one 10″ strip across the center; arrange 2 or 3 strips on each side of center about ½ inch apart. Cross these strips diagonally with the 5 or 6 remaining strips. Brush pastry edges with egg yolk, pinch ends of strips firmly to the edge of pastry, and cut off excess.

4. Bake at 350° F. for 45 minutes. If pastry is not browned enough, turn oven up to 400° F. for 5 minutes. Serves 8.

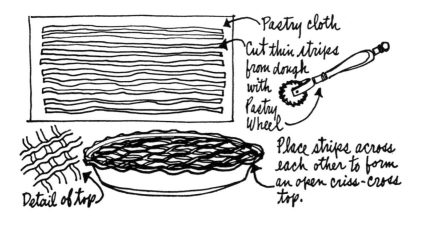

Pastry cloth

Cut thin strips from dough with Pastry Wheel

Place strips across each other to form an open criss-cross top.

Detail of top.

〰〰〰

Through the years, many of my friends who are fine cooks have sparked my food collection with their most unusual recipes. Credit goes to Alice Thompson for the next one. I am told that a charming inn in Martha's Vineyard features it for dessert. Guard the secret of its texture until all have eaten; you are sure to be questioned!

〰〰〰

Crunchy Meringue Pie ★ ★ ★

3 egg whites (room temperature)   ½ teaspoon baking powder
1 cup sugar   ⅔ cup walnuts, chopped
14 Ritz crackers, crushed

Grease a 9″ pie plate. Preheat oven to 350° F. Beat egg whites till frothy; add sugar gradually until stiff (3 to 5 minutes). Combine crushed crackers and baking powder and add to the meringue with the walnuts. Spread mixture all over the greased pan. Bake at 350° F. for 35 minutes. Serves 8.

FOUR WAYS TO SERVE:

Pile 3 cups of sweetened whipped cream over meringue to cover completely. Sprinkle shavings of dark sweet chocolate over all.

Hull 1 pint of strawberries. Cut in halves and soak in ¼ cup Kirsch for 1 hour. Blend strawberries with 3 cups of sweetened whipped cream and spread on the baked meringue. If teetotalers or children are present omit the Kirsch.

Place round scoops of ice cream all around edge of the pie. Fill the center with fresh berries or peaches. Pour the red or light glaze over fruit. With a decorating bag, pipe whipped cream around berries and ice cream.

Place scoops of ice cream around edge of the meringue. Fill the center with 2 cups of sweetened whipped cream. Dribble chocolate sauce over all.

PIE QUESTIONS ANSWERED

Q *How much cream should be used to make 1 cup of whipped cream?*
A Heavy sweet cream doubles in bulk when whipped. Use ½ cup heavy cream.

Q *What apples do you use for a covered apple pie?*
A Greenings are very good. I like to add a few McIntosh for sweetness and moisture. When greenings are not available use a combination of apples such as Roman Beauties, Baldwins and Cortlands.

Q *Why do my pie doughs always crumble when I am rolling them?*
A Usually this is caused by too little moisture. Don't be afraid to work the dough a little in order to make it more cohesive.

Q *How and which pies do you freeze?*
A I freeze unbaked pie shells and make the fillings fresh when the need arises. However, all pies freeze well except ones with custard.

Q *Do you refrigerate the cheese pie before serving?*
A No, it is superb when it is baked fresh and served at room temperature the same day.

LESSON 14

The Yeast Cake

I fell in love with baking the first time I made Danish pastry. It is time to confess that I had done very little baking before December, 1948 and I remember the date well because my joy was momentous. This experience was also instrumental in guiding me towards the great adventure of teaching cooking, a subject I had not formally prepared for.

Agda Larson, cook at our nursery school, was my teacher. Her unique recipe for Danish pastry and puff pastry were so simplified that I was astonished enough at the results to want to share it with others. After my first pastry success she and I decided to raise funds for our non-profit school. I taught, she baked. There is no cake dough more rewarding to the lay baker than a good yeast dough. It is almost enough satisfaction to smell the yeast aroma as to eat the cake itself.

Before giving you Agda's Danish pastry, I have included the plainer, everyday yeast doughs that you might like to try first. They are all used constantly in homes around my town. Kneading dough is no longer a thing of the past. The modern suburban woman is rediscovering the fun in baking with yeast. Her family and friends are constantly urging her on with compliments.

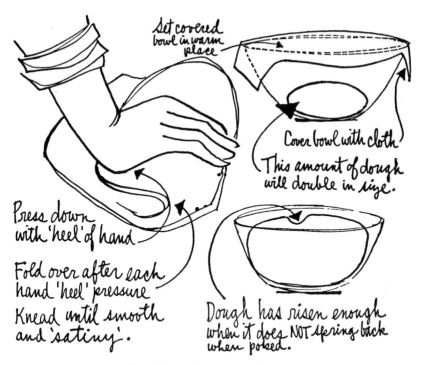

Set covered bowl in warm place

Cover bowl with cloth

This amount of dough will double in size.

Press down with 'heel' of hand

Fold over after each hand 'heel' pressure

Knead until smooth and 'satiny'.

Dough has risen enough when it does NOT spring back when poked.

Facts to Remember About Yeast Doughs:

1. Fresh yeast keeps very well in the refrigerator. A 2- to 4-ounce cake of yeast keeps up to 2 weeks. Larger pieces will keep longer.

2. When using dry yeast always follow directions on the package for dissolving it in warm water. Use this amount of water as part of liquid in the recipe (unless recipe calls for dry yeast and provision is made for the water).

3. Ingredients used in yeast doughs should never be warmer than lukewarm since the action of yeast is destroyed by high heat.

4. Yeast should always be dissolved before using. With fresh yeast, this may be done by mixing yeast with a little lukewarm water or milk. Sometimes the yeast is creamed with a small piece of butter and sugar (fresh yeast can be handled this way for the Danish Pastry).

5. Use all-purpose flour or, if you can find it, bread flour (which is high in gluten) for yeast doughs. Since flours vary in their ability to absorb moisture and develop gluten, it is impossible to give exact flour measurements. However, try to keep within ½ cup of the amounts given in the recipes.

6. Kneading develops the gluten. Gluten, in turn, helps to make

the dough elastic and light in texture.

7. Doughs should be kneaded until they are smooth and satiny.

8. A dough has risen enough when it no longer springs back after being poked in the center.

9. Yeast doughs may be refrigerated up to 3 days. If dough rises in the refrigerator, punch it down to remove the air. Cut off pieces and use as desired.

10. All yeast doughs should be brushed with one of the following mixtures to produce a shiny and brown crust. Egg yolk broken up with 1 tablespoon of water or cream produces the shiniest crust. Whole egg beaten with 1 tablespoon milk gives a moderately shiny brown crust. Egg white when beaten until frothy produces a brown crust without shine.

Old-Fashioned Yeast Cake

¾ cup sour cream	¼ cup warm water
¼ cup milk	½ cup sugar
5 tablespoons butter	2 eggs
3 packages dry yeast	1 teaspoon salt
or 2 ounces fresh	4½ to 5 cups all-purpose flour

1. Heat sour cream, milk and butter, just until butter melts. Set aside until lukewarm.

2. Place yeast and warm water in a large mixing bowl. Yeast will melt in a few minutes. Add sugar, eggs and salt. Combine with sour cream mixture. Blend in a little flour. Add more flour and mix well with your hand. Add up to 4 cups of flour. You may want to use more on your board or pastry cloth.

3. Turn dough on to floured cloth and knead for 8 to 10 minutes. Dough will become smooth and light. Place in a greased bowl (twice as large as dough). Cover and allow to rise in a warm place. I usually set the bowl on top of a warm oven. It sometimes rises to double within 2 hours. If the room is cool it may take longer.

FILLING

4. Combine and crumble with your fingers ¼ pound butter, 1 cup sugar, ¼ cup flour, ½ cup bread or cake crumbs, 1 teaspoon cinnamon, and 1 cup ground nuts (walnuts, pecans, filberts). Add ½ cup white raisins or currants. Set aside.

5. Prepare two greased 9″ x 3″ loaf pans.

6. When dough has risen to double, roll out the dough into a rectangle 18″ x 6″. Spread ¾ of crumbled mixture over dough. Sprinkle raisins all over. Roll up as a jelly roll. Cut into twelve 1½″ slices.

7. Place 6 slices in twos, cut side down, in each loaf pan. Sprinkle remainder of crumbs all over and set to rise for another 2 hours.

8. Bake at 375° F. for 45 minutes. Yield: Two loaf size coffee cakes.

Yeast cakes may take varied fillings. Sometimes the filling changes the flavor of the cake. The doughs of most yeast cakes do not have much sugar or flavor in themselves. A good deal of the final flavor depends on your filling. The following may be used with any of these doughs.

Fillings

NUT

Blend together 2 cups ground walnuts, ¼ cup sugar, 2 tablespoons warm milk, grated rind of ½ lemon. Yield: 2¼ cups.

APRICOT

Cook 1 pound dried apricots in water to cover until tender. Add 1½ cups sugar and cook till sugar dissolves. Strain or purée. Cool. Yield: 2 cups.

PRUNE

Use prepared lekvar. This may be bought at better food shops by the pound or in jars. To 8 ounces of the prune mixture add 1 tablespoon lemon juice, 1 tablespoon lemon rind and 1 tablespoon flour. Yield: 1⅛ cups.

CHEESE

Blend together 8 ounces softened cream cheese, ½ cup sugar, 1 egg yolk, 1 tablespoon orange rind, 1 tablespoon flour and 1 teaspoon vanilla. Yield: 1⅛ cups.

ALMOND PASTE

Blend 8 ounces almond paste with 4 tablespoons butter. Beat 2 whites with ¼ cup sugar until stiff. Add to almond paste. Yield: 1¼ cups.

NUT AND CHOCOLATE

Beat 2 egg whites until frothy. Add ¼ cup sugar and beat until stiff, then blend in 2 cups ground walnuts (pecans or filberts) and 4 ounces grated semi-sweet chocolate. Yield: 2½ cups.

CUSTARD

Heat 1 cup milk with ½ cup sugar. In the meantime beat together ¾ cup milk, ½ cup sugar, pinch salt, 2 eggs, 2 tablespoons cornstarch and 1 tablespoon flour in a 4-cup pyrex pitcher. Add second mixture slowly to the hot milk and sugar. Cook over low flame until mixture thickens. Cook 2 to 3 minutes. Flavor with 1 teaspoon vanilla. Yield: 2 cups.

Crescents

1 package dry yeast or ½ ounce fresh	¼ cup sugar
¼ cup warm water	¼ cup sweet cream or milk
½ pound butter	1 teaspoon vanilla
3 cups all-purpose flour	Filling:
½ teaspoon salt	1 egg white
3 egg yolks, stirred	1 cup ground nuts

1. Dissolve yeast in warm water.
2. In the meantime, blend butter, flour and salt together with a pastry blender or 2 knives. When mixture forms tiny beads of buttter, add egg yolks, yeast (already dissolved), sugar, cream and vanilla. Mix thoroughly into a ball of dough.
3. Knead dough on a floured board or cloth. Knead for about 5 to 7 minutes. This dough is firm not soft. Divide dough into 4 parts. Shape each into a round ball. Cover and refrigerate.
4. When ready to bake, make desired filling or use just a generous sprinkling of sugar, cinnamon, nuts and jam.
5. Roll each ball into a round about 9″ in diameter. Cut into 12 wedges.
6. Sprinkle sugar over surface of dough. Place a teaspoon of filling on the edge of each wedge. Roll up towards middle of circle.
7. Dip each crescent into slightly beaten egg white and then dip in ground nuts.

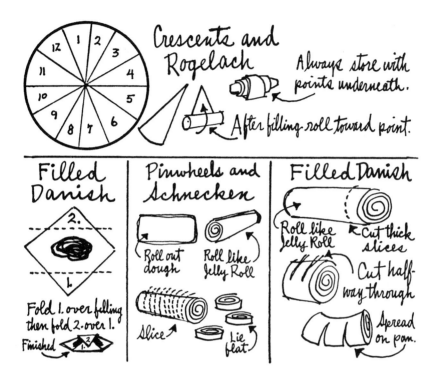

8. Allow these to stand at room temperature for 30 minutes. They rise just slightly.

9. Set oven in the meantime to 350° F. Bake crescents at 350° F. for 20 to 25 minutes. Yield: 4 dozen.

Teacher says:

Instead of dipping crescents into egg whites, you may simply brush each cookie with beaten yolk or egg whites and sprinkle them with nuts.

Make the dough and refrigerate it up to three days. It keeps very well.

These crescents may be frozen after they are baked. Be sure to reheat them directly out of freezer and serve.

~~~~~~~~

The following two recipes make use of the crescent dough. Apple cakes are always favorites. Try this with fresh or canned apples.

Dutch Apple Cake

½ recipe crescent dough
  (preceding recipe)
1 can sliced apples
  (without thickening)
2 tablespoons lemon juice
½ cup sugar

¼ pound butter
½ cup sugar
½ cup bread crumbs
½ cup flour
½ teaspoon cinnamon

Roll out dough and place into a 9″ layer pan, preferably with a loose bottom. Set aside to rise for 30 minutes. Mix apples with lemon juice and ½ cup sugar. Preheat oven to 375° F. Make crumb topping with last five ingredients, blending with fingers until large crumbs are formed. Place apples on dough. Spread crumbs over apples. Bake at 375° F. for 40-50 minutes. Serves 10 to 12.

~~~~~~~~

Surprise your family with this wonderful treat for a special breakfast. Pass the heavy cream around if they grow slim in your house. For a summertime dessert and a sure favorite, cut squares and top the kuchen with a fine vanilla bean ice cream.

Fresh Blueberry Kuchen

1 recipe crescent dough
1 quart fresh blueberries
½ cup bread crumbs
¾ cup sugar

¼ cup ground almonds
rind and juice of one lemon
4 tablespoons flour
4 tablespoons butter

Preheat oven to 375° F. Wash and dry blueberries. Grease a 17″ jelly roll pan. Blend together bread crumbs, sugar, almonds, lemon and flour. Roll out crescent dough to fit shape of pan. Place dough in pan. Allow to rise for 30 minutes. Sprinkle dough with ½ of blended mixture. Place berries evenly over dough. Sprinkle with remainder of dry mixture and dot with butter. Bake at 375° F. for 40 minutes. Yield: 18 squares.

Many of us are frequently requested to bake for organizations, teas and meetings. Whenever I see the petite crescent on a dessert table I know it must be Sylvia Allen's recipe. If they are tinier than petite, then I know the lady herself made them. Although we all use her recipe, Sylvia makes the smallest and the most crescents of anyone I know. Try these little delicacies and measure them to one inch!

Sylvia's Rogelach (Crescents)

½ pound butter, melted and cooled
1 package dry yeast
  or ⅗ ounce fresh
¼ cup warm water
2 eggs

2 cups all-purpose flour
2 tablespoons sugar
½ teaspoon salt
2 teaspoons cream
1 teaspoon vanilla

Melt butter and set aside to cool. Dissolve yeast in warm water. Mix all ingredients together, reserving a little flour for the end. Form a ball, roll in reserved flour. This is a very soft dough and must be refrigerated at least 6 hours, preferably overnight. It will last well, covered, up to 3 days in the refrigerator.

TO PREPARE ROGELACH

Mix 2 cups sugar and 2 teaspoons cinnamon. Prepare 1 cup ground nuts and 1 cup raspberry jam or English morello cherry jam. If you wish to form a tiny crescent, divide dough into 6 small balls. Preheat oven to 375° F. Roll each into an 8″ circle of dough. Sprinkle with sugar, cinnamon and nuts. Cut each circle into 10 to 12 wedges. Place a dot of jam at the outer edge and roll towards center. Bake on a greased cookie sheet at 375° F. for 25 minutes. Yield: 5 to 6 dozen.

Cooky Crescents (Rogelach)

See page 257.

Crescents

See page 208 for another yeast version not quite as rich as this.

〜〜〜〜〜

William Greenberg, Jr, has built up a fine reputation in Manhattan because his cakes have the homemade quality. How he can turn out so many wonderful baked goods from his tiny red and white shops is truly amazing! His mama's schnecken recipe has always been loved by New Yorkers; here it is for you wherever you live.

Schnecken (Honey Buns)   ★ ★ ★

3 packages dry yeast	3 egg yolks
or 2 ounces fresh	½ teaspoon salt
½ cup warm water	1½ teaspoons white vinegar
1½ cups butter (3 sticks)	1 cup sour cream
½ cup sugar	5½ cups all-purpose flour

Dissolve yeast in warm water and set aside. In a large bowl, cream butter and sugar. Add egg yolks and salt. Blend in vinegar and sour cream. Add dissolved yeast, then flour, and mix very well. Dough should be heavy not pasty. Knead the dough on a floured board or cloth. This takes about 10 minutes. Dough becomes smooth and elastic. Refrigerate for a minimum of 6 hours or a maximum of 3 days.

FILLING

1 cup butter (2 sticks)	whole pecans (48 to 96)
1 pound light brown sugar	cinnamon
1 teaspoon cinnamon	white raisins
1 tablespoon light Karo syrup	

1. Cream butter with ½ pound sugar (save ½ pound sugar for later use). Add 1 teaspoon cinnamon and 1 tablespoon Karo syrup.

2. Place 1 teaspoon of mixture in the bottom of each muffin tin. Set one whole pecan flat side down in each muffin tin. More broken nuts may be used too.

3. Prepare your pastry board or cloth and rolling pin. Take dough out of the refrigerator. Cut off ¼ of the dough. Roll into an oblong about ⅛″ thick. Lift dough after rolling so it is free from the board.

4. Sprinkle with brown sugar, cinnamon and raisins. (Bill uses them generously.)

5. Roll as for a jelly roll. Pull roll to elongate it slightly. Cut into ½″ slices for small muffin tins, 1½″ slices for large. Place each into

muffin tin on brown sugar mixture and nuts. The dough should reach almost to the top of the muffin mold.

6. Allow to rise in a warm place for 45 minutes. Preheat oven to 375° F. Bake for 25 minutes (small), 35 minutes (large). Yield: 4 dozen regulation muffin size; 7 to 8 dozen petite size (1½″).

~~~~~~~~~

Agda's Danish Pastry ★ ★ ★

3 packages dry yeast
   or 2 ounces fresh
½ cup warm water
1½ cups butter (3 sticks—
   cut each stick in eight parts)

½ cup sugar
4 cups all-purpose flour
3 eggs
½ cup milk
2 teaspoons vanilla

1. Prepare a pastry cloth or board and a rolling pin.

2. Soften yeast in warm water and set aside.

3. In a large bowl cream 4 pieces of butter (⅛ pound) with ½ cup of sugar. Add softened yeast, 3 cups of flour, 3 eggs, ½ cup of milk and vanilla. Beat this sticky dough vigorously with bare hand (some mixers have a special attachment for yeast doughs).

4. Notice that the remaining butter and 1 cup of flour have not yet been used. If the dough is very sticky, add ½ cup more flour.

5. Turn dough on to floured board or cloth using some of the remaining flour. Roll out dough lightly into a large sheet. Dot all over with pieces of the remaining butter. Fold dough from top and bottom to enclose butter. Roll out again.

6. In the rolling process use remainder of flour. Repeat rolling and folding 3 or 4 times or until dough seems to resist rolling pin.

7. If the atmosphere is warm, dough may stick. In that case refrigerate it between rollings, it will be easier to handle when chilled.

8. Work quickly! The method of folding is unimportant in this case as long as butter is blended into dough.

9. Set dough in refrigerator covered lightly. Keep overnight or up to 2 days.

DIRECTIONS FOR BAKING

The simplest way to make these is to make a shape similar to the schnecken and use just a sprinkling of sugar, cinnamon, nuts and raisins. This can be made in minutes. Other possible shapes are shown on page 209.

For all other fillings, use the fillings given on page 207 and 208.

1. Prepare the desired filling.

2. Cut off ¼ piece of dough. Roll it into a rectangle about ¼″ thick. Sprinkle all over with sugar, cinnamon, nuts and raisins. Roll up as for jelly roll. Cut down into 1″ slices and place cut side up on ungreased pans, ½″ apart.

3. If desired, a small amount of filling can be piped into the center of each bun. Use a decorating bag or drop it using 2 spoons.

4. Using the same directions as in step #2, make a long roll. Cut 1½″ slices. With a knife make three slits on one side of each slice. Place pastries on an ungreased sheet, curving each slice that slits open up like a fan.

5. For another shape, roll out dough into a rectangle and cut square 2″ x 2″. Sprinkle all over with sugar and cinnamon. Place 1 teaspoon of desired filling in the center. Bring the two opposite corners together, flapping one over the other.

6. Save any ends cut off and roll these in cinnamon and sugar. Form twists, snails or any shape your hands create. No matter how you handle this the result is always good!

7. After your forms are set on pans, brush each one with a mixture of 1 egg beaten with 1 tablespoon milk. Sprinkle all over with cinnamon, sugar and nuts.

8. Allow to rise at room temperature for 2 hours before baking.

9. Preheat oven to 375° F. Bake pastries for 15 to 20 minutes. Yield: 5 dozen medium Danish pastry.

YEAST CAKE QUESTIONS ANSWERED

Q *Do you find fresh yeast better than the packaged dry yeast?*
A Fresh yeast is very satisfying and activates quickly. However it is not readily available. Perhaps a friendly local bakery will sell you some. Otherwise the packaged product is also reliable. Watch the dates on the packages of dry yeast and keep them in a cool place.

Q *I have always been afraid to work with yeast. Is there any special knack that makes the end result a good one?*
A As a matter of fact, yeast is simple to work with and very rewarding. The special knack comes with a little practice. All dough-handling (pastry, breads, etc.) entails a certain amount of personal approach to the dough in front of you. It is more a matter of getting to know the dough rather than some special talent.

Q *Can yeast doughs be frozen raw?*
A   No, but they can be lightly baked, cooled and then packaged for freezing. Always heat cakes in the oven to defrost them before serving. Yeast cakes are one of the best cakes to freeze. They can be thawed in the oven immediately from freezer and so they recapture some of their freshness. They should be eaten warm.

LESSON 15

The Cake and the Festive Dessert

Baking can be the most rewarding cooking experience for the man, woman or child who loves to cook. Fill the house with aromas of freshly baked vanilla cakes or yeast-rising doughs and you are surely inviting smiles and compliments from family and friends.

The following recipes offer you a fine sampling of various categories in baking. Each recipe has been successfully performed over a period of years and acclaimed by cooking students and professionals alike. The following cakes include both vanilla and chocolate, all in the butter cake family. When we refer to a cake as a butter cake we mean that the cake has butter as well as eggs, but you may want to substitute a shortening other than butter. This may be done in all cases. Each cake has its own characteristic texture. This feature of baking, a constant incentive to try new recipes, is always of great interest to baking enthusiasts.

Cake Baking

With the advent of modern equipment and abundance of fine recipes, baking can be overwhelmingly successful for the novice and expert alike. Listed below are suggestions that are easy to follow. Read them thoroughly. Successful baking will greatly depend on your basic knowledge and preparation.

1. Study your recipe carefully: Do you have all the ingredients? Do you have the pans called for? Do you have the uninterrupted time required for preparation?

2. Use the finest ingredients for best quality. Fresh eggs, milk, cream and butter cannot be replaced.

3. In working with a new recipe it is unwise to make substitutions. Give the recipe the benefit of your utmost confidence. Be exact with measurements.

4. For best results, all ingredients should be at room temperature.

5. Use wax paper instead of bowls. Sift dry ingredients on to wax paper. Measure fruits and nuts and set aside on wax paper. This saves a great deal of washing later on.

6. Set up all ingredients measured, ready for use. Grease pans lightly but always line *only* the bottom with wax paper. This insures an easily turned out cake. Set your oven.

7. Concerning the speed of your electric mixer: Lighter weight and moist ingredients can take a faster speed. Heavier ingredients must be started slowly. Both dry and wet ingredients, unless beaten slowly, will spatter out of the machine.

8. Know your oven. Check its temperature by placing a thermometer inside. If it is not accurate, call your serviceman. Be aware of whether your oven bakes hotter in front or back. Try to center your cakes or space them evenly before baking.

9. Never fill a pan more than ½ to ⅔ full.

10. Always test for doneness. Insert a cake tester (or toothpick) in center. On removal the tester should be dry. Butter cakes usually come away from the sides of the pan when finished.

11. All recipes specify the type of flour to use. Caution! Watch for all-purpose flour, cake flour and self-rising cake flour. All-purpose flour can be used for all cakes, pastries, bread and rolls unless recipe otherwise specifies. Buy the unbleached variety which gives a natural and more nutritious product. Cake flour is a refined combination of flour and starch mainly used for delicate cakes. Self-rising cake flour is cake flour with the addition of baking powder and salt.

*One of the funniest experiences of my teaching career was at a pre-
miere of the men's class. Picture three volunteers, fresh and strange at
the mixing bowl, reading the "One Bowl Cake" recipe and puzzling
over the simplest terms. It worked into a satisfying lesson for all:
students loved the cakes, teacher enjoyed the noble amateur perform-
ance plus the fact that each man baked his cake with a different fruit
topping.*

One Bowl Cake for Every Occasion

BATTER

¼ cup butter (½ stick)	¾ teaspoon baking powder
½ cup sugar	⅛ teaspoon salt
1 egg	1 tablespoon milk
1 cup cake flour	2 teaspoons vanilla

Fruits: Either sliced fresh peaches, apricots, sliced apples, Italian
plums or dark bing cherries. (Use just enough fruit to make one
layer.)

TOPPING

¼ cup butter (½ stick)	3 tablespoons bread crumbs
3 tablespoons sugar	1 teaspoon cinnamon
3 tablespoons flour	nutmeg to taste

1. Grease one 8″ or 9″ square, a 9″ pie plate, or an 8″ layer pan.
2. Prepare topping first by blending all ingredients with a fork
until mixture falls in large lumps.
3. Prepare any one of the above fruits to be used.
4. Set oven to 375° F.
5. Prepare batter. Cream butter and sugar. Add egg and beat.
6. Sift in dry ingredients gradually, blending well. Add milk and
flavoring.
7. Spread batter into pan and place sliced fruit over top in one
layer. When using a round layer pan or pie plate, arrange fruit in cir-
cular fashion. Sprinkle topping over fruit.
8. Bake at 375° F. for 35 minutes. Cool in pan before tranferring
to cake plate. Serves 8.

Cake failures and their causes

Rises higher on one side
- Batter spread unevenly in pan.
- Racks or range not level.
- Warped pans.
- Pans placed too close to sides of oven, or to other pans on rack.

Cake burns on side and bottom
- Oven too full.
- Oven too hot.
- Pans too close to bottom of oven.
- Glass and black pans bake hotter.
- Pans too close.

Humps or cracks on top
- Oven too hot.
- Too much flour or wrong kind.

Falls and is soggy
- Insufficient baking.
- Too much shortening.
- Too much leavening
- Too much sugar.
- Too slow baking.

Tough
- Temperature too high.
- Too little sugar.
- Too little shortening.
- Overbeaten.

Soggy layer on bottom
- Insufficient mixing.
- Damp flour used.
- Insufficient baking.
- Insufficient leavening

Coarse-Grained
- Too much leavening
- Insufficient mixing.
- Temperature too low.

Cake runs over pan
- Too much batter in pan, fill only ⅔.
- Too much leavening
- Too slow baking.
- Too much sugar.
- Too much shortening.

Sticks to sides and bottom of pan
- Pan not properly prepared.
- Left too long in pan.
- Insufficient baking.
- Too much sugar.

The simple butter cake is not only simple to do, but superior in flavor. It becomes an exciting taste combination when coated with the sour cream icing. Students love the soft texture of this cake with its smooth unusual icing.

Simple Butter Cake

3 egg whites	1 cup sugar
¼ cup sugar	¾ cup milk
¼ pound butter, room temperature	1 teaspoon vanilla
2 cups self-rising flour	3 egg yolks

Grease 13″ x 9″ x 2″ pan and line bottom only with wax paper. Preheat oven to 350° F. Beat egg whites until frothy. Gradually add ¼ cup sugar and beat until stiff. Set aside. Place butter into a large mixing bowl. Sift flour and 1 cup sugar on to the softened butter. Pour in milk and vanilla. Blend mixture together and beat 1 minute. Add egg yolks one at a time and beat for 2 minutes. Fold in beaten egg whites. Pour batter into pan and bake at 350° F. for 40 minutes. Cool; remove to rack. Good with Vermont Sour Cream Icing (see index).

You can be old fashioned and beat the pound cake by hand, but when you finish, you will most likely be too exhausted to eat it. Both the pound cake and the torte take about 20 minutes of beating time in the electric mixer. They travel well, stay fresh for a week and are good to the very last crumb. Even toasted stale cake tastes good. Be sure to serve this type cake thinly sliced since the texture is tightly knit.

Old-Fashioned Pound Cake

2 cups sifted all-purpose flour	1¾ cups sugar
½ teaspoon nutmeg	5 eggs
½ pound butter	1 teaspoon vanilla

Preheat oven to 325° F. Grease a 9 x 5 x 3″ pan. Line the bottom and sides with brown paper. Sift flour with nutmeg. Cream butter and sugar thoroughly for approximately 8 minutes. Add eggs one at a time, beating well after each addition. Add flour gradually to creamed mixture. Blend well. Add vanilla and pour into prepared paper lined pan. Bake at 325° F. for 1½ hours. Cool in pan. Serves 16 to 18.

Various kinds of pans used in recipes

Layer Pan

Square Pan

Tartlette Pan

Pie Pan

Tube Pan

Cooky Pan (has no sides)

Removable bottom with tube

Turk's Head

Jelly Roll Pan (notice: narrow side edges)

Oblong Pan

Spring Form Pan

this spring tightens sides around removable bottom

9"

2"

13"

~~~~~~~~

Grand Marnier Torte ★ ★ ★

½ pound sweet butter
1¼ cups sugar
4 eggs
1 cup cornstarch, sifted
1 cup flour

1 teaspoon baking powder
2 teaspoons vanilla
2 tablespoons Grand Marnier
grated rind of an orange

Grease a 1½-quart Turk's Head mold and set oven at 375° F. Cream butter with sugar for about 10 minutes until light in color. Beat in first egg. Add ¼ cup cornstarch and blend well. Beat in second egg. Add ¼ cup flour and blend well. Beat in third egg. Add ¼ cup cornstarch and blend well. Beat in fourth egg. Add ¼ cup flour mixed with baking powder. Blend well. Add flavorings and rind. Bake in a greased cake mold at 375° F. for 40 to 50 minutes. When cool, remove from pan to rack and dust with powdered sugar.

Note: Our children love the torte when it has a coating or dribble of chocolate on it. Use your favorite chocolate icing or melt 4 ounces semi-sweet chocolate with 2 tablespoons strong coffee (1 tablespoon coffee mixed with 2 tablespoons water). Stir until the chocolate is smooth.

The addition of a little cream or milk helps the consistency (see index for Chocolate Coating).

~~~~~~~~

Sour cream turns out to be a wonderful ingredient whether added to cakes, cookies, sauces, meats and so on to dozens of different foods. In the next cake it adds flavoring, an additional richness, and moistness. Because sour cream embodies these three characteristics, it produces a moist and soft textured cake.

Sour Cream Cake

2 cups all-purpose flour
1 teaspoon baking powder
1 teaspoon baking soda
¼ teaspoon salt
¼ pound butter
1 cup sugar
2 eggs

1 cup sour cream
1 teaspoon vanilla
2 tablespoons sugar mixed with
  1 teaspoon cinnamon
  ¼ cup chopped walnuts
  4 ounces coarsely cut semi-sweet
    chocolate

1. Preheat oven to 350° F.
2. Grease a 1½-quart Turk's Head mold or tube pan.
3. Sift flour, baking powder, soda and salt.
4. Cream butter. Add sugar gradually and beat until mixture is blended (2 to 3 minutes).
5. Add eggs one at a time.
6. Beat in dry ingredients and sour cream alternately, beginning and ending with flour.
7. Add vanilla.
8. Sprinkle about one third of chocolate and nut mixture over greased pan. Pour in half the batter. Sprinkle more chocolate and nut mixture over batter, reserving some for the top. Pour remaining batter into pan. Smooth it out evenly and top with remainder of chocolate and nut mixture.
9. Bake at 350° F. for 45 minutes. Cool. Remove from pan to rack. Serves 12.

De Luxe Chocolate Nut Cake

3 cups flour
4 teaspoons baking powder
1 teaspoon salt
6 eggs, separated
2 cups sugar
¾ cup butter

1½ cups strong coffee
   (3 tablespoons instant and water)
½ pound ground hazelnuts
6 ounces coarsely cut semi-sweet
   chocolate
3 teaspoons vanilla

1. Preheat oven to 400° F. and grease a 10″ x 5″ spring form.
2. Sift together flour, baking powder and salt; set aside.
3. Beat egg whites until frothy, adding ½ cup sugar, 2 tablespoons at a time, until mixture holds up stiff; set aside.
4. Cream butter and add remaining 1½ cups sugar gradually. Add egg yolks one at a time and beat well.
5. Add sifted dry ingredients and coffee alternately, starting and ending with flour. Beat in nuts, chocolate and vanilla just until blended; and last, fold in whites by hand.
6. Place batter in pan, smooth out with spatula and bake at 400° F. for 10 minutes. Lower oven to 350° F. and bake for 1 hour.
7. Allow cake to cool for 30 minutes then remove to a rack. Serves 14 to 18. This is wonderful for hungry late evening snackers. Also very good after a light lunch or supper.

～～～～～

Statistics are hardly necessary here. We know for a fact that chocolate is an all-time favorite. Recipes for chocolate cake are overwhelming in number so I have made the choice for you. These two chocolate butter cakes are constantly praised and enjoyed by my students and friends.

Chocolate Cake No. 1 ★ ★ ★

3 ounces unsweetened chocolate
2¼ cups sifted cake flour
2 teaspoons baking soda
½ teaspoon salt
¼ pound butter
1 pound brown sugar

3 eggs
½ cup buttermilk
  (sour milk or sour cream)
1 cup boiling water
2 teaspoons vanilla

Preheat oven to 350° F. Grease a 13″ x 9″ x 2″ pan and line bottom with waxed paper. Melt chocolate in a bowl over warm water (in double-boiler). Sift flour, baking soda and salt; set aside. Cream butter, and, adding sugar gradually at first, cream well together. Add eggs one at a time and beat hard after each addition. Add melted chocolate. Beat in flour and buttermilk alternately, starting and ending with flour. Add boiling water and vanilla. This final mixture will be very thin. Pour into pan. Bake at 350° F. for 45 to 50 minutes. Cool before removing from pan. Yield: 24 squares.

TO SERVE:

1. Cut a stiff cardboard to fit the size of the cake.

2. Remove cake to the cardboard. Cut cake into 24 squares, using a wet knife. Do not separate pieces.

3. Cover cake completely with Chocolate Fudge Frosting (recipe on page 245). The frosting will camouflage the cuts in the cake.

4. Coat sides with chopped nuts or slivered almonds. Using a wax paper decorating bag, decorate the top of the cake with leftover frosting.

The presentation of this cake is a genuine surprise because guests never suspect it is already cut. This is excellent for a large party or organizational meeting. No last minute slicing to be done.

Chocolate Cake No. 2

3 ounces unsweetened chocolate	5 eggs
2½ cups sifted cake flour	1 cup sour milk
1 teaspoon baking soda	combined with
½ teaspoon salt	1 tablespoon hot water
½ pound butter	2 teaspoons vanilla
2 cups sugar	

Grease three 8″ layer pans lightly and line bottoms with waxed paper. Melt chocolate in a bowl over a pan of warm water. Cool slightly. Sift flour, baking soda and salt. Set aside. Preheat oven to 375° F. Cream butter, adding sugar gradually. Beat for 3 to 4 minutes. Adding eggs one at a time, beat each one thoroughly. Blend in melted chocolate. Add dry ingredients alternately with sour milk and vanilla mixture, beginning and ending with flour. Beat well. Divide batter into 3 layer pans. Bake at 375° F. for 25 minutes. Cool layers in pans. Serves 12.

FINAL PREPARATION:

Prepare *Orange* or *Mocha Whipped Cream*. Cut a cardboard to fit the size of the layer. If layers are very uneven, do not hesitate to shave off bumps with a sharp knife. Reserve the best layer for the top. Melt 2 ounces of semi-sweet chocolate with 1 tablespoon strong coffee and allow to cool slightly. Set one layer on cardboard. Spread whipped cream about ¼″ thick. Place second layer on top and spread whipped cream over it also. Place on third layer. Spread cream smoothly over top and sides. Reserve some whipped cream for decoration. Dribble cooled melted chocolate over top, allowing it to run down the sides. With a decorating bag, #2 or #4 star tube, pipe out rosettes of cream on the border.

Teacher says:

The following group of recipes are for the cakes leavened with eggs. Except for the Gênoise they do not contain butter. They are all light and delicate so that they combine well with creams and fruits. Learn these cakes well for they provide you with the base for all sorts of festive layer cakes, petit fours and ice cream cakes.

Since we depend almost entirely upon our eggs for leavening in these cakes it is most important that eggs be room temperature or slightly warmer.

Eggs beat to a greater volume when warm.

It is easier to separate the eggs when they are cold; whites are heavy when cold and come away from egg yolks easily. Place the bowls of whites and yolks either near a warm oven or even over a saucepan of warm water, but watch that they do not cook!

Basic Sponge Cake

6 egg whites (room temperature) in large bowl
⅛ teaspoon salt
½ teaspoon cream of tartar
1¼ cups sugar

6 egg yolks, room temperature
2 tablespoons orange juice
2 tablespoons lemon juice
finely grated rind of one orange
1¼ cups sifted cake flour

1. Prepare an ungreased 9″ or 10″ spring form with tube. Preheat oven at 325° F.

2. Beat egg whites with salt and cream of tartar until frothy. Add sugar gradually (3 minutes) and beat until very thick. This may take up to 5 minutes.

3. Stir yolks with a fork. Add juices and rind. Pour yolks on to beaten egg whites and blend in.

4. Gradually add flour, folding it in gently by hand.

5. Bake in an ungreased pan at 325° F. for 1 hour. Invert and cool.

This six-egg sponge may be baked in a 10″ deep layer pan or a 13″ by 9″ by 2″ oblong. For a variation, try adding ½ cup sour cream after flour is blended in. It lends a pleasant change of flavor and more moistness to the cake. Many thanks to my friend Elaine Ross for this hint.

The basic sponge roll is your practicing ground for the most delicate and delicious of all cakes, the Génoise. Perfect the sponge roll and the Génoise appears to be the most natural step ahead in baking. The preparation and beating method is the same for both; clarified butter is added to the Génoise not to the sponge roll.

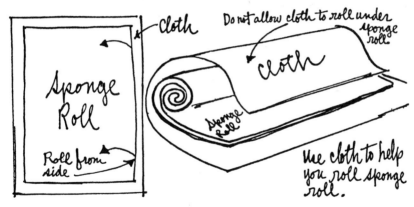

Basic Sponge Roll

6 eggs, room temperature
1 cup sugar

1¼ cups sifted cake flour
1 teaspoon vanilla

1. Preheat oven to 350° F. Grease and line bottom of pan with waxed paper. Grease again. Spread out a dish towel. Sprinkle it all over with confectioners' sugar.

2. Place whole eggs and sugar into large mixing bowl (of your electric mixer). Be sure eggs are room temperature (keep them in a warm place for a short while). Beat eggs and sugar for 12 to 15 minutes or until tripled in bulk.

3. Add flour gradually by sifting flour over batter. Fold in gently by hand. Add vanilla. Spread evenly onto lined jelly roll pan. Bake for 18 minutes.

4. Turn out onto prepared dish towel. Roll sponge cake immediately by holding towel at either end for leverage. Cover with towel lightly and cool on a rack. Serves 12.

When sponge is cool, unroll. It may be sprinkled with orange juice, cognac or Kirsch, if desired. Spread with prepared filling: Orange or Mocha Whipped Cream; raspberry or apricot jam; fresh strawberries or blueberries blended with Red Glaze; Custard. Slice off each end diagonally to show a neat roll. Serve on a wooden board or tray.

CLARIFIED BUTTER

To prepare clarified butter for the Gênoise, melt ¼ pound (1 stick) of butter over low heat. Allow butter to simmer gently until white sediment disappears. Small specks of brown may show at bottom of the pan. Butter should turn clear yellow. Do not allow it to brown. Cool the clarified butter while you organize your ingredients.

Gênoise

6 eggs at room temperature　　　6 tablespoons clarified butter
1 cup sugar　　　　　　　　　　　(page 227)
1¼ cups sifted cake flour　　　　　1 teaspoon vanilla

1. Prepare clarified butter. Cool.
2. Grease lightly and line the bottom of pan with waxed paper.
3. Place eggs and sugar in large bowl of electric mixer. If eggs are cold allow bowl to set in a warm place or over a saucepan of warm water. Stir eggs and sugar together with a spoon. Beat eggs and sugar for 12 to 15 minutes or until mixture reaches almost to the top of the bowl. The batter should be ivory in color and thick in texture.
4. Sift flour over the top of batter, a little at a time. Fold in by hand gently. Before adding the last ¼ cup of flour start folding in clarified butter, 2 tablespoons at a time. Finish the flour, alternately with butter. Last, add vanilla.
5. Spread batter evenly in pans and smooth top.
6. Bake at 350° F. Allow 25 minutes if baked in two layers; 35 to 40 minutes for 1 large cake. Cool slightly. Remove from pan and set on rack. Serves 10 to 12.

This cake may be baked in: two 9″ x 1½″ layers, one 10″ x 3″ round, one 17″ x 11″ x 1″, one 13″ x 9″ x 2″.

THE FESTIVE DESSERT

The lovely creations that line the shelves of a pastry shop are now within your reach. With basic recipes for the butter cakes and delicate egg cakes, with a small knowledge of decorating procedure and directions for creams and frostings, you are prepared to compose a variety of party cakes and desserts.

Here are some important facts:
1. Butter creams and frostings refrigerate and freeze well.
2. Chocolate-covered decorations keep well in the refrigerator or in a cool pantry.
3. All custards and toppings can be prepared well in advance.
4. Cakes may be baked weeks in advance, wrapped well and frozen.
5. Be sure to defrost butter creams at least 6 hours ahead of time. Even out of the refrigerator, butter creams need time to soften.

6. Only egg cakes make good bases for ice cream cakes. Cakes of this type defrost immediately and are edible out of the freezer. Butter cakes are too firm when they are frozen and should never be used for ice cream cakes.

7. Organized preparation is an absolute necessity for fancy layer cakes. The final task of composing and decorating is a job to be enjoyed.

Chocolate Layer Cake

1 recipe Simple Butter Cake
  (see index)
1 recipe Chocolate Fudge Frosting
  (see index)

4 ounces raspberry jam
4 ounces slivered toasted almonds

Bake Butter Cake in two 8″ layer pans. Cool and remove to rack. Make Chocolate Frosting. Set aside ½ cup in refrigerator.

TO DECORATE LAYERS

1. Place one layer, crust side down, on a clean round of cardboard to fit cake. If you own a turntable rest your cake on it.

2. Spread raspberry jam over layer and place second layer, crust side up on top of this.

3. With a steel spatula spread frosting evenly over top and sides of cake. Allow frosting to set for 10 minutes.

4. Make a waxed paper decorating bag. Remove chocolate frosting from refrigerator and fill waxed paper bag half full. Fold down securely and cut ⅛″ off tip.

5. Spread out a long sheet of waxed paper. Hold cake under cardboard with left hand and with the palm of your other hand place nuts all around sides of cake. Place cake on a serving tray.

6. Now use wax paper decorating bag to make diagonal lines going first in one direction, and then criss-crossed the other way. If you allow chocolate to press out freely the chocolate will fall into curved ribbons.

7. If you are using this cake for a birthday, decorate only around the edge and write your greeting in contrasting color. Serves 10 to 12.

Holiday Cake

1 recipe Gênoise Cake (see index)   1 recipe Heavenly Chocolate Cream
1 recipe Orange Cream (see index)   (see index)
                                       shavings of chocolate (3 ounces)

1. Bake the Gênoise in 2 layer pans measuring 9" x 2".

2. Prepare Orange Cream and Heavenly Chocolate Cream frosting.

3. Set each cooled layer of cake on a rack. Spread a thick coating of cream over each layer. Reserve at least ⅓ of cream for sides of cake. Refrigerate for at least 2 hours for cream to set.

4. When cream is firm, spread Chocolate Cream over one layer. Make this one your top layer.

5. If possible place cake on a cardboard cut to fit cake. This makes handling very easy. Coat some of the remaining Orange Cream thinly around sides, saving remainder of cream for the finishing touch.

6. With palm of your hand place chocolate shavings around sides of cake. Pipe out a border of cream around the top of the cake.

Betty's Dream Cake ★ ★ ★

1 recipe Gênoise cake   ½ recipe Chocolate Coating
1 recipe easy Chocolate Butter   (see index)
   Cream (see index)   1½ cups cream, whipped stiff

1. Bake Gênoise in three 8" layer pans. Cool thoroughly.

2. Cut a cardboard to fit size of cake. Place one layer on cardboard.

3. Spread about ⅓ of chocolate butter cream over the layer spread about ⅓ of whipped cream over second layer. Spread the chocolate coating on the third layer. Set your layers one on the other in that order. With a metal spatula smooth some of the remaining butter cream around the sides of the cake.

4. Using a decorating bag with a #5 tube, fill it with the remainder of butter cream and whipped cream, placing butter cream on one side and whipped cream on the other. In this way both creams will press out simultaneously.

5. Pipe rosettes of combined creams around the edge of cake. Place crystallized violets and mint in two rosettes on the cake. Serves 10 to 12.

Teacher says:

For larger parties and special occasions, bake the basic sponge in a 12″ by 3″ round baking pan. The large surface provides space for "greetings" and the quantity amply serves 24 portions. Of course, the basic sponge cake recipe should be increased to 9 eggs and so all other ingredients proportionately increased. Many students have been successful with the traditional strawberry and whipped cream fillings.

~~~~~~~

Seven-Layer Cake

1 recipe Basic Sponge Roll

Preheat oven to 350° F. Grease a jelly roll pan (17″ x 11″). Spread batter evenly on pan and bake for 18 minutes. Do not turn out. Allow cake to cool in pan. Divide the length of the pan in 4 and cut into 4 layers (about 4¾″ x 11″). Remove each layer to a board and split each one in half to make eight layers (one extra layer for the children for a bonus dessert).

Note: This is the easiest way to bake the seven layers. If you must have them all crisp (like the classic Dobos Torte), bake the sponge in two well-greased 16″ pans. Loosen them from the bottom of your pan immediately upon removal from oven. They harden rapidly because they are thin. You may need that extra layer!

MOCHA BUTTER CREAM

6 ounces semi-sweet chocolate	6 egg yolks
3 tablespoons strong coffee	¾ pound sweet butter, softened
1 cup sugar	2 tablespoons rum (optional)
¾ cup water	

Melt chocolate with coffee over warm water and set aside. Combine sugar and water in a saucepan. Cook over low heat stirring constantly only until sugar is dissolved. Stop stirring, cook syrup hard until syrup spins a light thread (238° F. on a candy thermometer). While syrup is cooking beat egg yolks until light in color. When syrup is ready, pour it slowly in a thin stream on to yolks, beating constantly. Continue beating for about 12 minutes. As mixture cools, it becomes thicker. Cream softened butter and add to egg mixture a little at a time. Beat for ½ minute. Add cooled melted chocolate and rum. Beat until blended (1 minute).

TO DECORATE SEVEN-LAYER CAKE:

Spread Mocha Butter Cream on six layers; set one on top of the other and refrigerate. Boil ½ cup sugar, 2 tablespoons water, ⅛ teaspoon cream of tartar. Stir only until sugar melts. Continue boiling without stirring. Place seventh layer on an oiled board. When syrup becomes amber quickly spread a thin coating over seventh layer. Cool. Place top layer on cake, coat sides with butter cream and decorate top with rosettes of butter cream piped from a decorating bag (#1 or #2 tube). Refrigerate for several hours or overnight. This magnificent cake freezes well too. Serves 14 to 16.

Special cakes deserve special acclaim. The chocolate roll has had rave notices from students who carry back tales of huge success. It is no wonder that only one constant complaint has been registered with me. How can one keep a lovely lean figure while baking such tempting cakes?

This chocolate roll is not as tricky to do as many of the other rolls. It is a one bowl cake, quickly made and, need I say, quickly eaten. When it is not rolled it may be used as a basic chocolate sponge sheet for petit fours, layers and ice cream cakes.

Chocolate Cream Roll

6 eggs, separated
½ teaspoon cream of tartar
1 cup sugar
½ cup sifted unsweetened cocoa
½ cup sifted self-rising cake flour
1 teaspoon vanilla

1. Grease and line with waxed paper and grease again a 17″ x 11″ jelly roll pan. Preheat oven to 350° F.

2. In a large mixing bowl, beat whites with cream of tartar until stiff. Gradually add sugar, beating until consistency is very thick (5 minutes).

3. Lower speed of machine. Add egg yolks, cocoa and vanilla beating only until blended (½ minute). Fold in flour, by hand, 2 tablespoons at a time. Spread on to pan and even batter out to all corners.

4. Bake at 350° for 18 minutes. While the cake is baking, prepare a clean dish towel. Dust it well with unsweetened cocoa. When cake is finished invert it on to towel, remove waxed paper immediately and roll up at once. Hold towel at either end and use it to push cake into a roll. Keep towel over cake and cool on a rack.

5. When cake is cool, whip 1 pint of heavy cream. If preferred, use 2 tablespoons of fine sugar or 4 tablespoons of confectioners' sugar to sweeten cream plus 1 teaspoon of vanilla. Gently unroll cake, spread all over with whipped cream and roll up again. Place cake on a long wooden or china tray. Cut ends off diagonally for a clean look. The children will be waiting anxiously for quick handouts! Yield: 12 to 14 portions.

Teacher says:

Try a dash of rum or cognac sprinkled on to cake before spreading it with whipped cream.

Bake the chocolate batter in 3 8″ layer pans. Cool and fill layers with whipped cream. Decorate with shaved chocolate and pistachio nuts.

The chocolate cream roll freezes very well. It may either be defrosted 2 hours before serving or it may be eaten with frozen cream.

Occasionally substitute mocha whipped cream for vanilla flavored cream.

This cake may be cut in half and rolled horizontally. Now you have two smaller rolls for 2 dinners. Coat the entire surface with a chocolate coating (see index) and decorate with crystallized violets and mint leaves. These rolls freeze very well. Wrap them after they are frozen solid.

Chocolate Ice Cream Cake

1 recipe Chocolate Cream Roll   1 pint heavy cream whipped
1 half gallon (brick form) ice cream   Chocolate Coating (see index)

Bake chocolate roll on 17″ x 11″ jelly roll pan, greased *without* waxed paper. Cool cake in pan, divide it evenly into three layers lengthwise and loosen it from pan. Cut a cardboard to fit one layer. Open ice cream and cut five 1 inch slices of ice cream. Place 1 layer of cake on cardboard; fit 2½ slices of ice cream on to cake. Place second layer on to ice cream; fit another 2½ slices of ice cream on to cake. Top this with third layer of cake. If you are working slowly and ice cream is melting, place cake back into freezer at this point. Decorate the cake when ice cream is thoroughly frozen. Spread top of cake with chocolate coating. Use whipped cream around the sides. Be sure to pipe rosettes of whipped cream all around top edge and bottom of cake. Yield: 20 servings.

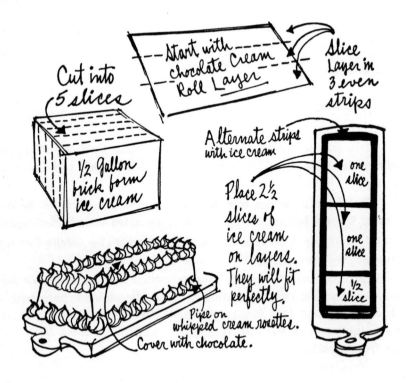

Teacher says:

I prefer to do the ice cream cake instead of the ice cream roll. For the roll, ice cream must be slightly softened and so loses its original texture. For ice cream cakes, this need not happen. Ice cream can be cut when it is frozen. Be sure to be completely prepared and organized. The ice cream cake may be divided into 3 parts and stored for family use or smaller dinner parties.

If you wish to prepare this well in advance with decorations, freeze the cake uncovered until very firm. Wrap well. When ready to use unwrap the cake when it is still frozen hard.

The basic sponge roll may be used for ice cream cake too.

Angel Delight

1 10″-Basic Sponge Cake (baked in tube pan)	¼ cup rum (or Kirsch if you prefer)
#2 can crushed pineapple	1 envelope unflavored gelatin
4 ounces marshmallow miniatures	¼ cup cold water
8 ounces maraschino cherries (cut in halves)	1½ pints heavy cream, whipped stiff
	½ cup slivered toasted almonds
	18 almond **halves**

Combine pineapple, marshmallows, cherries (reserve 4 or 5 halves) including juices and rum. Soak these for at least 2 hours. Soften gelatin in ¼ cup cold water and place cup in a saucepan of hot water until liquefied. Slice ¼″ layer off the top of cake and set aside. Scoop out inside of cake leaving a firm crust all around. (Keep the soft sponge for another dessert.) When gelatin is liquefied, cool it slightly. Mix fruit, gelatin, 4 cups of whipped cream (2 cups for later decoration) and ½ cup slivered almonds (halves of almonds reserved for top of cake); fill cavity of the sponge crust with this fruit mixture. Fit ¼″ top layer on. Pile more fruit mixture into the center space. Cake may be refrigerated this way overnight and decorated an hour or two before serving. Spread whipped cream over top and sides. Pipe rosettes of cream around the edge. In three or four spots on top of the cake, place a cherry for the center of a flower and arrange almond halves around it for petals.

~~~~~~

A good many years ago a student requested me to work over some inherited European recipes and translate them correctly for our comprehension of weights, measures and timings. Lucy's Apple Tart turned out to be one of our finest fruit desserts.

Lucy's Apple Tart ★ ★ ★

3 cups crushed zwieback (2 boxes)	3 tablespoons butter
4 tablespoons butter	3 tablespoons sugar
2 tablespoons sugar	6 whole eggs
1 teaspoon cinnamon	1 cup sugar
7 large apples, peeled and quartered	1 pint sour cream

Blend zwieback, butter, sugar and cinnamon. Prepare a buttered 9" x 3" spring form by lining bottom and sides with 2 cups of this mixture. Reserve the remainder. Set oven at 375° F. Place apples in a saucepan with 3 tablespoons butter and 3 tablespoons sugar. Simmer until they are tender. Beat eggs, sugar and sour cream. Add mixture to apples and simmer for 2 minutes. Watch carefully. Do not let sour cream curdle. Pour apple mixture into spring form. Top with remainder of zwieback crumbs. Bake at 375° F. for 45 minutes. Serve at room temperature. Serves 12.

~~~~~~

Coffee Soufflé Froid

1 envelope unflavored gelatin	1 cup strong coffee (2 tablespoons
¼ cup cold water	instant, 1 cup water)
1 egg	1 cup heavy cream, whipped stiff
3 egg yolks	coarsely grated chocolate
½ cup sugar	

1. Cut a piece of waxed paper 2 feet long. Fold it in half lengthwise to make a collar around a 1-quart soufflé dish; tie it with a string.

2. Soften gelatin in ¼ cup of cold water. Set cup in a pan of water and heat until gelatin liquefies.

3. Beat eggs; gradually add sugar. Beat until thick and lemon colored. Add cooled coffee and gelatin. Place in refrigerator until it thickens and starts to jell. Fold in whipped cream and pour into pre-

pared soufflé dish. Fill the dish over the top so that soufflé extends up along the waxed paper collar. Refrigerate at least 6 hours or overnight.

4. Decorate with coarsely grated chocolate. Pass more whipped cream around if you dare! Serves 6.

Peach Chanteclair

1 cup water	3 large fresh peaches, skinned,
⅓ cup sugar	halved and pitted
1 tablespoon lemon juice	6 tablespoons currant jelly
	2 tablespoons Kirsch

TOPPING

1 cup heavy cream	¼ cup confectioners sugar
¼ cup confectioners sugar	1 tablespoon Kirsch
1 egg white	

1. Bring water, sugar and lemon juice to a boil in a large skillet. Cook and stir until sugar clears. Place peaches into syrup when water is simmering. Simmer for about 10 minutes or until peaches are just tender. Cool and refrigerate.

2. Prepare 6 glass dessert dishes or one large crystal bowl.

3. Melt jelly and Kirsch over a low flame. Place 1 teaspoon of melted jelly in each dish or a thin layer at the bottom of the large bowl. Reserve the remainder of jelly in the saucepan to keep it melted.

4. Beat cream, adding ¼ cup sugar gradually. Beat stiff.

5. Beat egg white till frothy. Add ¼ cup sugar gradually until a meringue is formed. Combine cream and meringue.

6. Place a peach half, cut side down in each dish, over the jelly. Top with mixture of cream and meringue. If you are using one large bowl, arrange peach halves at the bottom and cover with topping as described.

7. To serve, add the 1 tablespoon of Kirsch to remainder of jelly. Warm slightly, ignite and pour hot syrup over the cream topping. Serve immediately. Serves 6.

Teacher says:

To skin fresh peaches, drop them into boiling water for 1 minute. If they are ripe freestone peaches, the fuzzy skin will peel off easily.

A good quality, canned freestone peach may be used for this dessert.

~~~~~~~~~

Orange Alaska

6 naval oranges
1½ pints vanilla ice cream

6 tablespoons Cointreau
(or other orange liqueur)

Cut one inch slice off top of orange. Scoop out pulp in one piece if possible. If orange does not stand straight cut a straight thin slice off bottom. Sprinkle inside of each orange with 1½ teaspoons Cointreau. Fill with vanilla ice cream. Sprinkle top of ice cream with 1½ teaspoons Cointreau. Cover and set in the freezer.

TO SERVE

2 egg whites
pinch of salt

¼ teaspoon cream of tartar
(or 1 teaspoon lemon juice)
½ cup confectioners sugar

Remove oranges from freezer and place them on a cookie sheet. Beat egg whites with salt till frothy and add cream of tartar. Add sugar gradually until the consistency is that of thick marshmallow. Cover top of orange with this meringue. Use a decorating bag or make a tall mound. Bake at 450° F. for 2 to 3 minutes. Serve with garnish of orange slices and fresh mint leaves. Serves 6.

~~~~~~~~~

If you own a punch bowl shaped like a brandy glass, fill it with ice cream for your next large party. The various ice cream flavors are most attractive when viewed through crystal.

Brandy Bowl of Ice Cream

1 cup heavy cream
2 egg whites
pinch of salt
¼ cup sugar

1 teaspoon vanilla
#2 can pitted bing cherries
½ cup cognac (you may substitute rum, kirsch, brandy)

Whip cream till stiff. Beat egg whites with salt until frothy. Add sugar gradually until mixture stands in peaks. Combine both mixtures with vanilla and refrigerate. Drain cherries very well of their juice. Pour cognac on to cherries and allow them to soak.

TO SERVE

Prepare different flavors of ice cream. Scoop out balls and place in brandy glass, distributing brandied cherries among them. Cover the top of ice cream with the cream or serve cream on the side. Serves 10 to 12.

OTHER PARTY DESSERTS

Apple Pancakes
Brandied Alaska
Crepes Suzette
Frozen Cream Crepes
Fruit Blintzes
Genoise Zabaglione Sauce
Hawaiian Fruit Dessert
Lemon Ices with Loquats
Soufflé Desserts

See index for recipes.

CAKE QUESTIONS ANSWERED

Q *What is self-rising flour?*
A Self-rising flour is cake flour to which baking powder and salt have been added. The box will specify "self-rising flour."
Q *May I substitute regular flour?*
A This is possible but in baking it is best to follow recipes to the letter. If you are making a substitution use 1 teaspoon baking powder and ¼ teaspoon salt to each cup of flour.
Q *How long after a cake is baked do you remove it from the pan?*
A As a general rule all cakes made with butter should not be removed from the pan until they are cool. Do not invert butter cakes! Set the pan on a rack until cake is cool. Cake whose leavening is mainly eggs such as the Sponge should be inverted onto a rack or hung to permit air to circulate around it.
Q *How much work can be done in advance in preparing festive cakes?*
A The baking and icings may all be done well in advance. Follow specific instructions with the recipe. Butter cream cakes can be decorated a day in advance if refrigerated well covered (so as not to absorb odors from other foods). Whipped cream cakes are best if they are decorated as close to serving time as possible (within 6 hours).

LESSON 16

The Cream, the Icing and the Decoration

Decorating a cake is akin to choosing the proper frame for a painting. The decorations are there to enhance the appearance of, and to spotlight, the cake. For all of us who are not professional bakers, it is wise to depend on a few very good recipes and ideas for creams, frosting and decorations.

First, consider the tools that will be needed. Actually, a bare minimum of decorating equipment need be purchased for carrying out the directions in this book. Both food platters and decorative cakes take on that finished look when the decorating bag is used.

Decorating bags may be bought either in canvas or in the more expensive nylon cloth. Metal 2″ tubes slip easily into either one of these bags.

If you are purchasing only one bag, buy the 16″ or 18″. This will comfortably accommodate everything from butter creams to mashed potatoes. Canvas bags may be washed and dried in automatic machines. Wash the nylon by hand. Occasionally, bags have to be boiled to rid them of odors.

#0 plain tube has an opening of ⅛″ and is used mainly for filling cream puffs or eclairs.

#0 star tube has a tiny opening which makes small decorations for petite pastries and cakes.

Large plain tube from #5 to #9, is used for shaping cream puffs, éclairs, drop cookies and the larger Pâte à Chou pastries. I have found that with the proper pressure the #5 tube can make shapes as small as the tiniest cream puff and as large as the swirl for the Paris-Brest.

Large star tubes #5 to #9 are used for dropping meringues and cookies onto a cookie sheet, for decorating with whipped cream, and for forcing mashed potatoes.

To use the cloth decorating bag:

1. Drop the metal tube into the bag, fitting it into small end. The decorating tip will protrude.

2. Holding bag in the left hand, fold top half of bag over the left hand to make a cuff.

3. Fill bag only ¼ to ¾ full. If the amount of filling is less than ¼, fold bag over to make an even larger cuff. In this way no filling is wasted along the sides of the bag.

4. Twist the unfilled portion of bag tightly until filling starts to show at the tip of the metal tube.

5. Use only your right hand for the pressure needed. Left hand may hold the bag lightly to guide it.

6. As the filling is used up, retwist the bag to force mixture towards tip.

7. If this is a new experience for you, practice piping borders and rosettes on waxed paper. Use soft vegetable shortening for practice. Experiment with different amounts of pressure. Make sharp releases. You will notice that you can control the size and shape with each tube. Control comes from *pressure* of your right hand and then the release.

8. You will find decorating a cake much easier if you can work on a turntable. Any flat lazy Susan will do.

How to Make a Paper Cornucopia

One of the handiest of all decorating tools is the homemade paper cornucopia. Use this "throw away" decorating bag for all small jobs such as writing messages (Happy Birthday, etc.), outlining shaped cookies, dribbling chocolate decoratively and adding small touches of color. Use in same way as cloth or nylon bag, but fold the top down: do not twist it.

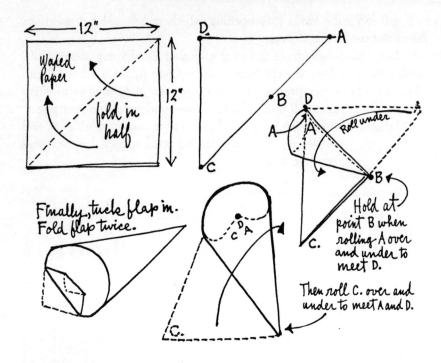

Make a decorating bag by cutting a 12″ square of waxed paper or parchment paper. If you are using waxed paper, fold it over to form a triangle. Waxed paper must be used doubled. For the heavier parchment paper, cut the square in half to make two triangles.

1. B is centered between A and C. This center will be the point of your decorating bag.

2. Holding the paper at B with your left hand, bring point A all the way over in a roll to meet point D.

3. Now hold partially made cornucopia at point A, D (now together) with the right hand. Roll point C all the way over to finally meet A, D.

4. A, C and D, should meet exactly. B should be a closed sharp point. Fold in A, C, D, to secure the cornucopia.

5. Fill the paper bag no more than ½ to ⅔ full.

6. Fold down the top to securely enclose the filling. Press filling towards the tip.

7. With a scissors, cut off tip to make an opening for the size of decoration to be used (generally ⅛″).

Simple Decorating Icing

½ cup confectioners' sugar
1½ teaspoons warm water

½ teaspoon vanilla
coloring if desired

Mix all together thoroughly. It must be thick or it will not hold its shape. Make a paper cornucopia. Fill it ⅓ full of icing. Fold top down securely. Cut tip. Test on a sheet of waxed paper to be sure that icing holds its shape. Use this icing essentially for writing messages, for outlining cookies or for a touch of color.

Many thanks again to my friend, Alice Thompson, tireless traveler on the road to the best in American cooking! Since sour creams differ in butter fat, boiling time for this icing may vary. Remember, all boiled icing becomes thicker when cooled and especially thick when beaten. The flavor of this one is unusual!

Vermont Sour Cream Icing

1 cup sour cream
1 cup sugar

1 teaspoon vanilla
½ cup chopped walnuts

Boil cream and sugar in heavy pot, stirring constantly until sugar dissolves. Boil mixture without stirring until it forms a soft ball when a sampling is dropped in cold water. A candy thermometer will register 238° F. Cool, add vanilla and beat to a spreading consistency. Blend in nuts and spread over cooled cake.

Easy Chocolate Butter Cream

8 ounces semi-sweet chocolate
¾ cup butter, softened
2 egg yolks

1 teaspoon vanilla
1 teaspoon instant coffee

Melt chocolate in a bowl over a saucepan of water. Cool. Cream butter till light in color and fluffy. Add cooled chocolate, egg yolks and flavorings. If too soft to spread, refrigerate for a while. Rum or brandy may be used for flavoring too (use 1 tablespoon). Yield: 1½ cups.

White Butter Cream

¼ cup water	2 egg whites
1 cup sugar	1 teaspoon vanilla
⅛ teaspoon cream of tartar	⅔ cup sweet butter, softened
pinch of salt	

Blend water, sugar, cream of tartar and salt in a saucepan. Place on low heat and stir until sugar melts. Stop stirring and allow mixture to boil until soft ball consistency (238° F. on candy thermometer). While syrup is boiling, beat egg whites until stiff. Pour hot syrup (soft ball stage) in a fine stream over beaten egg whites, beating constantly. Beat for 3 or 4 minutes until frosting is thick. Add vanilla and *cool*. Cream butter well and add cooled egg white mixture to butter a little at a time. Yield: 2¼ cups.

Note: This is a good butter cream, especially when a pure white cream is needed. It takes very well to colors but be sure to keep them pale. Without the butter the fluffy white meringue may be used as a frosting for chocolate cake or cup cakes.

Heavenly Chocolate Cream

4 ounces semi-sweet chocolate	¼ cup heavy cream
2 tablespoons strong coffee	

Melt chocolate with coffee. Beat sweet cream very stiff. When chocolate is melted, cool slightly. Blend whipped cream into chocolate. It is heavenly chocolate! Use as a topping or filling for cakes or desserts. Yield: 1¼ cups.

To make strong coffee allow 1 tablespoon instant coffee to 2 tablespoons water.

Praline Icing

1 cup brown sugar	1 tablespoon corn syrup
1 cup heavy sweet cream	1 teaspoon vanilla

Blend all ingredients in a saucepan. Stir sugar until it is melted. Stop stirring. Allow mixture to boil until it coats the spoon (238° F. on candy thermometer). This will form a soft ball when dropped into cold water. Cool. This is a delicious satin-textured coating for cream puffs, éclairs and is excellent on ice cream. Yield: 1¼ cups.

~~~~~~~

Mocha Whipped Cream

1 pint heavy sweet cream
3 tablespoons unsweetened cocoa
1 teaspoon instant coffee

5 tablespoons confectioners' sugar
1 teaspoon vanilla

If time permits blend all ingredients except vanilla in your mixing bowl. Cover and refrigerate for 4 to 6 hours. Beat mixture when ready to decorate cake. Add vanilla when cream is somewhat thick.

Note: If cream is prepared the last minute, add blended cocoa and sugar after cream is beaten slightly thick.

~~~~~~~

Orange Whipped Cream

1 pint heavy sweet cream
4 tablespoons confectioners' sugar

2 tablespoons orange juice
grated rind of one orange

Beat cream in electric mixer, watching it constantly. When mixture is somewhat thick, add sugar gradually. Occasionally use rubber spatula around edges of bowl so that cream is beaten evenly. Add flavoring. Beat cream very stiff.

~~~~~~~

Chocolate Fudge Frosting

4 ounces unsweetened chocolate
4 tablespoons butter
3 cups confectioners' sugar

½ cup warm milk
1 teaspoon vanilla
½ teaspoon almond extract

Melt chocolate and butter in a bowl (ready for the mixer) by placing it over a pan with 1 inch of simmering water. When chocolate and butter melt bring bowl to electric mixer. Add sugar and milk alternately. Watch for desired consistency. If you prefer a fudgy frosting use more sugar; a more moist frosting may need more milk. Beat well for smoothness. Yield: 2½ cups.

Note: An added egg yolk gives the frosting more shine and richness. An additional amount of softened butter will make it creamy. Flavorings of coffee, cognac or rum may also be used.

―――~~~~~―――

Chocolate Coating

4 ounces semi-sweet chocolate   ¼ cup heavy sweet cream
2 tablespoons strong coffee

Place all ingredients in a heavy saucepan over low heat. Allow chocolate to melt, stirring constantly. Cook slowly until chocolate is smooth and thick. Use the best chocolate you can buy and you will find this a most delicious coating over cream puffs and éclairs. Use it for cake toppings or as an ice cream sauce. Yield: ¾ cup.

―――~~~~~―――

One of the most attractive decorations for cakes are the chocolate shapes that you can easily make yourself.

Chocolate Wafers

Melt 4 ounces semi-sweet chocolate in a bowl over warm water. Keep heat low. When chocolate is almost melted remove it from flame. Stir it with small butter knife to remove all lumps of chocolate.

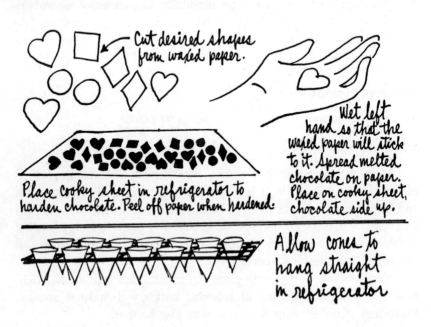

Cut desired shapes from waxed paper.

Wet left hand so that the waxed paper will stick to it. Spread melted chocolate on paper. Place on cooky sheet, chocolate side up.

Place cooky sheet in refrigerator to harden chocolate. Peel off paper when hardened.

Allow cones to hang straight in refrigerator

Cut desired shapes of waxed paper. You may want squares, rounds, hearts, diamonds, etc.

Keep a wet sponge handy. Moisten left hand so that waxed paper shape sticks to your hand as you hold it. With butter knife or spreader, spread melted chocolate to cover waxed paper shape completely. Place on a cookie sheet, chocolate side up. When they are all finished, refrigerate until chocolate becomes firm again.

When chocolate is firm they may be packaged and stored in a cool place for future use.

When ready to use, gently tear off waxed paper and you will have a thin chocolate wafer.

This may be placed on to frosting or cream around the side of a cake or as ornaments on top of a cake. The chocolate cone which follows this recipe may be used in the same way.

Chocolate Cones

Start with 6″ metal cone shapes or as many #2 to #9 metal tubes as you own.

Melt 4 ounces semi-sweet chocolate in a bowl over warm water. Heat on slow flame. Cut 6″ squares of waxed paper. Fold in half to make a triangle and proceed to make cornucopias as described at the beginning of this lesson. Drop each cornucopia into a metal tube. Make sure that the waxed paper point at the bottom is closed. Spread melted chocolate all around waxed paper to coat entire surface. Set tube on a metal rack so that it hangs straight. Refrigerate until chocolate is hard. Waxed paper will slip off easily if chocolate is very cold and firm. These may be filled with whipped cream or butter cream.

Teacher says:

Broken, slivered, crushed nuts provide fine coatings for the sides of cakes. Use pistachios for a different color. Change the variety of nuts for a different look and a different taste.

Among the simplest and prettiest decorations are crystallized violets, rose petals and mint leaves. They are attractive whole and equally attractive when crushed and sprinkled over surfaces.

I think my happiest moments in class are those seconds just after a decoration is completed. Even in this day of cake mixes there are still many of us sincerely interested in home baking. There is living proof of this fact because I encounter tremendous enthusiasm with every class. The students actually go home and bake!

CAKE DECORATING QUESTIONS ANSWERED

Q *What are the different chocolates used?*

A Unsweetened chocolate is bitter chocolate used solely for baking and cooking. Semi-sweet chocolate comes in bits or bars. Cocoa that is used in these recipes is unsweetened. The flavor of chocolate cake always depend greatly on the quality of chocolate and cocoa. There are subtle flavor differences in the chocolates themselves. Use the finest quality and the ones you like the best.

Q *What is the best method for melting chocolate?*

A Chocolate should be placed in a small bowl over water on low heat. It will melt rapidly. Take it off the flame and stir it before completely melted. Any lumps will disappear.

Do not heat chocolate directly on flame unless you have a heavy saucepan, a well controlled low heat and your eye on it constantly.

Chocolate may be melted in a 200° F. oven but watch it. Take it out before it is completely melted. You can stir out remaining lumps.

Q *Why does cream present problems in whipping?*

A Good whipped cream depends on several factors. First it depends on the quality of the cream itself. Cream whips best when it is *not* fresh. Use cream up to one week old. Cream must be very cold. It will have more body for whipping. In the warm weather months it may be necessary to refrigerate your mixing bowl and beaters before whipping. It is sometimes helpful if you put cream into the freezing compartment for 20 minutes. As a last resort, if the heat is blistering, you may have to beat cream by setting the bowl in another bowl of ice.

Most students are fearful of overbeating, but runny cream is not good-looking for decoration. Beat cream with a watchful eye and make it stiff.

Q *Sometimes melted chocolate loses its smoothness? Why? Can it be used?*

A Probably some moisture was added—even a wet spoon might do it. Salvage by adding 1 tablespoon Spry or similar shortening to 4 ounces chocolate.

LESSON 17
The Cookie and the Sweet

Cookies and pick-up squares are an absolute necessity for the busy household. The hostess who can prepare several varieties of delicious small goodies is never at a loss for dessert. A selection of any three of the recipes given in this lesson makes an attractive and mouth-watering sweet tray.

Cookies are not difficult to make if:

Ingredients are all room temperature (except for Danish Elephant Ears).

Preparation is organized and neat.

You can take the time to watch the baking (fast-baking cookies are also fast-burning).

You like to handle small things. Larger cakes and squares are less time-consuming.

You remember that almost all cookies can bake in a hot oven 375° F. to 425° F. Watch cookies with nuts or chocolate, they bake better at a more moderate temperature (350° F.) because nuts and chocolate cannot take high heat.

To store cookies: Undecorated cookies store best in tightly closed plastic boxes. Cookies taste better if they are not refrigerated; however, during hot weather months they may have to be.

249

To freeze cookies: All the cookies can be frozen but they have to be used immediately upon defrosting. They lose flavor very rapidly.

To keep the shine on the chocolate that is used for coating cookies, buy the best dark sweet chocolate and keep the cookies at about 65° F. to 70° F. Do not refrigerate them again after chocolate is set. Low temperatures dull chocolate.

～～～～～

The Meringue

3 egg whites, room temperature　　　½ cup sugar
¼ teaspoon cream of tartar　　　　　½ teaspoon vanilla

1. Grease a cookie sheet with vegetable shortening. Preheat oven to 225° F.

2. Place egg whites in a mixing bowl for electric beater. Add cream of tartar. Beat whites. When they become frothy start adding sugar very gradually. Whites should become very stiff and hold their shape. Beat in vanilla. This may take up to 7 minutes.

3. Using two teaspoons, drop onto a well-greased sheet. I like to use the decorating bag with #5 (to #7) star tube. Pipe out a rosette, or a cookie 2″ long (to look like a lady finger).

4. Bake at 225° F. for 40 minutes.

5. To test for doneness, remove one from the oven. Let it rest on a rack for 1 minute. If it does not fall, shows no beads of moisture and is dry enough for your taste (some like it chewy) remove the others from the oven. To dry them more thoroughly, turn off oven and allow meringues to remain in oven another hour. Remove meringues immediately when finished and cool on a rack. Yield: 3 dozen small meringues.

Teacher says:

Meringues are versatile. A mouth-watering confection, they are a fine accompaniment for ice cream or sherbet.

Use meringues as one cookie for a cookie assortment.

For an unusual presentation of meringue: Fill a decorating bag (using #3, #4 or #5 star tube), with sweetened whipped cream. Pipe a rosette of whipped cream on to the back of one meringue and place another meringue on top. A slice of strawberry may be inserted. The long meringues may be sandwiched this way too. These look elegant on a silver tray. They may also be placed next to or on top of ice cream.

Mound a quart of fresh strawberries. Sprinkle a few drops of Kirsch or cognac over them. Place these sandwiched meringues all around strawberries to form a border.

Would you like to make "meringue glacée?" Instead of making a cookie shape pipe out a circle of meringue (2" in diameter). Repeat another circle of meringue on top of first. Three layers should be sufficient to build up a shell. Bake at 225° F. for 1 hour, 15 minutes. Fill tart with ice cream, sherbet, or fruit (no bottom to this shell, only rim). This recipe will make 6 to 8 shells.

Did you notice that I used vegetable shortening for greasing pan? Meringues should stay white. Vegetable shortening does not brown the way butter does. The shortening can take long baking without a change in color.

Butter Cookies

1 cup butter, softened (½ pound)	sifted together with
¼ cup confectioners sugar	¼ teaspoon salt
2 cups all-purpose flour	1 teaspoon vanilla

Cream butter with sugar. Add flour, salt and vanilla. Mix ingredients by hand or machine. Dough should be soft. Divide into 3 or 4 pieces. Place 1 piece on a sheet of waxed paper. With the help of the waxed paper, shape cookie dough into a long roll, 1" in diameter. Refrigerate dough for 1 hour or wrap well and freeze. Preheat oven to 375° F. Cut cookie roll into ⅛" slices. Place on ungreased cookie sheets and bake for 10 to 12 minutes. Do not allow them to brown. Yield: 7 dozen.

Teacher says:

Shape dough by hand into little balls. Make a dent in the center and fill with ½ teaspoon raspberry or apricot jam.

Shape dough by hand into crescents or "cigarettes." Powder heavily with confectioners sugar upon removal from oven.

Add 4 tablespoons unsweetened cocoa to ½ the recipe. Roll out ½ recipe of white cookie dough ⅛″ thick between 2 sheets of waxed paper. Do the same with the chocolate dough. Brush slightly beaten egg white on plain dough. Place chocolate dough directly on to plain dough. Pat together. Roll up jelly roll fashion and stop when cookie is 1¼″ in diameter. Cut dough there. You may have enough for another roll. Wrap well, refrigerate or freeze.

These frozen cookie rolls are a tremendous help for unexpected guests. They may be sliced, baked and served within 15 minutes.

Butter Cookie #2

½ pound butter	2 cups all-purpose flour sifted with
½ cup sugar	¼ teaspoon salt
2 egg yolks	1 teaspoon vanilla

Cream butter and sugar. Add yolks, flour, salt and vanilla. Refrigerate dough for 1 hour or overnight. Preheat oven to 375° F. Roll out and cut shapes. For an easier cookie, make balls, flatten on a cookie sheet, brush with beaten egg white and sprinkle with cinnamon sugar. Bake for 10 to 12 minutes. Yield: 7 dozen.

Chocolate Decorated Cookies

Bake any butter cookie dough recipe. Bake some rolled into very thin rounds. Shape some rounds and make a cavity in the center, leave it empty.

Melt 6 ounces of semi-sweet chocolate. Prepare some well drained maraschino cherries with stems. Lay out a long sheet of waxed paper. On one side of paper place ground walnuts; on another section place slivered almonds, and on another, coarsely broken pecans or hazelnuts.

Prepare a bowl of raspberry jam. When cookies are baked and cooled, dip fork into chocolate and let chocolate drop in free lines over the cookie. Place on a tray.

Dip the ends of cookies into chocolate first then nuts.

Drop a cherry into chocolate and place it into empty cavities of cookies.

Sandwich 2 thin cookies with melted chocolate. Dip rim into hazelnuts.

Sandwich 2 thin cookies with jam. Dip into chocolate and then ground nuts.

Always place dipped cookies on to a tray and refrigerate until chocolate hardens.

By using a variety of nuts, differently ground or cut, each individual cookie takes on a different look.

My classes are always astonished when they see a completed tray of these decorated cookies. They are so beautiful!

Hold leaf stencil down flat on a cooky sheet. Spread batter evenly with spatula.

*Be sure to wipe excess butter off the stencil before lifting from cooky sheet. Repeat operation until cooky sheet is filled.

This requires a leaf stencil. It is well worth the investment!

Almond Leaf

½ pound butter, softened
⅓ cup sugar
6 ounces blanched almonds,
    finely ground
    (use electric blender)

1 cup all purpose flour
1 teaspoon vanilla
½ teaspoon almond extract

Cream butter and sugar. Add almonds, flour and extracts. Mix until very smooth. Preheat oven to 375° F. Hold leaf stencil (in left hand) flat against ungreased cookie sheet. Spread mixture with spatula on to cookie sheet, wiping off excess from stencil; remove stencil. Repeat this until pan is filled. Bake at 375° F. for 7 to 8 minutes. Remove from oven. Let it set for ½ minute. Remove cookies to a rack and cool. Yield: 6 to 7 dozen.

FOR DECORATION:

Melt 6 ounces semi-sweet chocolate in a bowl over water. Keep flame low. Spread chocolate over flat side of the leaf cookie. With a small spatula or butter knife make lines in the chocolate for the leaf veins. Refrigerate until chocolate hardens.

These cookies are very tender and short. Handle them gently, they are worth it.

Almond Crescents

See index for recipe.

Conga Bars ★ ★ ★

⅔ cup butter (1 stick, plus
  2⅔ tablespoons)
1 box brown sugar
3 eggs
2¾ cups all-purpose flour
2½ teaspoons baking powder

½ teaspoon salt
1 teaspoon vanilla
1 package (6 ounces)
  chocolate bits
¾ cup broken walnuts or pecans

Grease a 13″ x 9″ x 2″ baking pan. Set oven at 375° F. Cream butter. Add sugar gradually. Add one egg at a time beating constantly. Sift together flour, baking powder and salt; add a little at a time. Beat in vanilla, chocolate and nuts. Spread batter evenly in pan. Bake at 375° F. for 45 minutes. Cool before cutting. Yield: 24 squares or 30 smaller pieces.

Watch these; they disappear under your very eyes!

Pecan Squares ★ ★ ★

Cream ¼ pound (1 stick) butter with ½ cup brown sugar. Beat in 1 cup all-purpose flour. Spread mixture over bottom of 8″ square pan. Bake at 375° F. for 20 minutes.

In the meantime, beat 2 eggs with 1 cup brown sugar. Stir in 1 teaspoon vanilla, 1 cup chopped pecans, ¼ cup coconut, 2 tablespoons flour, and pinch of salt. Spread over baked crust and bake again for 20 minutes. Cool. Cut into squares or small pieces. Yield: 20 pieces.

———————

By consensus of opinion we voted these the best brownies on our side of the street. My friend Blanche tells me they originated with her Australian cousins!

Blanche's Brownies

2½ ounces unsweetened chocolate	½ cup all-purpose flour
⅓ cup butter (5⅓ tablespoons)	¼ teaspoon salt
2 eggs	⅛ teaspoon baking soda
½ cup sugar	1 cup chopped walnuts
¼ cup old-fashioned molasses	½ teaspoon vanilla
¼ cup light corn syrup	

Grease an 8″ or 9″ square pan. Preheat oven to 350° F. Melt chocolate and butter together in bowl over warm water. Keep it on low heat. Beat eggs. Add sugar, molasses, syrup, and melted chocolate. Sift together flour, salt and soda. Beat into chocolate mixture. Add nuts and vanilla. Spread in an 8″ or 9″ square pan. Bake at 350° F. for 25 minutes. Yield: 16 squares.

———————

Lace Cookies

½ cup butter	1 cup flour
½ cup light corn syrup	1 cup chopped walnuts
⅔ cup brown sugar	

Grease several cookie sheets. Preheat oven to 325° F. Place butter, syrup and sugar in a saucepan. Bring to a boil and immediately remove from heat. Stir flour and nuts into first mixture. Using two teaspoons drop batter 3″ apart on to a greased cookie sheet. Bake at 325° F. for 8 to 10 minutes. Cool for 1 minute before removing to a rack. Yield: 4 dozen.

To decorate: Melt 6 ounces of semi-sweet chocolate in a bowl over warm water on low heat. Dribble chocolate over cooled cookies and refrigerate them until chocolate hardens.

A young Danish girl who worked for my friend, Essie Davis, finally parted with this recipe when she returned to her native Denmark some years ago. This is almost like a puff pastry turned into a cookie. It is delectable and easily made if directions are followed carefully. Oddly enough, a meat tenderizer that rolls on a handle will be a useful gadget for this recipe. Without it you will have to use a fork and some physical effort.

Danish Elephant Ears ★ ★ ★

½ pound sweet butter,   2 cups all-purpose flour
   cold but pliable   7 tablespoons ice water

TO PREPARE DOUGH:

1. Break butter into large pieces. Add flour and blend well together. Use your hand. Add water (try not to use more than 7 tablespoons) and form dough into a ball. Divide into two pieces and refrigerate for 1 hour.

2. Prepare pastry cloth or board and rolling pin. Roll out one piece of dough ¼" thick. Cut out rounds with a cookie cutter or glass. Make them approximately 1½" in diameter. Place these on a plate; you may overlap them. Save scraps to reroll. Continue until all the dough is rolled out. Refrigerate these till firm (1 hour).

TO BAKE:

Preheat oven to 450° F. Grease 2 cookie sheets. Place a long sheet of waxed paper on your counter. Make a mound of sugar in the center. Place 3 rounds of dough, side by side on sugar. Roll them once to elongate them. Turn them over and roll again. Place these sugared elephant ears on a greased cookie sheet. Using a fork prick many, many holes in each cookie. (If you own a meat tenderizer with spikes on it, roll it back and forth over the cookie.) Bake the cookies at 450° F. for 5 to 6 minutes. After 4 minutes look at them. If they have started to glaze on the underside turn them over. Watch these with your quick eye. They burn rapidly! Yield: 6 to 7 dozen.

Teacher says:

After cookies are rolled and sugared place them on a platter or tray and refrigerate. You may also do this well in advance (6 to 8 hours) and bake them when you are ready. They bake better when they are cold.

When you are ready to bake, place sugared ears on greased pans, prick all over and bake.

It is good to know that these rounds of dough freeze very well. Freeze them at the end of preparation (before baking instructions). The raw rounds of dough may be used at a later date for either these dessert cookies or for "Piquant Hors D'oeuvres" (see index). Package these in single layers separated by waxed paper so that you may take out as many as you need at a given time.

My last cookie offering to you is the only one I remember from my girlhood. My mother made these with great enjoyment some thirty years ago. Students still ask for the recipe which is perhaps the simplest and the best of all the crescents.

Cookie Crescents (Rogelach)

1 cup butter (2 sticks)   2 cups all-purpose flour
½ pound cream cheese

Blend butter, cheese and flour all together with your hand. Mix it well until you form a ball of dough. Divide dough into 4 pieces. Form small balls of dough. Cover well and refrigerate overnight.

TO BAKE

Prepare shakers of sugar and cinnamon, and bowls of raisins, ground nuts and jam. Preheat oven to 375° F. Roll out each ball of dough to a round. Sprinkle it generously with sugar. Use cinnamon, raisins and nuts as desired. Cut into 12 wedges. Place a ½ teaspoon of jam on each wedge near outside rim. Roll each wedge towards center. Turn corners in to make a crescent, see drawing page 209. Place on a greased cookie sheet. Bake at 375° F. for 25 minutes. Remove and cool on a rack. Yield: 4 dozen.

Pretty Little Chocolates

6 ounces semi-sweet chocolate
24 small paper cups
1 cup stale cake
1 cup drained raspberries

2 tablespoons rum
(or your choice of brandy)
whipped cream for decoration

1. Melt chocolate in a bowl set over a saucepan of warm water. Keep heat low. As soon as chocolate is almost melted remove from the heat even if lumps are still there. You may stir these out with a spatula.

2. Use the tiniest muffin cups you can buy. Prepare a muffin pan for petite muffins.

3. Holding a double muffin paper cup in your left hand (use 2 cups to give body) spread melted chocolate on the inside surface of the paper cup. Spread it so that no paper shows through. Refrigerate in the muffin pan.

4. While chocolate is hardening, mix the stale cake with raspberries and rum. Set aside.

5. You should still have some melted chocolate. If you do not, melt another 2 ounces of chocolate.

6. If chocolate cups are now hardened remove them from refrigerator. Place some of the cake mixture into each cup to reach ⅛" below top. Spread on melted chocolate to cover top completely. Repeat until the dozen are finished. Refrigerate.

7. After 2 or 3 hours the chocolate should be very hard. Remove one at a time from refrigerator. Tear away paper cup gently. You will have a pretty little chocolate enclosing a delicious filling.

8. Serve with a tiny rosette of whipped cream on top.

9. These may be refrigerated for several days if they are well covered (of course without whipped cream).

Note: Make these with a filling of brandied cherries or softened almond paste. If you are a chestnut lover try a purée of sweetened chestnut and cognac for a filling.

Many students love these made as large krinkle cups, filled with ice cream, fruits or sherbets.

COOKIE QUESTIONS ANSWERED

Q *What shortening do you use for greasing the cookie sheet?*
A Generally, butter, but in the case of meringues, shortening is used (as explained in the recipe).
Q *When do you remove baked cookies from pan?*
A Cookies are allowed to rest for at least 30 seconds so that they set. Follow a recipe specifically if it mentions the time. This is especially important in the Almond Leaf and the Lace Cookie. If you allow the Almond Leaf to get too cold, it is so thin and short that it may break in lifting it from pan. The Lace Cookie must be lifted off the pan before it cools to the point of sticking.
Q *Can all of the cookies be made in double quantities?*
A Yes, all the butter cookies and meringues work out just as well made in bulk. Work only single recipes for the squares and the Lace Cookie.
Q *If chocolate is melted for cookie decoration can it be stored and reused when it is leftover?*
A Absolutely. As long as chocolate is not overheated it may be hardened (in the refrigerator) again. Store in a cool pantry (65° F. to 70° F.) and melt again when needed.

LESSON 18

The Barbecue Grill

In my barbecue course for men I have seen the enthusiasm that can be stimulated when men's skills as backyard chefs are brought out by a few instructions and a file of reliable recipes. Although outdoor cookery is indeed as simple as it looks there are some basic problems that heckle the beginner.

V.I.P.'s for Barbecue Cooks:

1 Barbecue cookery is *not* fast. It takes coals at least 30 minutes before they are hot enough to cook on.

2. To obtain good heat for proper grilling use a minimum of 4 pounds of charcoal; up to 8 pounds for large amounts of vegetables and meats. A homemade fire starter is shown opposite.

3. Coals are ready when they look gray ash on the outside and show a red glow within.

4. Keep a pail of water for emergencies. Keep a laundry sprinkler of water to douse flames.

5. Control of the heat is arrived at:
by lowering or raising grill above the hot coals.

by removing some hot coals if fire is too hot.

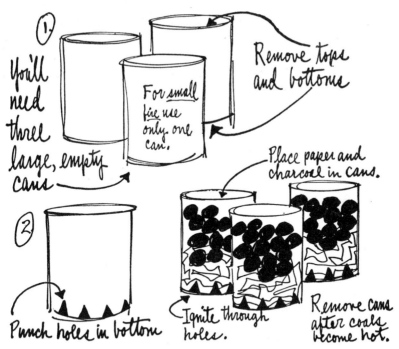

(1.) You'll need three large, empty cans

For small fire use only one can.

Remove tops and bottoms

(2) Punch holes in bottom

Place paper and charcoal in cans.

Ignite through holes.

Remove cans after coals become hot.

by spreading out hot coals for a lower fire or piling them for much concentrated heat.

by moving coals to one side of the fire box thereby leaving an empty space. Long-cooking meats and poultry can be broiled over empty space. They will obtain plenty of heat but will not be directly exposed to hot coals.

6. Much equipment can be bought for outdoor grilling. Start with the simplest. Use long-handled utensils, one pair of asbestos gloves, a few stainless steel bowls and perhaps a meat thermometer. (I test meat by making a small incision near bone.)

7. Always keep a sauce, marinade or a simple mixture of oil, butter and lemon juice on hand. Constant basting enhances all foods.

8. Your best knowledge of charcoal grilling comes from experience. Each cooking time will be another lesson if you make a few written notes each time you cook.

9. To be practical and organized, prepare a shopping list to be sure that all ingredients are on hand when you need them.

10. Keep your family or guests busy with a good salad while you prepare the main course to perfection.

11. Enjoy yourself! Provide yourself with a comfortable chair; cook when you have the time and the desire.

THE SAUCE AND THE MARINADE

Sauces usually are seasoned liquids to be served with meats. This is a fine point. For instance, beef may be marinated in the barbecue sauce and then grilled. Sauce may then be served accompanying beef.

If a marinade contains a great deal of tomato or sugar, wipe most of it off before grilling. Meat will char before it is completely cooked because sugar burns so rapidly.

~~~~~~~~~

Tomato Barbecue Sauce ★ ★ ★

1 can (8 ounces) tomato sauce
½ cup catsup
½ cup chili sauce
3 tablespoons brown sugar
2 teaspoons Worcestershire sauce
2 tablespoons wine vinegar

2 tablespoons oil
2 cloves garlic, crushed
1 teaspoon salt
½ teaspoon black pepper
½ teaspoon dry mustard

Stir all together. Use as a baste as well as a sauce. Excellent with steak, chicken, etc. Yield: 2½ cups.

Marinades and bastes are often interchangeable. Marinade indicates that the meat will rest in the mixture for a prescribed time. This liquid mixture may also be a baste which can then be used to brush on meat while it is cooking.

~~~~~~~~~

These sauces can be prepared in stainless steel bowls directly on your fire. Use a good canned gravy if you have none homemade. Leftover sauces can be refrigerated and used indoors as well as out.

Chateaubriand Sauce

1 cup brown **gravy**
1 cup white **wine**
6 tablespoons **butter**
2 tablespoons **lemon juice**

1 tablespoon parsley
¼ teaspoon salt
⅛ teaspoon pepper

Cook gravy and wine together until well blended and thick. Add other ingredients. Stir well to melt butter and serve when mixture is smooth. Good with barbecued steak. Yield: 2 cups.

Bordelaise Sauce

2 shallots or 1 onion, minced
2 tablespoons butter
1 cup beef gravy
½ cup red wine
1 tablespoon lemon juice

1 tablespoon parsley
¼ teaspoon salt
dash pepper
1 tablespoon butter

Cook shallots in butter. Add gravy and wine. Simmer until mixture cooks down slightly. Add all other seasonings and butter. Serve. Yield: 1½ cups.

Wine Marinade

1 cup red wine
½ cup olive oil
1 sliced onion
1 teaspoon salt

6 peppercorns
1 bay leaf
2 tablespoons chopped parsley

Blend all ingredients by hand. Pour over meats or poultry. Marinate for 2 to 24 hours. Yield: 1¾ cups.

Spicy Marinade and Baste

3 tablespoons soy sauce
2 tablespoons Worcestershire sauce

½ teaspoon dry mustard
4 thinly sliced onions

Stir all together and pour over beef or chicken. Yield: 2 cups.

Chinese Barbecue Marinade

2 cups chicken broth
2 tablespoons soy sauce
2 tablespoons brown sugar

1 tablespoon honey
2 cloves garlic crushed
½ teaspoon monosodium glutamate

Stir all together. Marinate spareribs or chicken overnight. Yield: 2½ cups.

————————

Each of these marinades is excellent. Chicken may be marinated from 2 to 24 hours or it may be broiled (just salted) and basted with any one of these marinades. Blend all ingredients by hand.

Three Good Marinades for Barbecue Chicken

1. Combine ¼ cup oil, ¼ cup soy sauce, ½ cup dry vermouth, and ½ teaspoon dry mustard.

2. Combine 4 tablespoons butter melted, ½ cup white wine, 2 tablespoons lemon juice, 1 tablespoon chopped tarragon (1 teaspoon dried), ½ teaspoon salt, and ⅛ teaspoon pepper.

3. Combine 1 cup chicken consommé, 2 tablespoons melted butter, 2 tablespoons oil, 1 tablespoon chopped parsley, fresh, 1 tablespoon chopped chives, fresh, 1 teaspoon chervil, and 1 teaspoon basil.

Should you prefer a tomato base sauce use the barbecue sauce for beef. Some of my men students tell me that they made it by the gallon for constant use all summer.

————————

Prepare and grill duck in the manner described for chicken. Duck can be a little tricky because the drippings of fat cause flare-ups of fire. Flames must be doused immediately. Keep water handy in a laundry sprinkler. Keep fire low and flames down. If the duck is browning too rapidly, move some of the hot coals to the side. Turn duck frequently and for the last 15 minutes baste with one of these recipes. Total cooking time should be about 2 hours (5 to 6 pounds).

Bastes for Duck

HONEY COATING

2 egg yolks
⅛ cup soy sauce

¼ cup honey
¼ cup chicken broth

BRANDY ORANGE SAUCE

1 cup orange juice
¼ cup tomato purée
1 cup white wine

2 tablespoons soy sauce
¼ cup brandy

Blend ingredients for each recipe by hand. In using one of these, grill duck until ¾ of cooking time has elapsed. Use these bastes only at the end. They are sweet and will encourage charring.

BARBECUED BEEF

Thick cuts of beef, whether they be sirloin, porterhouse or cross rib, should be purchased at least 1½ to 2 inches thick. Always bring steak to room temperature before grilling. While you are waiting for charcoal fire to become hot, allow steak to rest at room temperature with a sprinkling of soy and Worcestershire sauce. I use these seasonings instead of salt and pepper. Leave the salt and pepper to the discretion of each diner.

Timing on an outdoor grill can sometimes be a problem. Each grill is built differently; each fire has a different number of coals and is a different heat. For a thick 2″ steak, move hot coals to one section of the firebox. Place steak on grill over the section that is empty. Steak will cook through slightly but will not be exposed directly to coals. It will cook slowly and evenly without burning. Steak may be turned and allowed to remain in this warm section of the grill for 45 to 60 minutes. Fifteen minutes before dining, place steak directly over coals to brown rapidly on both sides.

Since beef is the favorite for most charcoal broiling, vary the beef cuts that appear in your household. Two-inch sirloin and porterhouse steaks are no doubt very fine but why not buy the flank steak, the cross rib, the butchers' hanger or the skirt steak? These more economical cuts cook deliciously on charcoal and provide you with different flavors and textures.

To prepare these less expensive cuts of beef, be wise enough to select a tasty marinade. With forethought, you can marinate these meats in advance. Marinades, which are combinations of oils, vinegars and spices, tenderize your meats and definitely make them more flavorful.

The Hot Sandwich

One of the most delicious of barbecued meats for really hungry eaters is the steak or hamburger sandwich. Fresh rolls or good bread make for happy partners with the sliced charcoal steak.

Economical cuts of meat should generally be sliced very thin on the diagonal. The other cuts may be sliced straight and about ¼" thick for sandwiches.

The Hamburger

Don't think for a minute that we ignore the hamburger! Freshly ground steak is a treat when quickly seared and is enjoyed when practically raw. In my barbecue class I always ask for a volunteer to create a recipe for hamburger. Men are truly imaginative and aggressive cooks. So far, no two men ever used the same combination of seasonings. Your guess is as good as theirs! Have fun with hamburgers, use anything or everything from salt to red wine. My one suggestion to you is the addition of 1 tablespoon of potato flour for each pound of meat. The potato flour binds the juices and makes the meat soft. Hamburgers can be elegant if served with one of the sauces given earlier in this chapter.

Tenderloin en Brochette

1 steak, filet or sirloin 1" thick
  (2 to 3 pounds)
½ cup red wine
1 tablespoon wine vinegar
¼ cup olive oil
1 teaspoon Worcestershire sauce
1 tablespoon chopped fresh tarragon

1 clove garlic crushed
½ teaspoon salt
¼ teaspoon pepper
4 onions, quartered
2 green peppers,
  cut lengthwise in 8ths
4 tomatoes, quartered

Prepare 8 long skewers. Cut steak into 1" cubes. Mix wine, wine vinegar, oil, Worcestershire sauce, tarragon, garlic, salt and pepper in a bowl. Stir meat into marinade. Marinate from 1 to 24 hours. Place meat on skewers, alternately with vegetables. Pour marinade into a large flat baking pan (jelly roll pan). Place skewers in marinade so that vegetables and meat will rest in seasoning. This may be prepared well in advance. Skewers should be placed on the grill over a hot fire about 3 to 4 inches over coals so that vegetables have a chance to cook without charring. Turn skewers frequently. Brochette should take no more than 10 minutes. Serves 4.

LAMB ON THE GRILL

Lamb may be used in this same way. Actually, I guess the beef dish came from the Shish Kebab but no matter which came first they are both excellent.

Shish Kebab

MARINADE

¾ cup olive oil
¼ cup lemon juice
1 tablespoon wine vinegar
2 cloves garlic, crushed
1 bay leaf

½ teaspoon **thyme**
½ teaspoon **oregano**
½ teaspoon **pepper**
1 teaspoon salt

TO PREPARE SHISH KEBAB:

Cut boned leg of lamb into 1″ cubes. Marinate meat at least 6 hours or overnight. Skewer meat with vegetables as for tenderloin en brochette. Figure about ½ pound meat per person (trimmed meat). Occasionally use mushrooms, zucchini and eggplant for your vegetables. Lamb takes the same timing as beef. It should be eaten medium rare but suit yourself!

Summer is the time for double lamb chops. Buy baby lamb cut in double or triple rib chops. Wait for an outdoor dinner night and enjoy this sweet meat grilled brown over charcoal.

Double Baby Lamb Chops

4 tablespoons butter
2 cloves garlic, crushed
½ teaspoon rosemary
1 tablespoon parsley
1 tablespoon lemon juice

¼ cup bread **crumbs**
½ teaspoon **salt**
⅛ teaspoon **pepper**
8 double rib chops

Mix all ingredients (except chops) to make a paste. Make a slit in each chop, cutting from outside fat of meat towards bone. This will make a pocket. Place one spoon of mixture into each pocket. Place chops on grill over hot coals. Broil chops about 4 inches over coals, 6 or 7 minutes on each side. To test for doneness make a tiny slit near bone. Serves 4.

BARBECUED PORK

Roast or grilled pork is probably the most succulent and flavorsome of all meats. The pork chop with its tendency to be dry when made under the kitchen broiler is sparked by the flavor of charcoal and the air around it. Soak the chop in tomato juice, basil, salt and pepper. Broil 4" over hot coals for at least 15 minutes on each side.

Spareribs are the all time favorite! Charcoal broil them with merely salt, pepper and garlic and the family will adore you for it.

It is worth a special trip to the nearest Chinatown to buy Hoisin sauce so you can prepare the pork and spareribs Chinese style!

Chinese Roast Pork

CHINESE PORK MARINADE

½ cup chicken broth, hot
4 tablespoons sugar
1 teaspoon salt
½ teaspoon monosodium glutamate
¼ cup soy sauce

1 tablespoon sherry
1 teaspoon brown bean sauce
 (crushed)
1 teaspoon red tomato coloring

Buy a loin or shoulder of pork; have it boned. Marinate it in the Chinese sauce for at least 3 hours. The boned pork may be cut into narrow strips to insure doneness and to make for more crisp surface. Grill meat for 35 minutes to the pound. What a treat for Chinese food lovers!

Note: All Chinese ingredients such as Hoisin sauce, brown bean sauce and red coloring may be purchased in any Chinese grocery.

If red coloring is omitted you may use 2 tablespoons tomato catsup.

Chinese Spareribs ★ ★ ★

4 pounds pork spareribs
 (1 or 2 racks)
3 tablespoons Hoisin sauce
4 tablespoons sugar
4 tablespoons soy sauce
¼ cup chicken broth

4 cloves garlic, crushed
1 teaspoon monosodium glutamate
1 tablespoon sherry
1 teaspoon red color
 (tomato color if available)

1. Marinate ribs in the sauce (made by combining the remaining ingredients) 5 to 6 hours up to 24 hours. Wipe sauce off before grilling over charcoal.

2. At first, place grill as far from coals as possible to allow ribs to cook without burning. You may also try clearing the firebox of coals just below ribs (as I suggested for thick steaks). Allow ribs to cook through without being closely exposed to hot coals.

3. For the last 15 minutes the rack of ribs can be browned more thoroughly. The total time may be from 45 to 55 minutes. It is best to cook them slowly so that they remain juicy. Turn them frequently and baste towards the end with leftover sauce.

5. Slice through individual ribs just before serving.

6. The heavier part of the ribs sometimes needs more cooking.

BARBECUED POULTRY

Chicken may be split or quartered before grilling. I generally prefer it split down the back so that the breast remains intact. Chicken keeps more moist if it is not completely cut up. Of course, it may also be grilled on the spit.

Chicken, like pork, requires longer slower cooking. Broil chicken flesh side down, baste and turn frequently. *Watch it carefully.* If fire is too hot and the chicken is charring, move coals to the side so that few, if any, hot coals remain directly under chicken.

Timing:

Most young broilers 1¼ to 2¼ pounds require no more than 45 minutes of broiling.

Fryers from 2 to 3¼ pounds require anywhere from 45 minutes to 1 hour and 15 minutes.

Roasters from 3 to 5 pounds require a minimum of 1 hour to approximately 1 hour and 30 minutes.

Add at least 30 minutes for chickens roasted on the spit.

Test for doneness by cutting into the joint at the leg. If chicken is not finished and dinner must be hastened, cut chicken into serving pieces. Continue to broil chicken for a short while, basting constantly to keep it moist. *Do not overcook chicken!*

Sea-food Kebab ★ ★ ★

½ cup olive oil
½ cup clarified butter, melted
2 tablespoons lemon juice
4 cloves garlic, crushed
¼ cup minced parsley

¼ cup mixed herbs
  (chives, chervil, tarragon)
2 teaspoons salt
½ teaspoon freshly ground pepper

Prepare marinade of above ingredients. Soak your choice of sea-food in the prepared marinade. Use the following amounts as your gauge to serve six.

2 pounds large shrimp (16 to 20)
3 lobster tails (1½ pounds)
1 pound scallops

Shrimp may be cleaned raw and deveined. The alternate methed is to clean shrimp in the shell. Slit shell to devein shrimp but leave shrimp in shell. Grill the shrimp in its shell.

Defrost lobster tails and remove meat. Cut it in chunks.

Soak sea-food in the marinade from 2 to 6 hours.

Skewer shrimp, lobster and scallops alternately. Grill over hot coals, at least 5 inches above flame for 10 minutes. Turn and baste frequently with marinade.

Teacher says:

Lobster tails may be split and broiled in the shell. Grill them shell side next to flame until edges of lobster meat look opaque. Turn flesh side down. This takes about 15 minutes on one side, 10 minutes on the other. Baste frequently with sea-food marinade.

Fresh Fish

If you are an outdoor man and a lucky fisherman, I need not tell you about the delicacy of freshly caught fish grilled on an open fire. If you are an indoor man but an outdoor chef, change your menu to fish one day, for an exceptional treat! To begin with, buy the best quality and freshest fish of the day. Be sure to wait for coals to become hot. Place a sheet of heavy aluminum foil on the grill. Brush it with oil or butter. Puncture the aluminum foil with a fork to make many holes.

Place fish on foil. Grill until sides of fish turn opaque. Brush with a mixture of olive oil or clarified butter, lemon juice, salt and pepper. Turn fish. Fish is finished when it flakes easily. Most varieties of fish cook from 10 to 25 minutes depending on their thickness. Try rainbow trout, halibut, salmon, mackerel, bluefish, fluke and red snapper.

FAVORED BARBECUE ACCOMPANIMENTS

Potato and Onion Packets

Figure 1 potato and ½ onion for each person. Slice potatoes ⅛″ thick. Slice onions thin.

Cut heavy aluminum foil into sheets of 8″ x 10″. Place peeled raw potato, onion, bits of butter, salt and pepper on aluminum foil (1 portion). Wrap package with a double fold. Make it fairly flat. Grill for about 30 minutes turning at least once or twice.

Corn on the Cob

There are two good methods for grilling corn. If corn is very fresh (picked within the hour), turn husks back, remove silk and cover corn with husks again. Soak corn in cold water until ready for grill. When fire is hot, place corn on grill about 4″ above coals. Turn frequently. Grill for 15 to 20 minutes.

For corn not quite so fresh, pull off husks and silks. Cut heavy aluminum foil sheets, large enough to enclose each corn individually. Melt butter. Place corn on aluminum foil. Brush with butter; salt; wrap tightly. Grill over hot coals for 20 minutes. Serve with freshly ground pepper.

Rice Pilaff

Lightly brown 1 cup of converted rice in a skillet or saucepan over hot coals. Use about 2 tablespoons of butter or oil to sauté rice. Add 2 cups of broth, cover tightly and cook for 25 minutes.

Frozen Vegetables

Wrap the solid frozen vegetables in heavy aluminum foil.
Enclose a few pats of butter in the package.
Peas cook rapidly in about 20 minutes.
Other vegetables take anywhere from 20 to 25 minutes.
Frozen as well as fresh vegetable may be cooked in saucepan directly over coals as though it were cooked indoors.

Zucchini (squash) is a fine accompaniment for poultry and fish.

Stuffed Baked Zucchini

4 medium zucchini (1½ pounds)	1 teaspoon salt
1 onion, minced	¼ teaspoon pepper
2 tablespoons softened butter	1 teaspoon chervil
¼ cup bread crumbs	1 tablespoon parsley

Cut off one layer (¼") of squash lengthwise and discard. Scoop out squash without tearing skin. Dice squash very fine and blend with all other ingredients. Re-stuff squash. Wrap each one in heavy aluminum foil. Grill for 30 minutes, turning occasionally.

Broiled Yams and Apple Rings

8 halves of cooked yams	4 tablespoons softened butter
8 apple rings (2 fresh apples, peeled, cored and sliced into rings)	2 tablespoons brown sugar
juice of a lemon	sprinkling of cinnamon

Spread a sheet of heavy aluminum foil over grill. Prick all over to make many holes. Place yams and apples on foil. Sprinkle with lemon juice and brush with butter. Cook for a few minutes, turning at least once. When apples start to soften, sprinkle sugar and cinnamon over yams and apples. Turn once. When sugar is melted, serve. Yams and apple rings also may be sautéed in a skillet over coals. They may also be sautéed on aluminum foil (without holes pricked).

~~~~~~~

Bananas are an unusual accompaniment when sautéed and served with grilled ham, poultry or pork. They provide an exciting finish when served as a hot dessert flambé.

Sautéed Bananas ★ ★ ★

2 tablespoons butter
4 firm bananas, sliced in half,
   lengthwise

2 tablespoons brown sugar
sprinkling of cinnamon

Spread a sheet of heavy aluminum foil over grill. Melt butter on foil. Sauté bananas in butter. Sprinkle all over with brown sugar and cinnamon. Turn at least once. Serve with meat or poultry.

Variations: Use the sautéed banana for a dessert. Sauté bananas in a skillet. This may be prepared in- or out-of-doors. When the bananas are hot sprinkle with brown sugar and cinnamon; pour on ¼ cup of rum. Set it ablaze. Serve with whipped cream.

The sautéed banana is excellent when flamed with banana or coffee liqueur and brandy. Serve with vanilla ice cream.

~~~~~~~

Comments and reports reach my ears about the menu favorites chosen by my men students for their charcoal cooking sprees. See index for recipes.

Al Fresco Menus

1

Green Goddess Salad
Flank Steak — Tomato Barbecue Sauce
Onion and Potato Packets   Hot Garlic Bread
Sautéed Bananas with Rum (above)

2

Sea-food Kebab
Grilled Chicken, Marinade No. 2
Corn on the cob   Tossed green salad
Hot herb butter bread
Cantaloupe with ice cream

3

Celery, carrot sticks, love tomatoes with
Bleu Cheese Dunk (page 14)
Mixed Grill of barbecued spareribs, roast pork and
duck bits (duck cut into small pieces)
Broiled Yams and Apple Rings (page 272)
Raspberry sherbet and cookies

4

Caesar Salad (page 165)
Shish Kebab (page 267)
Rice Pilaff (page 272)
Carrot and Pineapple Mold

Easy Rolls
Schnecken (page 212)

(To make mold: Dissolve 2 packages lemon-flavored gelatin in 2½ cups boiling water. Add ½ cup pineapple juice and 2 tablespoons lemon juice. Cool until mixture begins to jell. Stir in 1 cup coarsely grated carrots and 1 No. 2 can drained crushed pineapple. Pour into a 5- to 6-cup mold. Refrigerate until jelled. Unmold onto a serving platter and garnish with lemon slices alternated with carrot curls.)

BARBECUE QUESTIONS ANSWERED

Q *Will you explain the different cuts of steak suggested?*
A The sirloin and porterhouse steaks are expensive, tender cuts of meat. The sirloin is preferable for a family of 4 to 6 because it can be sliced to serve ample portions. The flank steak is a thin rectangular looking piece of meat with a long grain running through. It is excellent over charcoal. Slice it on the diagonal and in very thin slices.

The butchers' hanger is a thick, long piece of meat about 9″ x 3″. It is sometimes called a "tenderloin." Do not mistake it for a true *filet!* The hanger has a thick tissue running down the center of it. This is a very bloody, juicy cut of beef, good for hamburgers too. The skirt steak is a very thin cut of steak. It must be tenderized with aging or marinating.

The cross rib is a store name for shoulder steak. The so-called "London broil" could be any of the last four cuts of meats.
Q *Can meats that require longer cooking be packaged in aluminum foil to prevent fat from causing flare-ups of flame?*
A You may package meats such as pork and poultry but remember it will give you a steamed flavor rather than a broiled crisp flavor. If

you do use this method, package the meats with vegetables and seasoning.

Q *Is there any exact measure of heat?*

A You may purchase a thermometer to register heat but I should think that with a few cooking experiences at the fire, observation will eliminate the need to depend on anything other than your good judgment.

Q *Can wine marinades be reused?*

A No, usually the raw juices of meat and poultry have soaked into the marinade. This should not be used again. If a wine marinade has been used only for basting, it may be stored for a day or two.

Q *What is clarified butter?*

A Clarified butter is produced when butter is simmered slowly causing a milky sediment to rise to the top. Simmer it for about 10 minutes until it is clear and only small brown specks can be seen at the bottom. If any white sediment remains, skim it off. Pour off the clear butter. Store it in the refrigerator up to 8 weeks. It is excellent for all cooking purposes, especially grilling and sautéing. Clarified butter is always used as the dipping sauce for lobster. Also it makes an excellent baste for barbecued foods.

LESSON 19

The Party Menu

One of the questions most frequently asked by students is "what can I use for a menu? I am giving a dinner party." The mental strain of menu planning seems to be more of a hazard than the actual cooking. Usually this calls for a short conference with my puzzled student, during which I ask them the following questions:

> Is it a formal or informal party?
> How many guests?
> Do you know the likes, dislikes, allergies of your guests?
> What do you enjoy cooking most?
> What do you think you do very well?
> Are you afraid of doing even *one* thing the last minute?
> Are you daring or conservative in your entertaining?

These are the questions you might ask *yourself* before selecting a dinner menu. My questions obviously grope for the nature of the guests as well as the nature of the hostess. Once these are answered the next step is to decide on a main course and build the menu around it. Lesson 1, appetizers, discussed the composition of a menu regarding textures, flavors, organization and balance.

276

Remember too that the season of the year must influence your choice. A chilled soup is so appropriate for a summer meal and so wrong for a cold March evening. This is truly a matter of plain common sense.

Substitute: Consider these menus planned for you. Don't be afraid to borrow from one and omit from the other. They are frameworks upon which you can build menus with your personal touch. For instance in the menu using veal, substitutions of various veal recipes may be made. The suggested accompaniments will provide you with ideas for other main courses.

Rehearse: Follow carefully the direction given under Advance Preparation. To guide a maid, and to be sure that you do not forget anything, make a list with times noted for following the instructions.

MENU 1 FOR SIX
Aperitif: Beauvin Half and Half Vermouth
Melon Crabmeat Bowl
Melba toast   Crackers
Butterfly Veal Parmesan
Marruzine
Green Beans, Onions, and Capers, vinaigrette
Herb Butter Bread
Suggested wine: Meursault — Latour 1959
Chocolate Tartlette   Coffee

Melon Crabmeat Bowl

1 pound crabmeat (or 2 cans)	½ teaspoon salt
2 stalks celery, minced	¼ teaspoon pepper
3 tablespoons mayonnaise	½ pound prosciutto
2 tablespoons lemon juice	1 large honeydew melon
1 tablespoon chopped parsley	crisp chicory for garnish

1. Pick over crabmeat for bones.

2. Toss crabmeat with celery, mayonnaise, lemon juice, parsley, salt and pepper.

3. Chop two slices of prosciutto very fine. Add it to the crabmeat mixture. Refrigerate crabmeat until ready to use.

4. Cut off ⅓ of honeydew. At the bottom of larger piece, cut a thin straight slice so that the honeydew can stand firmly.

5. Scoop out balls (or wedges, if it is easier for you) from both shells. Discard smaller shell. Place balls of honeydew in refrigerator.

6. Trim the edge of the honeydew shell into points with a sharp knife or scissors. Sometimes I use the French fry potato slicer. This cuts a fancy edge very easily. Refrigerate.

7. An hour before serving, wrap half of the honeydew balls in slices of prosciutto. Hold together with picks.

8. Place honeydew shell in the center of a large round serving tray. Fill the cavity with crabmeat. Place honeydew balls all around the melon. Garnish with crisp chicory.

~~~~~~~~

Butterfly Veal Parmesan

6 rib or loin veal chops (¾ inch)	1 cup bread crumbs
1 teaspoon salt	¾ cup Parmesan cheese
¼ teaspoon pepper	1 onion, diced
¼ teaspoon paprika	1 cup white wine
6 tablespoons butter	2 tablespoons tomato paste

1. Have butcher slice through the meat of each chop and flatten it to form a butterfly. Season chops with a mixture of salt, pepper and paprika.

2. Prepare a flat casserole or baking pan. Place 4 tablespoons butter in pan and set into oven at 375° F.

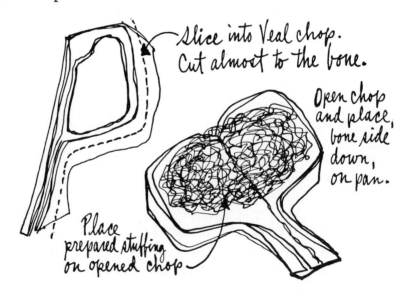

Slice into Veal chop. Cut almost to the bone.

Open chop and place, bone side down, on pan.

Place prepared stuffing on opened chop

3. Mix crumbs and cheese. When butter is melted in pan, remove pan from oven. Pour butter into crumbs and cheese, leaving a thin coating of butter on the pan.

4. Mix crumbs, cheese and butter well. Cover the concave side of the chop with this mixture, pressing down with your hand to make a compact topping.

5. Distribute diced onions over bottom of pan. Place chops side by side in the pan. Sprinkle with remaining 2 tablespoons butter, melted.

6. Add ½ cup of wine. Cover well and bake for 1 hour at 375° F.

7. During cooking time baste chops with more wine. Uncover chops for 10 minutes if they are not brown enough.

8. To serve, make a waxed paper decorator. Fill with tomato paste, pipe line marking of tomato paste over each chop. Place on a bed of macaroni shells.

Maruzzine

1 pound Maruzzine (small macaroni shells)	2 tablespoons oil
6 quarts boiling water	6 tablespoons butter or oil (or combination)
2 tablespoons salt	salt and pepper to taste

Immerse shells in boiling water with 2 tablespoons salt and oil. Cook for 10 to 12 minutes. Drain in a colander; run hot water through pasta. Immediately stir in 6 tablespoons butter or oil. Season to taste. This can wait about 30 minutes over a pan of hot water (double boiler fashion) as long as the pasta is separated with plenty of butter.

Green Beans, Onions and Capers, Vinaigrette

1 pound green beans, cut French style	¾ cup olive oil
2 onions, sliced thin in strips (not rounds)	¼ cup wine vinegar
	¾ teaspoon salt
2 tablespoons capers	½ teaspoon pepper
	¼ teaspoon dry mustard

Cook beans until tender, not mushy. Drain well and mix with onions and capers. Stir together the next 5 ingredients and blend with the vegetables. Refrigerate. This is best made 1 to 3 days in advance.

Herb Butter Bread

¼ pound butter, softened
2 tablespoons chopped parsley
1 teaspoon tarragon
1 teaspoon chervil

½ teaspoon salt
¼ teaspoon pepper
1 loaf Italian bread

Blend softened butter with all the herbs and seasonings. Cut bread into 1 inch slices. Spread each slice with butter, sticking each slice to the next to reshape the bread. Wrap bread in aluminum foil and heat for 15 minutes before dinner. Oven may be 350° F. or 375° F.

Chocolate Tartlette

6 baked tartlette shells
1 recipe Chocolate Mousse
¼ teaspoon cinnamon

2 tablespoons cognac or rum
1 cup whipped cream
¼ cup chopped pistachios

Prepare six individual pastry shells (see index) and cool. Prepare Chocolate Mousse (see index) adding cinnamon and cognac. Fill shells with mousse and decorate top with whipped cream. Sprinkle pistachios on to cream.

ADVANCE PREPARATION:

1. Make pastry for tartlettes as far in advance as you like. Freeze unbaked.

2. Prepare vegetable salad 2 or 3 days ahead of time.

3. One day in advance:

Prepare crabmeat; cover well. Refrigerate.

Prepare melon and melon balls, but do not wrap balls in prosciutto till day of dinner. Wrap well in Saran. Refrigerate.

Prepare veal up to and including step #5. Refrigerate. Bake it the day of dinner.

Make Herb Butter Bread. Refrigerate.

Bake pastries. Make mousse and fill tartlettes but do not garnish with whipped cream till day of dinner. Cover well and refrigerate.

DAY OF DINNER:

1. Early afternoon:

Take meat and bread out of refrigerator; leave at room temperature.

Put together melon crabmeat bowl onto serving tray. Cover with Saran and refrigerate.

Decorate tartlettes with whipped cream and pistachios. Refrigerate.

2. One hour before guests arrival:

Set oven at 375° F.

Prepare a large saucepan with water for macaroni.

Prepare serving dishes for meat and bread.

Place meat in the oven, 30 minutes before guests arrive.

Pasta may be boiled after first drink. Heat bread.

MENU 2 FOR SIX

Apértif: Lillet

Piquant Hors D'oeuvres

Rock Cornish Hens   Rice Apple Pecan Stuffing

Baked Belgian Endive

Port Wine Mold

French Bread

Suggested wine: St. Julien, Cruse, 1957

Génoise — Zabaglione Sauce   Coffee

~~~~~~

Piquant Hors D'oeuvres

18 rounds of unbaked pastry (Danish Elephant Ear Recipe) (see index)	6 thin slices tomato (no larger than rounds of pastry)
5 slices gruyere cheese	3 slices crisp bacon, crumbled
8 to 10 stuffed olives, sliced	6 anchovy filets
1 slice ham, cut in strips	6 strips pimento
	2 tablespoons mixed chopped parsley and chives

1. Fit rounds of pastry into the bottom of individual tartlette tins. Press against sides so that pastry will bake with a scalloped edge. Prick all over. Refrigerate.

2. Preheat oven to 400° F. Bake pastries for 12 minutes. Cool and remove to an ungreased baking sheet.

3. Cut cheese into small squares to just cover round of pastry. Place slice of cheese on each round.

4. On six pastries arrange sliced olives and strip of ham. On next six pastries place one slice of tomato on each and sprinkle with bacon. On last six, place 2 anchovy filets on each one and cross over with 2 strips of pimento. Sprinkle herbs over all.

5. Bake at 400° F. for 5 minutes. Serve piping hot.

~~~~~~~~

Rock Cornish Hen

6 Cornish hens (1 pound each)
juice of 1 lemon
1 teaspoon salt
½ teaspoon pepper
¼ pound butter
6 juniper berries,
  crushed with 1 teaspoon salt

1 cup dry vermouth
2 cups hot beef, chicken
  or veal broth
2 tablepsoons currant jelly
1 teaspoon Bovril
1 tablespoon cornstarch

1. Wash hens with cold water. Dry inside and out. Sprinkle lemon juice into cavities. Rub outside with lemon. Season with salt and pepper.

2. Stuff birds with the rice apple pecan stuffing below. Tie legs together.

3. Soften 4 tablespoons butter with crushed juniper berries and salt.

4. Rub outside of hens thoroughly with this mixture.

5. Roast on a shallow baking pan at 425° F. for 40 minutes. Baste frequently with remainder of butter, vermouth and ½ cup broth. Turn birds to brown evenly.

6. Remove birds from pan. Pour all pan juices into a saucepan, being sure to scrape pan thoroughly.

7. Set hens on baking pan again and return to the oven while you prepare sauce.

8. Add 1½ cups remaining broth, currant jelly and Bovril to sauce. Adjust seasoning and thicken with cornstarch blended with a little cold water.

9. Spoon some of the sauce over the hens. Lower oven to 350° F. Roast for another 25 minutes.

Rice Apple Pecan Stuffing

4 to 6 tablespoons butter
2 onions, diced fine
1 Roman Beauty apple,
  peeled and diced
1 cup cooked rice

¾ cup chopped pecans
2 tablespoons orange liqueur
  (Cointreau or Triple Sec)
½ teaspoon salt
dash pepper

Melt 2 tablespoons butter in a skillet. Sauté onion until it is lightly browned. Add apple and cook with onion for 2 minutes, adding more butter as needed. Remove from heat and blend in all other ingredients. Taste and adjust seasoning. Cool stuffing. Stuff birds.

Port Wine Mold

2 packages black raspberry
  flavored gelatin
2 cups boiling water

1½ cups port wine
crisp chicory

Place gelatin in a 4 cup measuring glass. Add boiling water to reach the 2 cup mark and stir until all the gelatin is dissolved. Add port wine and blend. Rinse mold with cold water. Pour gelatin into mold and chill until firmly molded. To unmold, run a knife around the edge of the mold. Immerse mold in few inches of lukewarm water for 30 seconds. Wipe the bottom of mold. Place tray on top of mold and reverse. Mold should slide out. Garnish all around mold with crisp chicory.

Baked Belgian Endive

6 heads Belgian Endive
1 tablespoon butter
½ cup chicken broth

2 tablespoons heavy sweet cream
¼ teaspoon freshly ground pepper

Wash endive and trim the base. Cut each head in half vertically, through the center. Grease a shallow casserole with butter. Preheat oven to 350° F. Place endive, cut side down, in the casserole. Set the halves of endives one next to the other in one layer. Pour broth and cream over all. Sprinkle with pepper. Cover and bake for 25 minutes.

~~~~~~~~

Gênoise Zabaglione Sauce

1 recipe Gênoise (see index)   ½ cup Marsala
6 egg yolks, room temperature   1 cup stiffly beaten cream
¼ cup sugar

Bake Gênoise in a 9" x 3" round pan. When cool dust with confectioners' sugar. Place yolks and sugar in a pottery bowl. Set bowl on a pan of water (do not allow water to touch the bottom of the bowl). Beat yolks and sugar with a hand electric mixer. Keep flame low so that water underneath just simmers. When mixture becomes frothy and thick (about 5 minutes) beat in Marsala. Remove bowl from water and beat for a few minutes more. When this mixture is cool, fold in whipped cream. Serve individual slices of Gênoise with a topping of sauce.

ADVANCE PREPARATION:

1. Prepare pastry for Danish elephant ears well in advance and freeze.

2. Bake Gênoise; cool, wrap very well and freeze for one week.

3. One day in advance:

Make mold.

Prepare stuffing.

Follow step #1 for Cornish hens.

Follow steps #1 and #2 for hors d'oeuvres; cool pastries and store for next day if you have not frozen them.

DAY OF DINNER:

Morning:

1. Prepare Piquant Hors D'oeuvres, up to and including step #4. Cover and refrigerate.

2. Unmold wine mold on to serving tray and refrigerate.

Afternoon:

1. Stuff birds and place on baking pan and set aside until 1 hour 15 minutes before dinner.

2. Cut bread in 2-inch slices. Wrap in aluminum foil for last minute warming.

3. Prepare Zabaglione sauce. Refrigerate.

4. Prepare endive in casserole and set aside until 25 minutes before dining. The timing and temperature of your oven will coincide for the Cornish hens and the endive. Defrost Gênoise. Set on to a serving tray.

MENU 3 FOR SIX

Baked Stuffed Shrimp   Dry Sherry
Sweet and Sour Spareribs   Pineapple, green pepper and carrots
Beef Curry with Onions   Chinese steamed rice
Chinese Tea
Lemon Ices with Loquats
Almond Crescents   Coffee

Baked Stuffed Shrimp

8 ounces fresh crabmeat (or 1 can)	¼ teaspoon dry mustard
1 shallot minced	¼ teaspoon salt
or 2 tablespoons minced onion	few grinds of black pepper
1 tablespoon lemon juice	1 pound medium shrimp,
2 tablespoons mayonnaise	cleaned and deveined raw
2 tablespoons dry sherry	sprinkled with juice of a lemon
¼ cup bread crumbs	

1. Mix all the ingredients (except shrimp) for the stuffing. Split each shrimp down the curved side, almost to the other side. Open each one to form a cavity for the stuffing. Fill each shrimp with a tablespoon of stuffing. It's easiest to do this with your hand.

2. Prepare a shallow baking pan. Mix the following and spread on baking pan, then place shrimps on pan.

3 tablespoons butter or olive oil	1 tablespoon chopped fresh chives
3 cloves garlic, crushed	1 teaspoon mixed dry herbs
2 tablespoons chopped fresh parsley	(chervil, basil, tarragon)

3. Preheat oven to 400° F. Bake shrimp for 10 minutes, just until they become opaque white. Do not overcook. Serve immediately.

Note: Try to obtain the shrimp that run 15 to 18 to a pound. These are a perfect size. Allow 2 or 3 per person for a first course.

This same shrimp may be used for a main course. Serve at least 5 or 6 per person in that case.

Sweet and Sour Spareribs

1. 1 rack spareribs—have butcher cut ribs in 1 inch pieces.
2. Sprinkle 2 tablespoons of sherry over ribs. Coat ribs with 2 tablespoons cornstarch.
3. Prepare the following:

1 #2 can pineapple chunks, drained   2 carrots sliced
2 green peppers, cut in eights

Parboil green pepper and carrots for 2 minutes. Drain; reserve.

4. Combine the following ingredients for sauce mixture:

1 cup chicken broth   1 tablespoon soy sauce
½ cup white vinegar   ½ teaspoon monosodium glutamate
2 tablespoons sherry   cornstarch solution of ¼ cup
2 cloves garlic, crushed   cornstarch and ½ cup water
½ cup sugar

5. To cook spareribs:

Heat 1 quart oil (peanut or vegetable) in a deep fry kettle or Chinese wok (an electric skillet is good too). When oil is hot, add meat. Do not crowd the pot. Separate the pieces if they stick together in the oil. Meat will float when it is finished. They are cooked in about 8 minutes. Drain on absorbent paper, repeat as needed.

6. Five minutes before serving, pour prepared sauce mixture into a large skillet. Add ½ teaspoon salt. Heat and bring mixture to a boil. Slowly add some of the cornstarch solution until desired thickness is obtained. Add vegetables to sauce, then add ribs and pineapple. Heat thoroughly and serve with rice.

Beef Curry with Onions

As prepared for my cooking class by Mr. Sou Chan, House of Chan.

1 tablespoon curry powder   1½ pounds steak, sliced ⅛ inch thick
2 tablespoons oil   4 onions, sliced in strips
½ teaspoon salt   1 tablespoon soy sauce
1 slice ginger root   1 cup chicken broth
1 clove garlic, crushed   2 tablespoons cornstarch, mixed with
¼ teaspoon pepper   ¼ cup water

Heat a large skillet or a Chinese wok. Place curry powder in the hot skillet. *Lightly* brown curry, stirring it constantly. Remove curry to a side dish. Add oil to skillet. Drop in salt and heat oil. Sauté ginger root, garlic and pepper. Discard ginger root. Add meat, stirring constantly until every slice is browned, but still pink inside. Remove meat to a side dish. Add onions to the skillet. Stir and fry until onions are slightly cooked. Add soy and chicken broth. Cover pan and cook for 2 minutes. Uncover skillet. Blend in meat and curry powder. Pour in cornstarch mixture gradually until thickening is correct for your taste. Stir constantly. Serve immediately with Chinese rice (see index).

Lemon Ices with Loquats

3 cups cold water	1 tablespoon finely grated
1¼ cups sugar	lemon rind
¾ cup light corn syrup	⅔ cup fresh lemon juice
	1 can loquats, drained of syrup

Place water, sugar, syrup and rind in a heavy saucepan. Heat and stir until sugar dissolves. When mixture comes to a boil stop stirring. Boil for 5 minutes. Add lemon juice. Cool syrup thoroughly. Place in 2 refrigerator trays. Freeze until firm. Remove from freezer. Cut into chunks and place into mixing bowl (of electric mixer). Beat until ice is of mushy consistency. Place into any bowl or container. Cover well and freeze again. Serve a ball of lemon ice and 2 loquats for each serving.

Almond Crescents

½ pound butter	pinch salt
⅓ cup confectioners sugar	6 ounces finely ground almonds
¼ cup granulated sugar	(blanched)
1¾ cups all purpose flour, sifted	2 tablespoons brandy

Cream butter with both sugars. Add flour, salt, nuts and brandy. Roll a small ball of dough between the palms of your hands. Shape into crescents and place on a cookie sheet. Bake at 375° F. for 12 minutes. Remove cookies to a rack and dust heavily with confectioners' sugar while still warm. Makes 5 or 6 dozen. This batch of cookies is more than you'll need to serve six. Freeze leftovers for another occasion.

Since the main course of this dinner is Chinese, there is a certain amount of last-minute preparation. It is well worth the effort if you know your guests enjoy Chinese food. The loquats are a Chinese fruit, available in the Chinese groceries. They are lovely in flavor and pretty to look at.

ADVANCE PREPARATION:

Bake cookies a few days in advance. Store them in closely covered plastic boxes. They may be made weeks in advance and frozen.

ONE DAY IN ADVANCE:

1. Prepare shrimp completely but do not cook them. Cover them very well with Saran wrap and refrigerate.
2. Make lemon ices and store in the freezer overnight.

DAY OF DINNER:

1. Slice vegetables and prepare all ingredients for Sweet and Sour Spareribs. Prepare ribs up to and including step #5. When ribs are fried, set them aside on a baking sheet.
2. Prepare all ingredients on a tray for the Beef Curry. Have everything precisely cut and measured so that only last minute cooking is necessary.
3. One hour before serving, cook rice. Do not uncover. Rice will stay hot enough even with flame off. For six servings, cook 1¼ cups raw rice.
4. Preheat oven to 400° F. Place shrimp into oven when guests arrive. They take a short time and will be ready just when guests start settling and sherry is poured.
5. Five minutes before serving main course, complete Sweet and Sour Spareribs.
6. Seat your guests. While spareribs are being served, complete the Beef Curry dish. Serve it piping hot. Pass rice around. If you own rice bowls, rice could be placed before each guest in advance. Tea should be placed on the table. Now you may sit down and enjoy the dinner with your guests.
7. Lemon ice may be served just following the main course, before the coffee. It is most refreshing.
8. For a change, take your coffee and crescents in the living room.

MENU 4 FOR SIX
Apértif: St. Raphael
Avocado with Lobster dressing
Norwegian Flat Bread
Rolled Boned Duck
Wild Rice
Asparagus-Lemon Crumbs
Watercress, Lettuce and Radish Salad
Easy Butter Rolls
Corton Charlemagne, 1959
Hawaiian Fruit Dessert

Avocado with Lobster Dressing

Prepare dressing by blending together:

2 cooked lobster tails, finely minced	1 tablespoon chopped chives
¾ cup mayonnaise	1 tablespoon chopped dill
2 tablespoons olive oil	¼ teaspoon salt
2 tablespoons lemon juice	⅛ teaspoon pepper
1 tablespoon capers	pinch cayenne
1 tablespoon chile sauce	

For individual service place ½ ripe avocado on a leaf of Boston lettuce. Fill cavity of avocado with lobster dressing. Garnish with lemon wedges. For buffet service, set on one large tray. Cut avocados in quarters. Cover tray with lettuce leaves. Make a circle of avocado quarters all around tray. Fill cavities with dressing. Place black olives in the center of tray.

Rolled Boned Duck

STUFFING

1 duck, cleaned and boned	½ cup bread crumbs,
2 tablespoons lemon juice	soaked in 3 tablespoons red wine
2 tablespoons butter	1½ slices white bread, soaked
½ pound mushrooms, minced	in ¼ cup heavy sweet cream
1 onion, minced	12 water chestnuts, sliced
½ pound ground beef	1 teaspoon salt
½ pound ground veal	¼ teaspoon pepper
¼ pound chopped boiled ham	¼ teaspoon ground clove
	¼ teaspoon thyme

1. Bone the duck, or ask your butcher to do the job. Be sure to keep the skin intact. Lay the duck out flat, skin side down. Sprinkle with lemon juice.

2. Melt butter in a skillet; add mushrooms and onion. Sauté until lightly browned.

3. Remove from flame. Mix in raw meats, bread crumbs, bread water chestnuts and all seasonings. Cool mixture.

4. Place the mound of stuffing down the center of duck. Bring both sides of duck over, one overlapping the other. Tie duck at 3 places with clean white string. Salt the duck lightly all over. Now it is ready for the roaster.

ROASTING

2 carrots, diced	½ teaspoon salt
2 stalks celery, diced	freshly ground pepper
1 large onion, diced	1 cup red wine
1 green pepper	1 cup brown sauce
1 sprig parsley	¼ cup port
1 bay leaf	½ cup Cointreau

1. Lay the vegetables over the bottom of the roasting pan. Add 1 sprig of parsley and 1 bay leaf. Sprinkle the vegetables with ½ teaspoon of salt and freshly ground pepper (5 turns).

2. Preheat oven to 425° F. Roast duck on bed of vegetables for 20 minutes uncovered, then cover with 1 cup of red wine.

3. Lower heat to 350° F. Cover pan and cook for 1 hour.

4. Take duck out and remove to a dish. Strain off drippings; discard vegetables.

5. Place duck into roasting pan and set it into the oven uncovered while preparing sauce.

6. If possible, pour off all the fat and reserve about 4 to 6 tablespoons drippings. Place drippings into a saucepan with 1 cup sauce and ¼ cup port wine. Simmer slowly until ready to serve.

7. When duck has roasted for 1¾ hours in total, baste it with ½ cup Cointreau or substitute chicken broth if you prefer. Set the oven up to 400° F. for 15 minutes. This will crisp and brown your duck. Coat with sauce for shininess.

8. Serve the duck with a border of wild rice.

Note: Do not prick the skin of the duck. It remains crisper without pricking. For the brown sauce use 1 cup of beef broth thickened with ½ tablespoon of cornstarch mixed with 2 tablespoons water. If you happen to have leftover homemade gravy (beef, chicken or veal) that is better still!

Wild Rice

1 cup wild rice	2 tablespoons butter
¼ cup consommé	salt and pepper to taste
¼ cup orange juice	

Keep a filled kettle of boiling water. Place wild rice in a pyrex bowl. Pour boiling water over it to cover it completely. Let it stand till water cools. Strain off water. Repeat the same. Pour clean boiling water over rice. Let it stand till water cools. You'll find that rice is practically cooked. This may be repeated as many times as you wish till rice is soft. After the second or third soaking, I prefer to add the consommé, orange juice, butter, salt and pepper. Bake in the oven at 350° F. covered until moisture is evaporated. This takes about 15 minutes. This last step may also be done on top of the stove in a saucepan.

Asparagus — Lemon Crumbs

3 pounds fresh asparagus	4 tablespoons lemon juice
or 2 boxes frozen	½ teaspoon salt
4 tablespoons butter	¼ teaspoon pepper
1 cup bread crumbs	

Melt butter. Brown bread crumbs lightly; add lemon juice, salt and pepper. Set crumbs aside. Steam asparagus. Serve on a flat dish. Sprinkle crumbs over asparagus.

Watercress, Lettuce and Radish Salad

Wash and dry greens very well. Place in a covered container overnight. Rub a wooden bowl with garlic. Toss greens and thinly sliced radishes in bowl. Pass the oil and vinegar for individual helpings.

~~~~~~~~

Easy Butter Rolls

2 packages dry yeast	2 teaspoons salt
½ cup warm water	2 eggs
½ cup milk (room temperature)	4½ cups flour
½ cup sugar	¼ pound butter

1. Place yeast and warm water into a large bowl. Stir yeast and allow it to soften for 2 or 3 minutes.

2. When yeast looks dissolved, add milk, sugar, salt and eggs.

3. Gradually beat in 3 cups of flour. Add butter and fourth cup of flour. Reserve ½ cup for the board.

4. When dough is well blended, remove it to a floured board. Knead it for about 10 minutes. It will become smooth and satiny.

5. Place it in a greased bowl and cover. Allow it to rise until double in bulk.

6. Punch down and knead briefly. Cut dough in half. Place ½ covered into the refrigerator. This dough may be kept up to 3 days in the refrigerator.

7. Cut the remaining dough into 12 pieces.

8. Roll each piece on a floured surface. Roll with the palms of your hands. Dough will roll out to a narrow roll about 8 inches long. Cut it in half.

9. Twist each 4 inch length into a knot and place on a buttered baking sheet. Brush with mixture of beaten egg yolk and 1 tablespoon water.

10. This ½ batch of dough makes about 24 small rolls. Place them 1 inch apart on a cookie sheet. Allow to rise about 1 hour.

11. Bake for 20 minutes at 375° F.

~~~~~~~~

Hawaiian Fruit Dessert

3 small pineapples	2 cups port wine
2 cans pitted bing cherries,	¼ cup brown sugar
well drained	½ cup kirsch

Slice pineapple lengthwise (with leaves) and scoop out fruit. Chill the shells. Cut pineapple into bite size pieces. Combine pineapple and cherries and marinate for several hours or overnight in wine, sugar and kirsch. When available use *fresh* cherries or strawberries.

TOPPING

1 cup heavy cream, whipped stiff	¼ cup rum
1 tablespoon brown sugar	1 pint vanilla ice cream,
1 cup guava or currant jelly	cut in small cubes

Fold sugar, jelly and rum into whipped cream. Lastly add chunks of ice cream.

TO SERVE:

Prepare a very large round tray (24″ in diameter). Place bowl of topping in the center of tray and surround the bowl with pineapple halves. Fill each cavity with marinated fruit. Serve each person a half pineapple and a few tablespoons of cream topping.

Note: The small chunks of ice cream may be wrapped and put away in the freezer. Do not place them in the whipped cream till ready to serve.

ADVANCE PREPARATION:

1. Rolls may be baked in advance, frozen, and reheated the day of the dinner.

2. Buy avocados early in the week so they may ripen at room temperature. If they become soft before they are needed, refrigerate them.

ONE DAY AHEAD:

1. Prepare lobster dressing. Cover well and refrigerate.

2. Prepare stuffing for duck. Set in a bowl. Cover and refrigerate.

3. Salt duck and sprinkle with lemon juice. Cover lightly till the next day. Refrigerate.

4. Wash greens; dry well. Refrigerate them closely covered.

5. Cut pineapples. Cover shells and refrigerate. Marinate fruit overnight in the refrigerator.

DAY OF DINNER:

Morning:

1. Prepare wild rice up to and including step #5.
2. Wash and clean asparagus if they are fresh.

Early Afternoon:

1. Stuff duck; prepare roasting pan.
2. Set duck in the oven at least 3 hours before dinner. When duck is finished, remove it from the oven.
3. Place salad in bowl. Cover with Saran. Refrigerate.
4. Prepare lemon crumbs. Set aside.

ONE HOUR BEFORE DINNER:

One Hour Before Dinner:

1. Cut avocados and arrange on individual plates or a large platter. Fill cavities with dressing. Garnish with olives. Refrigerate.
2. Complete the cooking of the wild rice about 20 minutes before guests arrive. Keep on low flame.
3. Cook asparagus after guests arrive.
4. Reheat duck in 400° F. oven 10 minutes before serving.

If your refrigerator is large enough you may want to set up the fruit tray ahead of time. If not it will take 2 minutes to fill shells of pineapple and place them on a tray. Blend the bits of ice cream into the bowl of whipped cream topping the last minute.

This dessert is a sparkling finale for any dinner.

MENU 5 FOR SIX

Cheese Fondue   Crusty Bread Chunks   Neuchatel
Chicken Breasts Riviera
Duchess Potatoes
Glazed Baby Carrots
Salade Mimosa
Brandied Alaska   Coffee

Cheese Fondue

1 pound Swiss cheese
2 cups Neuchatel wine
2 teaspoons cornstarch
2 tablespoons water

salt, pepper, dash nutmeg
2 tablespoons kirsch
1 crusty Italian bread,
    cut in 1 inch chunks

1. Grate cheese on a coarse grater. If cheese is sliced, cut it into thin strips.

2. Heat cheese and wine over very low heat. You may use chafing dish.

3. When cheese begins to melt and wine starts simmering, add mixture of cornstarch and water.

4. Season with a sprinkle of salt, 4 turns of the pepper mill and about 4 turns of the nutmeg grinder (⅛ teaspoon). Add kirsch.

5. Stir cheese and wine. When cheese starts blending with wine ask each person to pierce a chunk of bread with his fork. Let them each stir the cheese with their bread and remove it well coated with cheese.

6. Serve slightly chilled Neuchatel wine.

Note: As cheese cooks it absorbs all the wine and gets heavier. You may continue to add wine. If there is any leftover, immediately remove it to a greased dish. Refrigerate. Reheat over low heat within the next few days, adding a little more wine if necessary.

According to the Swiss the rules of the fondue game are as follows. Each person spears his own bread and stirs the cheese. Any guest who drops his bread off the fork into the pot, owes his host a bottle of wine.

Chicken Breasts Riviera

6 breasts of chicken boned	¼ cup flour
6 tablespoons of butter	2 eggs beaten with ¼ cup water
2 cloves of garlic, crushed	6 scallions (green and white),
½ teaspoon each savory and chervil	chopped fine
1 tablespoon parsley, chopped	3 ripe tomatoes, peeled and sliced
½ teaspoon salt	½ cup red wine
¼ teaspoon pepper	2 tablespoons olive oil
½ cup seasoned bread crumbs	2 tablespoons butter

1. Pound chicken breasts once or twice to flatten them somewhat. Lay them skin side down one next to the other on wax paper.

2. Blend butter, garlic, herbs, salt and pepper. Place 1 lump of this mixture on each chicken breast. Divide the mixture evenly.

3. Roll the ends of the chicken breast so that one overlaps the other. You may skewer the end or tie the roll.

4. Roll each breast in the crumbs and flour, which have been tossed together. Refrigerate the chicken or partially freeze before cooking. This makes them very easy to handle. Reserve any leftover crumbs.

5. When ready to cook, place crumbs on a sheet of wax paper. Add more if you think you'll need it. Place eggs and water in a shallow pan (pie tin).

6. Prepare a shallow (oven to table dish) casserole with scallions and tomatoes.

7. Prepare a skillet with 2 tablespoons of olive oil and 1 tablespoon butter.

8. While skillet and fat are heating, dip chicken breasts into egg then crumbs. Fry them in fat until all sides are brown. The six breasts can all be done at one time in a large skillet.

9. Transfer chicken breasts on to the bed of scallions and tomatoes. Pour red wine over all. Bake for 45 minutes at 350° F.

Duchess Potatoes

2 pounds potatoes	3 tablespoons butter
(regular, not baking)	2 egg yolks
water to cover	salt and pepper to taste
2 tablespoons salt	

Peel potatoes; wash well. Cut into large pieces. Cover with water and salt. Cover saucepan and cook until potatoes are tender. Drain potatoes well. Place them over flame for a few seconds to dry them. Beat in an electric mixer with butter, egg yolks and seasonings. If you have the muscle for it, sieve the potatoes and beat by hand. They are even more fluffy when beaten vigorously this way. Prepare your large decorating bag fitted with a #6 or #7 star tube. Fill the bag half full with potatoes. Pipe a lovely border of potato all around the border of the chicken breasts 15 minutes before serving. Potatoes will brown in the oven while chicken is completing its' baking time.

Glazed Baby Carrots

2 tablespoons butter	1 tablespoon lemon juice
4 tablespoons brown sugar	1 can baby carrots

Melt butter with sugar and lemon juice in a skillet or any baking dish suitable for carrots. Place drained carrots into sugar mixture. Heat in skillet on stove for about 15 minutes, turning occasionally. This may be baked in an oven dish along with chicken for the final 15 minutes.

Salade Mimosa

1 head Boston lettuce (bibb if you can get it)	1 teaspoon chopped chives
½ head iceberg lettuce	½ teaspoon tarragon
⅓ cup olive oil	1 teaspoon chopped parsley
¼ cup wine vinegar	½ teaspoon salt
1 tablespoon heavy sweet cream	⅛ teaspoon freshly ground pepper
	1 hard-cooked egg

1. Wash lettuce well. Drain and dry with paper toweling. Store in a plastic box and refrigerate overnight until crisp.

2. When ready to use salad, place it into bowl.

3. Measure all ingredients, except egg, in a 2 cup measuring glass. Stir vigorously. If you own a blender, use it for this dressing. The blender produces a very creamy mixture.

4. Sieve egg yolk and white together, or mince them with a knife.

5. Toss salad with dressing. Sprinkle egg all over the top. This is a classic salad which may be served with the main course or just after it.

Brandied Alaska

6 balls of ice cream

STRAWBERRY SAUCE:

1 ten-ounce package frozen strawberries	1 8-inch round layer of basic sponge cake (see index)
2 tablespoons cognac	1 pint strawberries, hulled and sliced
1 tablespoon cornstarch mixed with ¼ cup water	4 tablespoons cognac or brandy

MERINGUE:

6 egg whites, room temperature	1 cup sugar
½ teaspoon cream of tartar	1 teaspoon vanilla

1. Scoop out balls of ice cream and place them back in the freezer.

2. Cut out a double round of heavy aluminum foil to fit the sponge cake.

3. Prepare sauce. Heat frozen strawberries with cognac. Blend in cornstarch and water to thicken sauce. Set aside.

4. Place sponge on aluminum foil. Lay slices of strawberries on to cake, 1 inch in from the edge. Sprinkle 2 tablespoons of cognac over strawberries and cake. Pile remaining sliced strawberries in the center. Sprinkle 2 tablespoons of cognac over these berries.

5. Preheat the oven to 450° F.

6. When ready to serve, make the meringue. Beat egg whites with cream of tartar till frothy. Add sugar 2 tablespoons at a time, beating well after each addition. When sugar is all beaten in and mixture is very stiff add vanilla.

7. Use a large pastry bag fitted with a #7 star tube. Fill the pastry bag no more than ½ full. Refill when you need to.

8. Set ice cream balls on to the cake around the mound of strawberries. Be sure ice cream balls are close together.

9. Set cake and ice cream on the back of a wooden steak plank (or a board). Pipe out meringue to cover the ice cream and cake completely. Do not leave any air spaces. Set immediately into hot oven. Bake for 3 or 4 minutes on the center rack.

10. In the meantime heat the prepared strawberry sauce.

11. Place Alaska on a serving platter. Bring to the table with hot strawberry sauce. If you wish to serve it flaming, save ½ an eggshell. Set the eggshell into the top peak of the meringue before baking. Pour 2 tablespoons warmed cognac into eggshell when serving. Ignite!

ADVANCE PREPARATION:

1. Bake the sponge layer and freeze it.

2. Two or three days before dinner, wash and dry greens. They will be very crisp if they are refrigerated in a plastic closely covered box.

3. Two days before dinner, prepare chicken up to and including step #4.

ONE DAY BEFORE DINNER:

1. Prepare chicken breasts up to and including step #8.

2. Prepare carrots, completing step #1.

DAY OF DINNER:

AFTERNOON:

1. Cut Swiss cheese. Place it into the pot to be used, preferably a blazer pan of a chafing dish. Special fondue outfits are sold but they are not necessary. Arrange chafing dish on a large metal tray. Set out all necessary ingredients.

2. Scoop out balls of ice cream. Set back into the freezer.

3. Arrange salad in the serving bowl. Cover with Saran and refrigerate. Sieve the hard boiled egg and· set it aside.

4. Peel potatoes and allow them to soak in cold salted water.

TWO HOURS BEFORE GUESTS ARRIVE:

1. Boil and mash potatoes. Fill the decorating bag and keep it near a *warm* place.

2. Allow chicken and carrots to reach room temperature.

3. Mix salad dressing and set aside.

Allow egg whites for meringue to rest in mixing bowl at room temperature.

THIRTY MINUTES BEFORE GUESTS ARRIVE:

1. Cut French bread into chunks. Place them around chafing dish if tray is large enough. Set out fondue forks.

2. Add wine to cheese in the blazer pan and start warming the cheese and wine on the stove over very low heat. This will give the fondue a head start. It will be practically ready for completion when the guests arrive.

3. Set the chicken breasts into the oven at 350° F.

4. Arrange sponge layers with berries on wooden board; preparation up to and including step #4.

5. After first glass of wine has been served, pop carrots into the oven. Pipe duchess potatoes around chicken and place into the oven. Dinner will be ready in 15 minutes.

6. Toss salad with dressing and sprinkle sieved egg on top.

7. While guests are eating salad, preheat oven to 450° F. Set strawberry sauce to warm. Whip up the meringue and finish the alaska.

OPEN HOUSE FOR FIFTY

Holiday Hors D'oeuvres Tray
Pâté Maison   Artichokes à la Grecque
Crackers, melba toast, party rye

Hot buffet
Swedish Meat Balls   Imperial Crab Baltimore
Toast Points
Onion Pie   Cheese Pie
Assorted cookies   Coffee

Quantities:

1. Holiday hors d'oeuvres tray.

> 4 Lobster Aspics
> 6 pounds shrimp
> 5 dozen eggs
> 12 grapefruits
> 6 large avocados
> 3 recipes for Cucumber and Onion Relish
> 3 cans ripe olives

2. 4 terrines of Pâté Maison.
3. 3 recipes Artichokes à la Grecque.
   8 ripe tomatoes, capers and 3 cans anchovy filets for garnish.
4. 3 Cheese Pies.
   3 Onion Pies.
5. 2 recipes Swedish Meat Balls.
6. 4 recipes Imperial Crab Baltimore.

See index for all recipes.

ADVANCE PREPARATION:

1. Pie crusts should be frozen unbaked weeks in advance. Cookies may be baked and frozen.

2. Pâté and Swedish Meat Balls may be frozen well in advance. If I made them fresh I would prepare the Pâté 5 days ahead and the meat balls 3 days ahead of time.

3. Two days before the party:
Wash greens for garnishes (parsley, chicory, watercress).
Prepare Artichokes à la Grecque.
Prepare Cucumber and Onion Relish.
Prepare Lobster Aspics.

4. One day before the party:

Cook shrimp.

Prepare deviled eggs—cover well with Saran.

Segment grapefruits.

Prepare Imperial Crab Baltimore. Store in a pyrex bowl that can be heated over hot water.

5. Day of the party:

Defrost Pâté, Swedish Meat Balls, cookies.

Arrange cookies on serving trays.

Set up 2 chafing dishes; one for the meat balls and one for the crab Baltimore.

Arrange 2 trays with Artichokes à la Grecque, garnished with sliced tomatoes, capers, anchovies and greens.

Arrange "Holiday hors d'oeuvres" using the ingredients for one recipe. Replenish the tray as the food is eaten.

Bake the cheese and onion pies one hour ahead. They will keep warm at low tempearture when finished.

Heat crab Baltimore and Swedish meat balls in the kitchen. These are both best when heated slowly in bowls over warm water (double boiler fashion). Keep replenishing chafing dishes on serving table.

MENU FOR JULY 4th BRUNCH

(See Barbecue chapter for additional menus for outdoors.)

1. Start charcoal grill.

2. While coals are becoming hot, set the table outdoors.

3. Prepare a skillet for bacon and eggs. Have heavy aluminum foil for other cooking.

> Orange juice
> Scrambled eggs
> Grilled ham steaks
> Sautéed bananas wrapped in bacon
> Hot buttered rolls
> Cinnamon toast   Coffee

Partially render bacon in skillet. Remove and drain on paper. Use the same skillet for eggs. Slice rolls, butter them, wrap in aluminum foil and place on grill. Wrap each whole banana in partially rendered bacon. Set out a sheet of heavy foil on grill. Prick holes in foil. Grill ham and bananas on foil. In the meantime prepare eggs. Prepare buttered white bread in advance. For second cup of coffee, toast bread directly on grill and sprinkle with cinnamon sugar.

MENU-MAKING QUESTIONS ANSWERED

Q　*Is it necessary to serve a cooked vegetable with every dinner?*

A　No, there are times when a salad is sufficient to replace a vegetable.

Q　*Is it proper to serve salad with the meat course?*

A　Most hostesses serve salad with the meat course for easier service, however there are many times when a crisp salad can be better enjoyed after or before the main course. Crisp greens provide a change of texture before a creamy dessert.

Q　*For a buffet dinner, what other hot main course could be served with a baked or roast chicken?*

A　If the chicken has no sauce, why not serve Swedish meat balls or stuffed cabbage? Sea-food dishes blend very well with poultry too. Use any one of the shrimp or lobster recipes.

Q　*What is an interesting menu for a late supper?*

A　One of my favorites is the Cheddar Cheese Pie, served with fresh fruit, a bottle of dry wine, and of course hot coffee.

If you like to be the center of attraction, prepare apple pancakes and flame them in front of your guests. Serve Danish pastry and coffee for a fine finish.

LESSON 20
Herbs, Spices and Spirits

Port | Madeira | Sherry.

Fortified drinking wines will last indefinately.

You may also store Brandies and Liqueurs.

All drinking wines of low alcoholic content should be used very quickly.

Herbs and spices provide us with the means to improve and change the most ordinary dishes. Our personal tastes should direct us to adjust the flavoring and seasoning of every prepared dish. Experimentation with a new herb or combination of herbs will create a delectable new taste sensation for you. This necessitates practice, a small amount of daring and a few facts to guide you:

1. The word spice is popularly used to mean "hot" or "sharp," but actually there are sweet, spicy-sweet and hot spices. Cinnamon and sweet paprika are sweet spices; ginger is spicy-sweet, cayenne is hot.

2. Herbs and spices should be stored in a cool place and tightly covered.

3. Freshly minced herbs and spices always add a better flavor than the already-prepared variety.

4. Dried herbs may always be substituted for fresh herbs and vice versa; however, use ½ to 1 teaspoon of dried herbs for 1 tablespoon of fresh. This may vary too, because dried herbs diminish in flavor as they stand.

5. Do not use more than one robust herb in the same meal. Strong-flavored herbs include marjoram, sage, mint, dill, savory.

303

6. When using fresh herbs, mince them fine; when using dried herbs, crush them with your fingers before mixing them into foods. Mincing and crushing before use brings out aromatic oils and individual flavor.

7. The flavor of dried herbs can be further heightened by steeping them in warm liquids (milk, butter, both or water) before using.

Herbs

Basil—With eggs, fish chowders and all tomato recipes. I like fresh basil leaves on baked lamb and pork chops.

Chervil—Mild cousin to parsley, so combine for omelets, over baked fish and in salads. Use just before serving; one of my favorites for subtle sauces.

Chives—Perennial plant used with mild cheese, eggs, salad dressings and sauces. My garden is always abundant with chives (April to November), so I constantly have a garnish for soups, salads and vegetables.

Dill—Fresh dill is aromatic for broth, white sauce, salads; blended with butter, it adds zest to cooked potatoes and vegetables.

Garlic—You know about this!

Marjoram—Combine with other herbs for egg dishes, fish, poultry and vegetables. Add ¼ teaspoon to bisques just before serving.

Mint—Use fresh as garnish for fresh fruits and beverages. Use dried for stews and sauces.

Oregano—Use for spaghetti sauces veal, lamb and pork roasts. I like oregano in Marinara sauce (see index), especially with sea-food.

Parsley—Use fresh at all times because it is available all year; use for flavor in soups, stews, sauces, sea-food dishes, salads and vegetables. Use as garnish for fish, sea-food and salads. Like chives, parsley is rewarding for the home garden—no trouble at all.

Rosemary—Used on lamb roast, the aroma is pleasant, not overwhelming.

Sage—Use for pork dishes and stuffings. I find it easy to grow and the fresh leaf so much milder than the dried. Try fresh sage and veal!

Savory—Combine with parsley, marjoram and basil for hamburger, stews and tomato sauce. I like savory on broiled chicken, of course with plenty of butter.

Tarragon—Use for poultry (see index) and if you grow a few

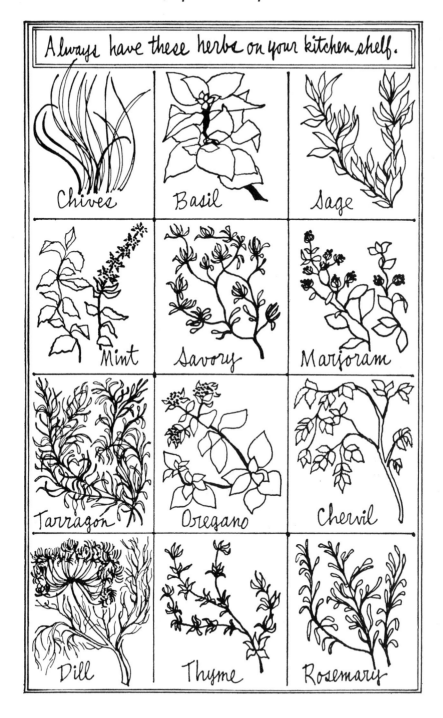

Always have these herbs on your kitchen shelf.

Chives   Basil   Sage

Mint   Savory   Marjoram

Tarragon   Oregano   Chervil

Dill   Thyme   Rosemary

plants in the garden, do make tarragon vinegar. Steep 2 cups freshly chopped tarragon to 1 quart good-quality vinegar. Allow to stand for at least 1 week. Shake occasionally.

Thyme—Use for stews, soups, chowders and stuffings. Sprinkle thyme over sliced, garden fresh tomatoes!

Spices

Allspice—Whole for pickling, poaching fish and sea food. Ground for stews, tomato sauce, fruit preserves and baked goods.

Bay Leaf—Use 1 or 2 leaves for fish stock, for marinades and stews. Try an occasional leaf on the skewers with shish kebab!

Chili Powder—This blend of chili pepper and spices is used for Mexican dishes, but is excellent in sharp sauces and stews.

Cinnamon—Use the stick for coffee, hot chocolate, apple sauce and fruit compotes. Use ground for coffee cakes, cookies, custards and puddings. Use a pinch in the Chocolate Mousse (see index).

Cloves—Use whole for pork and ham roasts, pickling and spicy preserves; ground for baked goods, stews and vegetables. Stud an onion with 1 or 2 whole cloves—perfect for soups and stews.

Curry—Use ground for eggs, fish, poultry and vegetables. Curry blends are fascinating—try blending your own with ¼ teaspoon red pepper, ⅛ teaspoon turmeric, 2 cloves, ½ teaspoon ginger, stick cinnamon and 1 teaspoon salt. Some like it hot—some like it mild.

Ginger—Use ground for cakes, spicy syrups and fruit compotes. Use in sweet-sour stews (see index—Stuffed Cabbage). For a real delight buy fresh ginger root at the Chinese grocery—one thin slice will perfume your next try at an Oriental dish.

Nutmeg—Buy whole and grind or grate it fresh—the flavor is superior. Use for fruits, eggnog, puddings, cakes, vegetables and don't forget Swedish Meat Balls (see index).

Paprika—Use sweet paprika for egg dishes, poultry and fish. It is worth a trip to a good food store to purchase fine-quality paprika. What color and flavor!

Pepper—Use freshly ground at all times. Black whole pepper (peppercorns) may be used in all dishes—an absolute *must* for all cooking. White pepper, the inner kernel of black pepper, is especially good for light broths and white sauces.

Saffron—Use very sparingly for chicken dishes (see index for Arroz con Pollo). Try a pinch in yeast doughs for a lovely yellow color!

Turmeric—Use for relishes, mustards and flavoring for salad dressing. Do not forget it when you blend your own curry!

Vanilla—Use the bean in your sugar bin for heavenly-scented sugar to flavor custards, cookies and cakes. The bean may be cut and scrapings used for ice cream. Extract is fine for desserts and baked goods.

Seeds

Anise—Whole for cheese canapés and on sweet rolls. Ground for beverages, fruits and cookies.

Caraway—For appetizer dips, breads, rolls, cakes and cookies. Sprinkle into buttered noodles, excellent in stewed cabbage.

Cardamom—Ground for bread and coffee cake; add to fruit salad or compote. Try a whole seed in demi-tasse!

Celery Seed—Use for pickling, salads, vegetables and stews. Just ¼ teaspoon to 4 cups of poultry stuffing gives added flavor.

Coriander—Use ground in cookies and gingerbread. Add ¼ teaspoon to fruits before stewing. Rub surface of pork roast with small amount before roasting.

Dill—For pickling, sauces and salads.

Fennel—Use with mild cheese; sprinkle over rolls. Try a light sprinkle in a chicken or sea-food stew.

Mustard—Use ground for preparing sharp (Chinese-type) mustard. Always excellent in salad dressings, cream sauces and stews.

Spirits

Since most of us do not have proper facilities for storing quantities of wine, it is best to keep just enough for cooking and a supply for a few dinners.

For cooking you will need:

1. Dry red and white wine, for marinades or in the liquid for poaching and stewing. The quality of this wine does not have to be vintage but it must always be good enough to drink.

2. Fortified wines (wines strengthened with brandy), used for flavoring food at the end of cooking time. These include Sherry, Madeira and Port.

3. Liqueurs and brandies used for flavoring and flaming desserts.

Liqueurs—Grand Marnier, Cointreau, Curaçao, Triple Sec are sweet and have an orange flavor.

Brandy, Cognac, Kirsch, Rum are unsweetened 80 to 100 proof liquors that flame very well when warmed slightly.

A minimum cupboard should stock:

2 bottles red wine	1 bottle Madeira
2 bottles white wine	1 bottle orange liqueur
1 bottle medium dry sherry	1 bottle brandy

The wines listed for cooking are named in the broadest terms, red and white. Specific suggestions are made in the lesson on menus. The pleasures of enjoying wine with meals should impel you to taste and test the tremendous varieties available. Make use of the facts laid down by the wine experts; benefit by their many years of experience but allow your own palate to be your final guide.

SEASONING QUESTIONS ANSWERED

Q *What is the difference between a spice and herb?*

A Spices are the roots, bark, stems, berries, seeds or buds derived from aromatic plants which generally grow in the tropics; on the other hand, herbs are the leaves of plants which grow mostly in the temperate zone.

Q *I have a small herb garden but always have more herbs than I need, at least in the summer. Can herbs be frozen?*

A Most herbs freeze well. Package them in small amounts before freezing.

Q *What is a bouquet garni?*

A A combination of herbs and spices—usually three or more—often wrapped in cheesecloth and then tied. Used to flavor soups and stews. A good basic combination is parsley, bay leaf and thyme.

Index